Human Potential

Throughout time, people have explored the ways in which they can improve some aspect of their performance. Such attempts are more visible today, with many working to gain an 'edge' on their performance, whether it is to learn a new language, improve memory or increase golf handicaps. This book examines a range of techniques that are intended to help improve some aspect of performance, and examines how well they are able to achieve this.

The various performance-enhancing techniques available can be divided into those where the individual remains passive (receiving a message, suggestion or stimulus) and those where the individual needs to take a more active approach. *Human Potential* looks at a range of techniques within each of these categories to provide the reader with a sense of the traditional as well as the more contemporary approaches used to enhance human performance. The techniques covered include hypnosis, sleep learning, subliminal training and audio and visual cortical entrainment, as well as meditation, mnemonics, speed reading, biofeedback, neurofeedback and mental imagery practice.

This is the first time such a broad range of techniques has been brought together to be assessed in terms of effectiveness. It will be useful to all psychology and sports science students, practising psychologists, life coaches and anyone else interested in finding out about the effectiveness of performance enhancement techniques.

David Vernon is Senior Lecturer in Psychology at Canterbury Christ Church University. He has a wide range of research interests covering a variety of performance-enhancing techniques, in particular the use of neurofeedback to alter brain activity as a mechanism for improving cognition and behaviour.

Human Potential
Exploring techniques used to enhance human performance

David Vernon

Routledge
Taylor & Francis Group

LONDON AND NEW YORK

First published 2009 by Routledge
27 Church Road, Hove, East Sussex BN3 2FA

Simultaneously published in the USA and Canada
by Routledge
270 Madison Avenue, New York, NY 10016

*Routledge is an imprint of the Taylor & Francis Group, an informa
business*

© 2009 Psychology Press

Typeset in Times New Roman by
RefineCatch Limited, Bungay, Suffolk
Printed and bound in Great Britain by
TJ International Ltd, Padstow, Cornwall
Paperback cover design by Andy Ward

This publication has been produced with paper manufactured to strict
environmental standards and with pulp derived from sustainable
forests.

British Library Cataloguing in Publication Data
A catalogue record for this book is available from the British Library

Library of Congress Cataloging in Publication Data
Vernon, David, 1964–
  Human potential : exploring techniques used to enhance human
performance / David Vernon.
    p. cm.
  Includes bibliographical references and index.
  ISBN 978-0-415-45769-9 (hb) – ISBN 978-0-415-45770-5 (soft
cover) 1. Performance–Psychological aspects. 2. Performance–
Physiological aspects. 3. Performance technology. I. Title.
  BF431.V394 2009
  158′.9—dc22
  2008050952

ISBN 978-0-415-45769-9 (hbk)
ISBN 978-0-415-45770-5 (pbk)

For Grażyna,

who helps me reach for the stars
but keeps my feet firmly on the ground

Contents

PART III
Peak performance   225

Acknowledgements

First, I would like to say a very special thank you to Ruth Woods, who pains-takingly read every chapter, making numerous comments and suggestions to help make clear what was often ambiguous. There is no doubt in my mind that the book benefited greatly from her dedicated and conscientious approach, ensuring a level of clarity that I often, mistakenly, assumed was inherent. Thanks Ruth; so that's another bar of Green and Blacks, then, is it? Thanks also to Chris Pike for providing support and inspiration to develop the idea when it initially emerged from one of our many coffeehouse conversations about the nature of psychology. Thank you to Sabina Hulbert for providing helpful comments, particularly on the latter section, as well as the much-valued support given throughout. Heartfelt thanks to Grażyna, whose support and belief in me never wavered, even when listening to all my doubts and concerns during the writing of this book, dzienkuje bardzo moja ukohana zona.

I would also like to acknowledge the support of my colleagues in the Psychology team as well as the helpful comments from external reviewers and the editorial team at the Psychology Press: Sharla, Tara and, in particular, Lucy for the initial positive response. I am also grateful to Canterbury Christ Church University for providing me with the support and academic freedom to pursue my research. It has always been about asking interesting questions.

Finally, to the memory of James Adamson, who helped to make my life more interesting than I would have believed possible. Thanks Jim.

The following quotes appear with permission. The quote from Carl Sagan (1981) is reprinted with permission from the Little Brown Book Group and Druyan-Sagan Associates, Inc. Quotation by William James (1890) reprinted with permission from Dover Publications Inc. Quotation by Charles E. Boklage reprinted by permission of the publisher from *Cerebral Dominance: The Biological Foundations*, edited by Norman Geschwind and Albert M. Galaburda, Cambridge, MA: Harvard University Press, © 1984 by the President and Fellows of Harvard College. Quotation by Miller (1974) from N. E. Miller, T. X. Barber, L. V. DiCara, J. Kamiya, D. Shapiro and J. Stoya (eds), *Biofeedback and self-control 1973: An Aldine annual on the regulation of bodily processes and consciousness* (pp. 11–20), Chicago, Aldine Publishers. Reprinted by permission of Aldine Transaction, a division of Transaction Publishers.

1 Introduction

The untapped potential of the human species is immense.

(Carl Sagan 1981)

Human potential

The concept of human potential stems from a movement which began in the 1960s cultivating the belief that there remains a large degree of untapped potential in people, which, if accessed, would help them break through any barriers and perform at their peak. Implicit within such an approach is the belief that everyone has the *ability* and the *desire* to be more than they are at present.

The idea that an individual is motivated to strive and develop their full potential is related to the notion of self-actualisation, a central tenet of humanistic psychology. A core concept within this approach is the idea that the behaviour of each individual is driven by a hierarchical set of motives (see Figure 1.1), which are fundamentally oriented towards self-actualisation, enabling the individual to perform at their full potential, but only when the more basic physiological needs, such as hunger and thirst, have been met.

Inherent within the notion of human potential is the belief that in reaching their full potential an individual will be able to lead a happy and more fulfilled life. Such ideas form the basis of much of the interest shown in the arena of personal growth and self-help.

To help people achieve their full potential a number of techniques have been developed to enhance some aspect of performance. The aim of this book is to examine some of these techniques in an attempt to discern whether or not they are effective. However, before I embark upon this pursuit it is important to outline what is meant by the term 'enhancing performance' and why such an aim might be deemed desirable. In addition, it is necessary to identify what evidence can and should be used to evaluate the effectiveness of such techniques, particularly given the exuberant and optimistic claims made by those within the field of self-development. There is also the issue of which techniques to include and which to exclude. For those interested, it should be

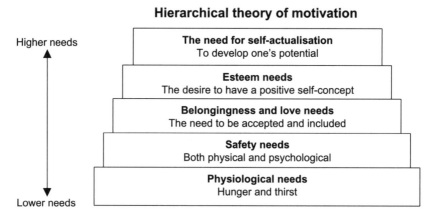

Figure 1.1 Maslow's hierarchy of needs. Ranging from the lower physiological desires to the higher goals of self-esteem and self-actualisation.

noted that the gender pronouns 'she' and 'he' will be used alternately throughout the book, with odd-numbered chapters adopting the female version and even-numbered chapters the male version.

Enhancing performance

Each individual throughout life is capable of performing any number of distinct behaviours. These can range from simple behaviours, such as remembering a shopping list, to more complex behaviours, such as playing a musical instrument or learning a new language. The individual's ability to complete such tasks can fall anywhere on the spectrum of performance from poor to peak (see Figure 1.2).

Such a classification may be overly simplistic but it highlights the point that behaviour can be classified, and that the performance of a behaviour that falls towards the peak end of the spectrum is likely to be more efficient, effective and produce better results. Thus, the aim of enhancing performance, or peak performance training, is not to bring individuals from the negative to the normative region of the spectrum of performance, but to encourage non-pathological healthy individuals to move beyond the normative level to achieve peak or optimal levels of performance.

In order to help people achieve such peak levels of performance, Seligman and Csikszentmihalyi (2000) have suggested that psychological science may need to shift its focus. Traditionally psychology has been interested in attempting to understand and explain human behaviour and the mental processes that underlie it. However, Seligman (1990) has repeatedly argued that psychology focuses too much on pathology and human health in an attempt to bring individuals up from the negative to the normative region of performance, with little or no effort expended trying to understand how, if at all,

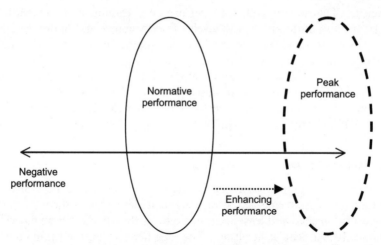

Figure 1.2 Classifying the spectrum of human performance from negative, through
normative, to peak performance. The aim of performance enhancement
training is to move individuals from the normative range up towards the
peak range.

it is possible to raise individual performance from the normative to more
optimal levels. However, this is changing due to the emergence and growth of
positive psychology (Seligman and Csikszentmihalyi 2000). Positive psychology represents an attempt to take a more coherent and in-depth look at the
measures and behaviours that encourage people to achieve their full potential. The idea of encouraging people to enhance their abilities is directly
reflected in the aims and ambitions of positive psychology, which, according
to Gable and Haidt (2005), examines the 'processes that contribute to
the flourishing or optimal functioning of people, groups and institutions'
(p. 104). This shift in focus may help provide a more coherent approach to
understanding the positive aspects of human psychology, leading to
increased attempts to understand what peak performance represents. For
many within the field, peak performance represents the superior use of
human potential which results in a level of behaviour that is more efficient
and effective than traditional behaviour (Privette 1983; Seligman 1990). The
idea here is that, when carrying out any behaviour, the individual uses her full
potential and performs at an optimal level. Thus, peak performance is a *way*
of functioning rather than a type of activity.

According to Privette (1983), there are a number of components that may
influence an individual's ability to perform at their peak. These include the
desire to achieve a goal, which acts as a behavioural motivator, and the ability
to produce a state of inner calm, thereby reducing stress and anxiety and
the negative effects they engender. In addition, the individual may view obs-
tacles as a potential challenge, thinking of new and efficient ways of dealing
with them, exhibiting what Csikszentmihalyi (1990) refers to as 'creative

optimism'. The aim of enhanced performance training is to increase the occurrence and duration of peak levels of performance and in doing so help people to reach their full potential. Such training may involve the use of specific techniques or new learning patterns to encourage more effective use of the brain's potential. However, before we look at such techniques it is worth spending a little time addressing one of the more pervasive myths concerning the notion of peak performance, and this is that an individual uses only 10 per cent of her brain.

The 10 per cent myth

The notion of untapped potential is often so strong and so pervasive that over time myths have emerged to support such ideas. One of the most enduring, most often cited and least accurate myths is the notion that an individual uses only 10 per cent of her brain. The idea here is that the brain contains hidden resources, or latent innate abilities, that are unused and that with training the individual can tap into these and enhance her performance. This myth is often used as a 'hook' to entrap the unwary into paying to gain access to a particular technique, or take part in a training programme or self-help seminar.

It is not clear where this myth came from but there are several lines of evidence which question the notion that vast regions of the brain remain unused. The first suggests that the brain is ever hungry to receive input and that it will reorganise itself in order to achieve this. An elegant and insightful study by Merzenich *et al.* (1984) focused on the identification of somatosensory cortical maps in adult monkeys before and after the surgical amputation of one finger. Before amputation, each finger was represented individually in the cortex (see Figure 1.3, top). However, a reassessment of the map a few months later following amputation of the third digit showed that the area of cortex originally given over to the third digit had disappeared (see Figure 1.3, bottom) and had been taken over by surrounding cortical areas.

This remarkable demonstration shows that the cortex is able to reorganise itself following alterations to sensory input. It is not the case that the region of the cortex initially given over to the third digit remained unused simply because it no longer received any input. Rather, it seems that the brain craves stimulation to such an extent that it is capable of restructuring itself in order to obtain it. Such findings suggest that it is unlikely that a large proportion of the brain simply remains dormant awaiting activation.

Furthermore, a plethora of research using a variety of brain imaging techniques shows that the vast majority of the brain does not lie dormant during the cortical processing of a particular stimulus. Although certain functions may utilise one region of the brain to a greater extent than another, complex tasks will invariably result in the activation of multiple cortical regions (see, e.g., Gazzaniga *et al.* 2002). Thus, there is no evidence that a large dormant section of the brain remains unused and is simply waiting to be stimulated in

Before amputation

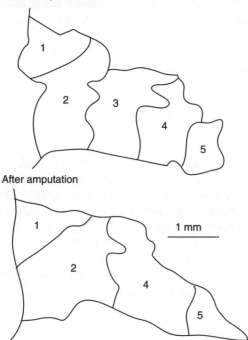

After amputation

1 mm

Figure 1.3 Maps of the somatosensory area of monkey cortex, showing the region devoted to the fingers of one hand before (top) and after (bottom) amputation of finger 3. Re-drawn from Merzenich *et al.* (1984) (with permission).

a particular manner, which will lead the individual to develop greater abilities and insights.

This doesn't mean, of course, that brain functioning cannot be altered. The research outlined above by Merzenich *et al.* (1984) shows that this is not the case. Nevertheless, enhancing performance doesn't simply translate into attempting to use *more* of the brain, but invariably means attempting to use it *more effectively*. As such, the myth that an individual uses only 10 per cent of her brain is at best a misguided interpretation of what is known about the brain and the way it works.

The desire to enhance performance

There could be any number of reasons why an individual adopts a particular approach or technique to enhance her performance. For example, she may be interested in acquiring a new skill or maintaining and improving a current skill or ability. As such, the decision to embrace a particular technique that purports to aid such enhanced development may be seen as a cost-effective approach that holds the possibility of producing rapid results. The results-oriented approach to business can also be seen to influence many different arenas encouraging individuals to work harder in an attempt to gain some form of advantage. In addition, there are the increasing pressures of working and living in a modern technological society where there is an implicit need to perform well and succeed. Individuals from all walks of life are under increasing pressure to gain an edge to their performance, whether it is improving memory or a golf handicap. Furthermore, there is the assumption that peak performance is associated with the ability to lead a happier and more fulfilled life (Csikszentmihalyi 1990).

Given this, it is unsurprising that people spend large sums of money on techniques purported to enhance performance. Natale (1988) estimated that in 1987 consumers within North America alone spent \$250 million on self-help tapes, self-instruction tapes and subliminal products. In contrast, Druckman and Swets (1988) estimated that approximately \$30 billion a year is spent in the US on training and development courses aimed at enhancing human performance. This would suggest that many people are highly motivated to improve some aspect of their behaviour and see the use of a particular technique as offering them the potential to achieve this – and they are willing to pay for it. It is therefore critical that the efficacy of such techniques is rigorously evaluated.

Evidence

The veracity of evidence used to support the various techniques represents a fundamental issue that serves as a recurring theme throughout the book. Of course, when examining any sort of evidence the key question soon becomes what information should be used as evidence and from where? When looking for evidence of an effect, one can obtain information from a number of sources. These can include testimonials, magazine articles, radio/media reports and/or scientific research published in peer-reviewed journals, to name a few.

Putting media reports to one side, as they invariably represent secondary sources, a clear distinction can be made between testimonials and scientific evidence. Testimonials remain a popular form of evidence, used with very good effect on the websites of many providers of various performance-enhancing techniques. They often represent a useful starting position when looking for answers to questions, but they should not be seen as the final answer. Testimonials have little if any scientific value and can oftentimes be rather ambiguous. The following example represents a testimonial used to support hypnopaedia:

Last night I used your CD and had the best night's sleep I've ever had.

It is unclear what the provider must have thought about such a claim, or why they deemed it supportive, given that the aim of sleep learning is to facilitate the learning of material presented *during* sleep, not learning how to sleep per se. Thus, while testimonials may encourage belief in a technique, they are inherently subjective, inaccurate, unreliable and biased. Even if testimonials provide compelling support for a particular technique, they may represent only a small proportion of the total sample and as such represent a self-selected bias. Furthermore, individuals who invest in a particular approach to enhancing performance may be highly motivated and actively desire a particular change. Any change in behaviour could therefore simply emerge from these motivational factors rather than the actual technique itself.

In contrast, scientific research adopts specific and agreed-upon methods to help develop and/or refine a particular theory, incorporating precise controls to limit the influence of possible confounding effects. The most dominant approach is the hypothetico-deductive approach, which involves the scientist/ researcher formulating a theory, which is then used to make a prediction and this prediction is then tested. If the results of the test support the theory, all well and good; if not, the theory is modified. An alternative is the inductive approach, which is often used as a precursor to the hypothetico-deductive approach as it begins with the collection of data. Once the data have been collected, information derived from them is used to formulate a theory that can then be tested using the hypothetico-deductive approach. Both approaches provide some clue as to the importance of a theory in the development of any idea. Without a clear theory an idea may lack structure, which in turn means that it is difficult to formulate any predictions. This can set up a negative feedback loop whereby the lack of a coherent theory results in few if any predictions being made, leading to a lack of explicit testing and, as a consequence, there is an absence of feedback to update or modify original ideas.

In addition, research assessing a particular performance-enhancing technique should compare a treatment group with a non-treatment control group to identify whether an effect is evident and ideally report the magnitude or size of the effect. The inclusion of a control group is essential to address issues of bias, as well as the *Hawthorne effect* (Landsberger 1958). The Hawthorne effect refers to the notion that participants taking part in an experiment may alter their responses simply because they are receiving the attention of an experimenter, or because they *believe* that the intervention will enhance their performance. One possible way of dealing with this is to conceal the nature of the study; another is to lead all participants to believe that their performance will be enhanced but to give the facilitating message/ technique only to some, providing a neutral message or technique to others. The often cited gold standard approach in terms of controls is the double-blind placebo controlled paradigm.

Once an effect has been established, it is also important to identify its magnitude. Reporting effect size is simply a way of quantifying the size of any difference found and can be used to help interpret the effectiveness of a particular technique. For example, a specific technique may elicit a difference when compared to controls but the size of that difference may be small. For instance, many people may try a technique that reportedly improves memory by 20 per cent, but few would give the same consideration to one that offered only a 2 per cent improvement. Thus, it is not simply about whether a particular technique elicits a difference when compared to controls but whether the magnitude of that difference is meaningful. Sadly, despite the American Psychological Association encouraging researchers to identify effect sizes, this method is not used widely (Wilkinson and APA Task Force 1999).

Thus, while the field of enhanced performance training may sag under the weight of an increasing number of glowing testimonials, the focus of the evidence provided in the following chapters is based on scientific research that incorporates some, if not all, of the above-mentioned components of research and has been published, where possible, in peer-reviewed journals.

The range of techniques

Any selection of techniques used to enhance human performance will inevitably include some methods and exclude others. Yet the selection was made with a particular rationale in mind, providing the reader with a balanced view of techniques across two dimensions (see Figure 1.4). The first dimension refers to a distinction that can be made between passive and active techniques. The second relates to the dimension of time, distinguishing between traditional and contemporary techniques.

Passive techniques are those that treat the individual as a passive recipient, subjected to a suggestion, message or stimulus that is assumed positively influence behaviour to. Traditional approaches include hypnosis, hypnopaedia and subliminal perception, with audio and visual entrainment providing a contemporary contribution. Techniques classified as active require the individual to adopt a more involved approach by learning how to focus their

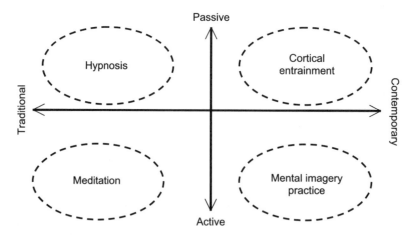

Figure 1.4 The two dimensions used to select specific techniques which include the distinction between passive and active approaches as well as between traditional and contemporary techniques.

attention in a particular way, or learn to become consciously aware of some aspect of their own physiology in an attempt to obtain some measure of control and enhance their performance. Traditional approaches include meditation, the use of mnemonics and speed-reading, with more recent contributions from the domain of biofeedback and mental imagery practice.

Selecting a sample of traditional and contemporary techniques from both passive and active domains provides the reader with a range of interesting and distinct approaches to enhancing performance. Some may be more familiar, and certainly more available, whilst others may offer new and novel insights into the realm of enhanced performance training.

Part I
Passive techniques

2   Hypnosis

The intimate nature of the hypnotic condition, when once induced, can hardly be said to be understood.

(William James 1890)

This chapter launches the exploration of passive techniques by focusing on the use of hypnosis. Hypnosis aims to enhance performance by encouraging the individual to relax whilst repeatedly providing positive or encouraging suggestions. The chapter begins by outlining what hypnosis is and provides a brief history of its development from mesmerism. This is followed by a summary of the hypnotic procedure, including the measurement of hypnotic susceptibility, the relaxation/induction stage and the suggestion stage. The chapter then covers the two main opposing theoretical perspectives of hypnosis encapsulated as non-state versus state approaches. Following this there is an examination of the evidence from various settings assessing whether hypnosis can enhance human performance. Finally, the chapter examines some of the factors known to influence the effectiveness of hypnosis.

What is hypnosis?

Although Hypnos represents the Greek god of sleep and the Greek word *hypnoun* refers to the process of putting one to sleep, researchers and clinicians alike agree that hypnosis does not actually mean putting a person to sleep. On the other hand, precisely what it does mean is a little more difficult to pin down. This may be a result of the different applications of hypnosis, with those in health-related fields identifying hypnosis as something distinct from those in the performance-enhancement arena. Nevertheless, there is continued debate surrounding precisely what hypnosis is, with some disputing its very existence, whilst others, particularly from the clinical domain, insist that it has therapeutic value.

Hilgard (1965), one of the pioneering researchers in hypnosis, has suggested that it is a process which involves the individual setting aside critical judgement whilst responding to suggestions from a hypnotist. Such a process may represent a distinct psychological state, which is induced by certain ritualistic procedures, during which the individual reduces his level of attention to external stimuli and, as a consequence of direct suggestions from the hypnotist, may experience changes in perception, memory and behaviour. Hypnosis is also thought to increase the level of cognitive flexibility of the individual, enabling him to see things in new and different ways and accept as possible things that he would not normally accept. Such behavioural changes have encouraged the popular belief that hypnosis represents a special state of consciousness in which the individual may be endowed with abilities to complete various mental and physical feats that would normally be difficult, if not impossible.

Whilst the debate continues as to what precisely hypnosis is, there is a common misconception that a hypnotised person gives up his free will and control as part of the hypnotic process and can easily be forced to carry out what he may normally consider to be abhorrent acts, or divulge personal information. Such a view is almost certainly the result of the unusual and often bizarre things that people are encouraged to do as part of a stage hypnotist's act, but there is no direct empirical evidence to support this idea.

From mesmerism to hypnotism

Hypnosis stems from work conducted by Franz Anton Mesmer, an Austrian physician, who put forward the idea of a universal fluid present in all living things that responded to magnetic vibrations. Mesmer proposed that illness was caused by an imbalance of these invisible magnetic fluids, which could be restored by gesturing with his hands, placing magnets over specific regions of the body and waving a wand at the source of the discomfort. Such claims raised certain sceptical concerns and, in 1784, a royal commission set up by Louis XVI investigated the concept of mesmerism and found that the cures were mainly the result of imagination on the part of the patient.

Later, in the early part of the nineteenth century, a surgeon by the name of James Esdaile attempted, with some degree of success, to use mesmerism to help relieve the pain of one of his patients during an operation (Gauld 1992). From then on, interest in hypnosis has waxed and waned, with contributions from a range of clinicians, including Freud. In 1933, Milton Erikson published a book on hypnosis, which many have argued provided the most scientific treatment of the topic at the time. This led to a resurgent interest in the use of hypnosis, particularly within clinical settings, which over time led to the setting up of various societies in Britain and America to oversee training and provide information on the topic.

Since then, the use of hypnosis has expanded beyond its original therapeutic domain into areas of peak performance. Today, there are a plethora of hypnotic recordings available on audiotape as well as in video format, and increasing numbers of practitioners who argue that hypnosis represents a powerful tool for personal development.

The hypnotic procedure

Many hypnotists follow a similar hypnotic procedure, which goes through a number of stages. First, the participant is screened to identify his level of hypnotic susceptibility. This is followed by the hypnotic relaxation or induction stage, which gives way to specific suggestions or instructions relating to performance.

Hypnotic susceptibility

The rationale for measuring hypnotic susceptibility is that this will let the hypnotist know how well, or not, he can expect the participant to respond to the suggestions made. Table 2.1 lists a range of tasks that the individual may be asked to carry out during hypnosis to assess their level of susceptibility.

For example, the first task of hand lowering involves asking the hypnotised participant to hold their arm out straight in front of them. They are then told that their arm is becoming heavier and heavier, and that it is taking more and more effort to hold it up. Suggestions to lower the heavy arm are then given and if the participant complies with these he scores a 'yes' for that task. The hypnotist then proceeds through the various tasks, scoring the participant's response to each. The more often the participant responds positively to each of the suggestions, the higher their hypnotic susceptibility. Those with scores in the top quartile represent highly susceptible individuals and those with scores in the lower quartile are classified as low-susceptibles.

Table 2.1 A summary of the Stanford Hypnotic Susceptibility Scale showing tasks carried out during hypnosis to identify level of hypnotic susceptibility

Item	Task	Response
1	Hand lowering	Yes/No
2	Hands moving apart	Yes/No
3	Mosquito hallucination	Yes/No
4	Taste hallucination	Yes/No
5	Arm rigidity	Yes/No
6	Dream	Yes/No
7	Age regression	Yes/No
8	Arm immobilisation	Yes/No
9	Anosmia	Yes/No
10	Auditory hallucination	Yes/No
11	Negative visual illusion	Yes/No
12	Posthypnotic amnesia	Yes/No
	Total score: _____	

Adapted from Stanford Hypnotic Susceptibility Scale (Weitzenhoffer and Hilgard 1962)

Relaxation/induction stage

Most people are familiar with the media image of a hypnotist gently swinging a watch on the end of a chain in front of a recumbent person while issuing instructions to 'look at the watch' and 'feel sleepy'. However, it is much more likely that a person undergoing hypnosis will be asked to stare at a spot on a wall or ceiling and, after a period of time, be encouraged to simply close his eyes and relax. This said, there is no clear consensus on what the requirements are for an induction procedure to produce an effective level of hypnosis. Nevertheless, the broad consensus is that the induction encourages the individual to achieve an intensely focused state of consciousness. In this way, the procedure is designed to heighten the readiness of the individual to follow suggestions given by the hypnotist.

The induction procedure itself may incorporate the use of detailed suggestions as well as the use of imagery to encourage the individual to reduce his level of reality testing. Reality testing refers to the natural process that involves an individual comparing his internal perceptions and beliefs with information from the world outside to see whether they match or not. A good example of reduced reality testing can be seen when someone is deeply involved in playing a video-game, particularly one that involves driving a car. Such a player, it is possible to notice, tends to lean to one side when driving their 'virtual car' around a corner at high speed. It is unlikely that such physical movements aid their performance but the point is that they do this because, at that moment in time, the 'reality' of the virtual world of the game seems more real to them than their surroundings. Thus, by encouraging the participant to reduce their level of reality testing, the hypnotist hopes he will become absorbed by the positive suggestions made.

Suggestion stage

Once the induction stage is complete, the participant is guided by the hypnotist to respond to a range of suggestions encouraging him to experience changes in subjective experience, perception, emotion and/or behaviour. The specific suggestions vary according to the goals of the procedure and may include the idea of enhanced memory or improving a specific skill. Such suggestions can also be linked to a 'trigger' provided during the hypnotic process.

Triggers can be words, sounds or images, or a natural part of the routine of the individual, which, when encountered, will trigger a response usually obtained during the hypnotic procedure. For example, a trigger which represents a normal part of the routine may be holding a golf club for a golf player, holding the ball for a basketball player or holding a pen for a student. Thus, a golfer may be given the suggestion that when he next grips his golf club he will feel completely relaxed and perform his best ever shot. In this way, the positive feelings of relaxation experienced as part of the hypnotic process can be linked to events outside the hypnotic procedure.

Theoretical perspectives on hypnosis

Many of the theories of hypnosis revolve around the issue of whether it represents a distinct state of consciousness or not. For the sake of convenience, these have been divided into *non-state* and *state* approaches (see Figure 2.1).

The non-state approach

The idea here is that hypnosis does not reflect an altered state of consciousness but is more readily explicable in terms of attitudes to authority figures, and a combination of beliefs and motivation to comply (Wagstaff 1991). In other words, the hypnotised person is simply following the instructions of the hypnotist because this is what is expected of them.

According to Wagstaff (ibid.), the behaviour of hypnotised individuals goes through three main stages. First, the hypnotised person makes assumptions about what is expected. Second, he adopts a number of strategies to ensure his behaviour falls into line with these expectations. Finally, if such a compliant approach proves ineffective, he may simply fake the experience. Wagstaff suggests that experiments that utilise a 'real–simulator' method, in which hypnotised individuals are compared to a non-hypnotised group who are told to *pretend* to be hypnotised, find that both groups report similar experiences and exhibit similar behavioural responses. For example, Spanos (1992) found that during a hypnotic procedure that encouraged participants

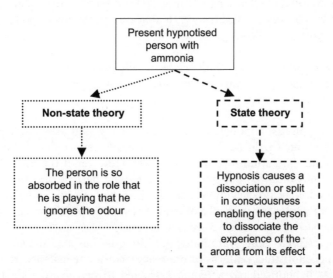

Figure 2.1 Theoretical approaches to hypnosis. If a person under hypnosis receives the instruction that he will be unable to smell anything, what happens if he is then presented with ammonia? Both non-state and state approaches offer possible solutions.

to fail to see a visually presented number, many reported not being able to see it. However, when they were then told that truly hypnotisable individuals would be able to see the number, albeit briefly at the onset, a large proportion altered their responses to indicate that they could now see it. These findings have led to the argument that motivation to comply with the suggestions of the hypnotist is a major factor in responsiveness.

The hypnotic state

State theorists believe that hypnosis represents an *altered state of conscious-ness*. However, the precise definition of what constitutes an altered state is itself a matter of debate. One of the most prominent advocates of this view is Ernest Hilgard (1992), who put forward a neo-dissociation theory of hyp-nosis. This theory suggests that hypnosis is best characterised by a change in the normal cognitive processes of memory, attention and perception in such a way that these processes become dissociated from a centralised control (see Figure 2.1).

According to Hilgard (ibid.), evidence for this proposal can be seen in the *hidden observer phenomenon*. This is when the experiences of one part of the hypnotised person's mind differ from the rest of his mind. An example of this can be seen when a hypnotised person is given the 'cold pressor' test, which involves him keeping his hand submerged in ice-cold water for as long as possible. In general, a non-hypnotised person can maintain this for about 25 seconds. In contrast, a hypnotised person, once given the suggestion that they will no longer feel any pain, can keep their hand in the water for about 40 seconds. The key point, however, is that during the hypnotic process the hypnotist gives the following instruction:

> *When I give you a cue I shall be able to talk to a hidden part of you that is aware of any physiological/behavioural changes that the part I'm now talking to is unaware of.*

When the hypnotist conducts the cold pressor test and asks the hypnotised person how much pain he feels, he will typically report significantly lower levels of pain than a non-hypnotised person. However, if the hypnotist then gives the individual the cue and asks the hidden part of him that is aware of any physiological/behavioural changes how he feels, the individual often reports a very intense experience of pain. Thus, the hypnotic process seems to divide the participant's sense of consciousness.

Recent research using brain imaging techniques has also shown that hyp-nosis can elicit distinct patterns of brain activity. In one instance, researchers found that hypnotised participants instructed to perceive colour, irrespec-tive of whether they were shown coloured or grey scale stimuli, exhibited greater levels of activity in the colour processing areas of the brain (Kosslyn *et al.* 2000). Interestingly, such areas showed a decrease in activation when participants were hypnotised and told to see grey scale images, irrespective of whether the stimulus was grey or coloured. In contrast, when participants who were not hypnotised were instructed to perceive colour, there was no effect on the level of brain activity. These findings suggest that the alterations in subjective experience brought about by hypnosis are associated with changes in the brain, providing convincing evidence that hypnosis represents a distinct state of consciousness.

Although there is little doubt that social influences and expectations play a role in hypnosis, the evidence also shows that hypnosis can produce distinct changes in the level and region of activation of an individual's brain. However, Kihlstrom and McConkey (1990) maintain that it is possible to see such views as complementary rather than competing. They, along with an increasing number of others, are now attempting to move beyond a *non-state* versus *state* debate and adopt a multi-level approach which incorporates socio-cultural, psychological and biological influences in an attempt to provide a more comprehensive understanding of the nature of hypnosis (see Figure 2.2).

Enhancing performance using hypnosis

Over the years hypnosis has been used in a wide variety of applications. These include health and therapeutic settings as well, with victims and witnesses of crime. Here, however, the focus will be on its use to enhance performance. Its alleged benefits for enhancing performance include improved memory recall, enhanced academic ability, improved motor speed and coordination, and enhanced sporting skills. This section examines the evidence from each of these areas in turn.

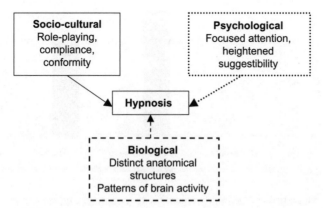

Figure 2.2 Multi-level approach to hypnosis, incorporating socio-cultural, psychological and biological influences.

Hypermnesia

Hypermnesia refers to the facilitation of memory as a result of hypnotic suggestion and is based on the view that hypnosis facilitates recall in therapeutic settings, where it has been used to help patients come to terms with experiences they may otherwise be unable to remember consciously (see, e.g., Spiegel and Spiegel 1987). Such findings led others to suggest that hypnosis may be used to enhance normal everyday memory processing. However, the research in this area has produced mixed results.

White *et al.* (1940) found that hypnosis aided recall for meaningful material but not for meaningless nonsense material (see Figure 2.3).

They compared recall of nonsense paired associates (e.g. PQS paired with TXB), a selection of verse and some visual scenes across two groups. Following the encoding of the material, participants from one group underwent a hypnotic induction procedure, which involved suggestions for enhancing memory recall. They found that participants in the hypnosis group recalled more information than those in the non-hypnotic control group, but only for poetry and visual scenes. Such a pattern was thought to be due to the individual's ability to process the information, with meaningful material being processed more comprehensively than nonsense material.

Such findings imply that hypnosis can produce hypermnesia for material that is processed in a deep and meaningful way. Shields and Knox (1986) tested this idea by presenting lists of words to three groups of participants and requiring them to process the words in either a deep or shallow fashion. Deep processing involved semantically categorising each of the words, while shallow processing required participants to identify whether each word contained a specific letter. Each group then received different instructions. One group was played a hypnotic tape with suggestions to encourage hypermnesia, another was given a relaxation tape and asked to simulate

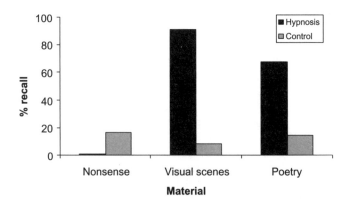

Figure 2.3 Mean percentage improvement for three different types of material following hypnosis.

(Adapted from White, Fox and Harris 1940)

hypnosis, and the final group was simply played a relaxation tape (see Figure 2.4).

They found that all groups recalled more words when they were processed deeply and that this difference was much greater for those who had received the hypnotic suggestion of hypermnesia. This led them to conclude that the 'depth of processing is critical in determining whether hypnotic hypermnesia can take place' (p. 363).

Others have suggested that highly susceptible people may be more prone to exhibit hypermnesia following hypnosis (Crawford and Allen 1996; Dhanes and Lundy 1975). For instance, Dhanes and Lundy (1975) found that only highly susceptible participants who had received a hypnotic induction exhibited an improvement in memory recall (see Figure 2.5).

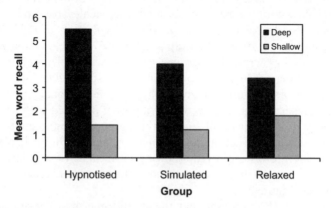

Figure 2.4 Mean word recall as a function of level of processing, for hypnotised, simulated and relaxed groups.

(Adapted from Shields and Knox 1986)

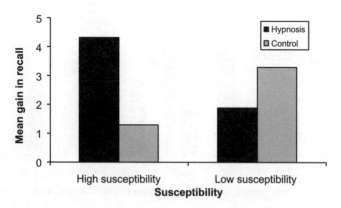

Figure 2.5 The average gain in recall for high and low hypnotically susceptible participants within hypnosis and control groups.

(Adapted from Dhanes and Lundy 1975)

Crawford and Allen (1996) suggested that the reason highly susceptible individuals are capable of exhibiting hypermnesia is because they have a greater level of cognitive flexibility and are able to alter the way in which they process information. This is based on the idea that, when attempting to complete a specific task, an individual will have recourse to various different possible strategies and that the greater the number of strategies available, the greater the possibility of correctly completing the task. Crawford and Allen (ibid.) argue that hypnosis enables an individual to shift his cognitive processing strategies from a predominantly verbal, detail-oriented approach, to a more visual holistic approach, which increases the number of possible strategies available facilitating the completion of the task at hand.

However, despite such findings, the effects of hypnosis on memory are far from consistent. Many researchers have shown that hypnotic procedures do not reliably improve memory beyond that achievable under normal non-hypnotic conditions (Dinges *et al.* 1992; Nogrady *et al.* 1985; Sheehan 1988; Wagstaff *et al.* 2004). Nogrady *et al.* (1985) compared the recall of simple line drawings across three groups, each receiving different instructions, with equal numbers of high and low hypnotically susceptible participants in each group. The first group were given a hypnotic induction, containing suggestions for hypermnesia. The second group were provided with an imagination strategy to aid their recall and the third group, acting as controls, were given no particular instructions as to what strategy to adopt. Performance across all three groups improved, showing clear signs of a practice effect. However, there was no difference in the amount of material recalled between the groups (see Figure 2.6).

Nogrady *et al.* (1985) admit that the stimuli may have lacked meaning, thereby reducing the possible enhancing effects of hypnosis. Nevertheless, neither hypnosis nor the use of imagination produced any benefits in terms of improved recall.

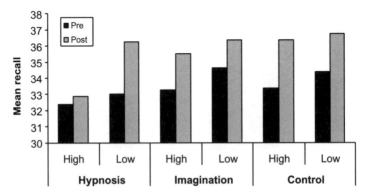

Figure 2.6 Mean recall for high and low hypnotically susceptible participants from each of the three groups before and after their specific intervention.

(Adapted from Nogrady *et al.* 1985)

Others found that, whilst hypnosis may lead to an increase in the amount of information recalled, such information is predominantly inaccurate (Dywan 1988; Dywan and Bowers 1983). For example, Dywan and Bowers (1983) gave two groups a set of pictures to learn and recall. One of the groups received a hypnotic induction to help them improve their memory, whilst the other received no such induction. They found that those in the hypnosis group recalled over twice as many items as those in the task-motivated control group. However, the majority of these items were incorrect (see Figure 2.7).

Thus, hypnosis elicited only a small increase in accurate recall but a three-fold increase in incorrectly recalled information. Dywan and Bowers (ibid.) suggested that the hypnotic induction altered participants' criterion for reporting accurate memories, making them less cautious in what they were likely to report as accurate memories. Such a shift may be the result of demand characteristics, social cues or changes in expectation as a result of the hypnotic induction. This is consistent with the view put forward by Register and Khilstrom (1987), who proposed that the effects of hypnosis interact with the specific requirements of the task. They suggest that when hypnotised participants are actively encouraged to guess or produce a set number of responses, this leads to greater levels of recall, but at a large cost to the accuracy of the material recalled. In contrast, when allowed to freely recall as much of the material as possible, little or no effect can be seen concerning the hypnotic induction. Thus, what hypnosis appears to do is to increase the level of incorrect material produced. Such findings led Register and Khilstrom (ibid.) to conclude that, 'hypnosis is an unreliable technique for enhancing memory' (p. 166).

Indeed, it has been shown that not only does hypnosis lead to the production of more errors but also that participants often exhibit a high level of misplaced confidence in the accuracy of such errors (Nogrady *et al.* 1985; Whitehouse

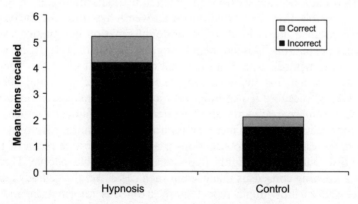

Figure 2.7 The average number of correctly and incorrectly recalled items for the hypnosis group compared to the control group.

(Adapted from Dywan and Bowers 1983)

et al. 1988). For instance, Nogrady *et al.* (1985) reported that, when asked to note how confident they were in their responses, participants who underwent a hypnotic induction to facilitate memory reported high levels of confidence for incorrect items that they rated as correct. Thus, it seems that hypnosis encourages a false sense of accuracy in the information recalled. This may be because hypnosis engenders a degree of confusion between real and imagined memories, or leads to an adjustment in the individual's report criterion. A *report criterion* represents the level at which an individual would normally recall information with confidence in its accuracy. If hypnosis leads the individual to relax his report criterion, thereby allowing him to report information he would not normally provide, this may lead to the confident reporting of one or more accurate guesses. It could also account for the increase in confidence seen when hypnotised individuals produce errors.

Dinges *et al.* (1992) examined the effect of hypnotic suggestions on memory recall using a forced-recall procedure in an attempt to control for possible changes in report criteria. A forced-recall procedure requires the participant to recall a set number of items, usually the same as the number of items encoded, and well above what would be expected using free recall. Testing the recall of low and high hypnotically susceptible participants, they found improved accuracy of recall for both groups, suggesting a practice effect, but there was no evidence that hypnosis contributed to this effect. In addition, they found that highly hypnotisable participants were more confident when rating their errors as correct.

A further attempt was made by Dinges *et al.* (ibid.) to examine whether hypnosis could facilitate recall once an individual had been given ample opportunity to recall information consciously. The rationale behind such an approach is that, once an individual has reached a ceiling level in terms of the amount of information recalled, if hypnosis can facilitate memory then simply by using such a technique he should be able to recall more information. However, following six trials in which individuals attempted to recall as much as possible, they found that during a seventh hypnotic trial participants not only 'recalled' lower levels of accurate information but greater levels of incorrect information. This led them to suggest that there is clearly no advantage in using hypnosis to aid in the recall of correct information. They also voice the concern that hypnosis may in fact have a detrimental effect on memory recall because it not only produces a large increase in errors, but highly susceptible participants report greater levels of confidence in such errors.

In general, it seems that memory improvements resulting from hypnosis are more or less confined to situations that require the free recall of highly meaningful material for highly hypnotically susceptible people. However, there is a growing consensus that even in such cases overall accuracy may not be increased as individuals report more erroneous information and their confidence in both accurate and inaccurate information increases. Thus, the evidence for hypnotic hypermnesia is at best equivocal.

Academic performance

Hypnotic training programmes have also been used to help improve students' academic performance. For instance, De Vos and Louw (2006) used hypnotic training to improve student learning. This involved placing participants into four different groups, with two receiving hypnosis, the third exposed to a relaxation intervention, and the fourth acting as non-contingent controls. Participants' average academic grades were noted before and after the intervention, and De Vos and Louw found that the students in the hypnosis groups exhibited higher academic grades following the training than either the relaxation-only group or the non-contingent control group (see Figure 2.8).

These findings led them to suggest that mental training regimes based on hypnosis have the potential to enhance the academic performance of students. Such programmes are thought to contribute towards student learning by encouraging a more focused attention span combined with an improved ability to concentrate.

Whilst the results are encouraging, there remains the difficulty of identifying precisely which component of the training procedure elicited the enhanced academic performance. This is because the hypnosis training programmes also contained other elements thought to benefit learning, including imagery and relaxation. A methodology that combines distinct components to ascertain their effect on learning is highly problematic as it remains extremely difficult, if not impossible, to pin down with any degree of certainty precisely which component produced the effect. A clearer methodology needs to be adopted which separates out the various components to ascertain the effect each component has on performance. Once this has been accomplished, the

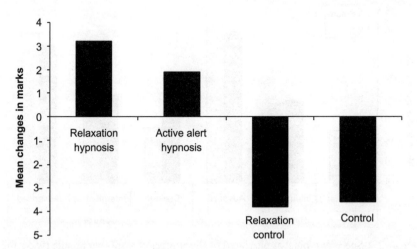

Figure 2.8 Mean changes to exam scores following hypnosis and relaxation interventions.

(Adapted from De Vos and Louw 2006)

various components can then be re-combined in a step-by-step manner to identify whether a combined approach is more effective.

Motor performance

Outside sport, the use of hypnosis to enhance motor performance has produced some mixed results. For example, post-hypnotic suggestions for enhancing vigilance given to pilots from the Royal New Zealand Air Force found that such suggestions led to significant reductions in error correction times when the pilots made in-flight manoeuvres (Barabasz 1985).

Others, however, have reported less success when using hypnosis to enhance motor performance. For instance, Jacobs and Salzberg (1987) examined whether hypnotic suggestions for improving motor performance could enhance the typing speed of individuals classified as beginner, intermediate or advanced typists. Half the participants from each typing group received hypnotic instructions to facilitate their typing speed, whilst the remaining half received motivating instructions without hypnosis. As would be expected, performance corresponded closely to skill levels, with advanced typists producing more words per minute than intermediates and beginners. However, neither the hypnotic suggestions nor the motivating instructions given to the control group had any positive effect on speed of typing (see Figure 2.9).

In fact, both the beginners and intermediates produced fewer words following the intervention. Such findings cast doubt on the effectiveness of hypnosis to enhance motor performance. Jacobs and Salzberg (ibid.) point out that much of the supporting evidence suggesting that hypnosis benefits motor

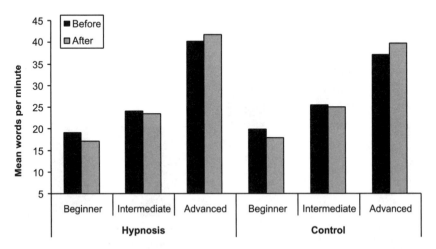

Figure 2.9 Speed of typing, as measured by the number of words per minute typed, for those classified as beginner, intermediate and advanced, receiving either hypnotic or control instructions.

(Adapted from Jacobs and Salzberg 1987)

performance is based on anecdotal reports and that such reports are often based on individuals specifically requesting hypnosis. They suggest that such individuals are likely to be highly motivated to change their behaviour and improve performance, unlike those taking part in an experiment. As such, it may be possible that an individual's level of motivation represents a mediating factor in terms of the effectiveness of hypnosis. To some extent this may account for the positive effects reported by Barabasz (1985), as air force pilots would be expected to exhibit high levels of motivation to improve their performance. However, this is a speculative possibility that remains as yet untested.

Sport

Hypnosis is widely used in sport to encourage athletes to remain physically calm and mentally relaxed, both characteristics of peak performance. More specifically, it has been used to induce behaviours and emotions that are consistent with optimal performance. This may include the rehearsal of visual motor actions, as well as attempts to reduce the negative impact of analytical thinking – what is often termed 'paralysis by analysis'.

Hypnosis has been suggested to enhance performance in a range of sports, including, *inter alia*, the shooting performance of basketball players (Pates *et al.* 2002; Schreiber 1991), archery skill (Robazza and Bortoli 1994) and golf putting scores (Pates *et al.* 2001). However, many of the studies exhibit methodological flaws that restrict the interpretation of their findings.

Pates *et al.* (2002) proposed that hypnosis can help athletes relax and re-live previous optimal experiences, allowing them to bring their peak performance state under volitional control. They tested this idea by examining the effect of hypnosis on the shooting performance of five basketball players. This involved establishing an initial baseline level of performance for each participant, followed by a hypnotic induction that focused on encouraging participants to learn how to relax and re-live a previous best performance, which was then associated with a trigger, such as the ball. This hypnotic procedure was repeated over a number of days using a taped recording, after which participants once again practised shooting basketballs. Pates *et al.* (ibid.) found that, following the hypnotic induction, participants showed a significant improvement in the accuracy of their shooting performance (see Figure 2.10).

Whilst it is clear from Figure 2.10 that all five participants showed an improvement in the accuracy of their basketball shooting, it is not clear that this improvement is the result of hypnosis. The lack of a control group would suggest that such a pattern of results can more easily be accounted for in terms of a simple practice effect.

Schreiber (1991) also attempted to show that hypnosis can enhance the shooting performance of basketball players and had the foresight to include a control group as part of his approach. Shooting performance for each of the participants was monitored across a number of games and compared to each

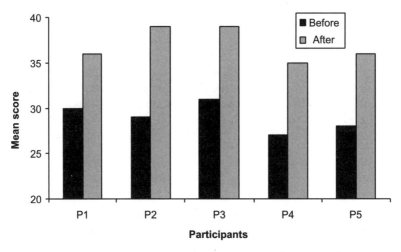

Figure 2.10 Mean basketball-shooting scores before and after hypnosis.
(Adapted from Pates *et al.* 2002)

athlete's performance during the previous season, resulting in their being identified as either low, middle or high scorers. Schreiber found that the hypnosis group produced more high and intermediate scorers compared to the control group (see Figure 2.11).

The pattern of results seen in Figure 2.11 is encouraging. However, given that there were more participants in the hypnosis group (N = 14) compared to the control group (N = 10), such a distinct distribution is in no way conclusive of a hypnotic effect. Schreiber (ibid.) does indicate that those within the hypnotic group showed higher cumulative scores relative to those in the control group, but no analysis was provided to support this testimony.

Similar problems plague the findings of Pates *et al.* (2001), who suggest that hypnosis can improve golf putting performance. They examined the effect of hypnosis on golf putting performance by initially establishing a baseline of performance for five participants and then providing a typical hypnotic induction to help them relax and recall previous best performances. Following hypnosis, they found that across a number of repeated trials the accuracy of the participant's golf putting improved (see Figure 2.12).

Although these findings led them to suggest that hypnosis can improve the accuracy of golf putting, once again the lack of any apparent controls leaves open an alternative explanation in terms of a simple practice effect.

Overall, whilst the results from studies examining the effect of hypnosis on sporting performance are suggestive, due to various methodological problems they are by no means conclusive. In particular, there is a lack of stringent controls. Furthermore, as many of the participants in such studies are not blind to the outcome of the study, any changes in performance may also be the result of participant bias, as demand characteristics could influence

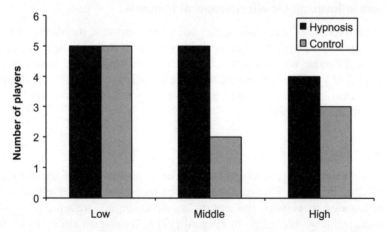

Figure 2.11 Number of players identified as low, middle or high scorers from the hypnosis and control groups.

(Adapted from Schreiber 1991)

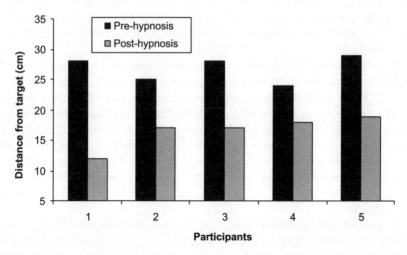

Figure 2.12 Mean distance from target of a putted golf ball before and after hypnosis.

(Adapted from Pates *et al.* 2001)

motivational levels. Many participants also completed multiple post-hypnotic induction test trials which do more to illustrate the effects of practice than the potential benefits of hypnosis. For any enhancing effect to be linked to hypnosis per se, a control group would need to complete a similar relaxation procedure, recall positive memories but not be given any hypnotic trigger. Then a comparison between the two groups would help to elucidate the potential impact of hypnosis on sport. So far, however, no study of this form has yet been conducted.

Factors influencing the effectiveness of hypnosis

The effectiveness of hypnosis seems contingent upon a number of factors and, as such, it is worth briefly examining some of the more salient of these to try to understand what, if any, effect they have. One of the most obvious is the level of hypnotic susceptibility of the participant. Other factors include the hypnotic induction procedure itself, the specific task and the level of arousal of the individual.

Hypnotic susceptibility

Hypnotic susceptibility refers to the level of responsiveness of the individual undergoing hypnosis. This can be measured using one of a variety of standardised scales to classify the person as either highly susceptible or of a low susceptibility. According to Hilgard (1979), a person's ability to become hypnotised develops with age, peaking at around 16 years and then remains fairly constant. The population distribution between high and low is reasonably normative, with approximately 10 per cent of the population exhibiting behavioural symptoms associated with levels of high hypnotisability, a further 10 per cent failing to show any response to hypnosis and the remaining 80 per cent falling somewhere in between these two extremes (Shor and Orne 1962).

Despite some popular beliefs to the contrary, hypnotisability is not correlated with personality traits such as suggestibility, hysterical character or intelligence (Hilgard 1979). There are, however, a number of factors that do appear to dispose an individual towards higher levels of hypnotisability. For example, both vividness of imagery ability and absorption are related to hypnotisability, so that those with poor imagery tend to exhibit low levels of hypnotisability (ibid.), whereas those who score high on absorption are more hypnotisable (Tellegen and Atkinson 1974). Absorption refers to the ability to become deeply involved in an experience with a low level of distractibility.

Consistent with what one would expect, hypnotic suggestions often produce a differential effect on those classified as highly susceptible compared to low susceptibles (Crawford and Allen 1983, 1996; Dinges *et al.* 1992; Nogrady *et al.* 1985). Thus, it would seem essential that research attempting to clarify the nature and effects of hypnosis needs to measure and identify the susceptibility levels of those taking part.

The hypnotic induction

There are a range of aspects within the hypnotic induction procedure that could potentially influence the effectiveness of the outcome. However, there is little research that has focused directly on such issues.

One seemingly obvious point would be the length of the hypnotic induction and the amount of hypnotic practice. A short induction may provide little opportunity to engage fully with the hypnotic suggestions, whilst a longer induction may produce more robust effects. Nogrady *et al.* (1985), for example, incorporated a 15-minute induction procedure and found that this had no effect on visual recall. Others reporting more positive effects have utilised induction procedures that comprise sessions lasting from 40 minutes per day over a period of seven days (Pates *et al.* 2001) to a one-hour session each week for a period of eight weeks (De Vos and Louw 2006).

Beyond the length of the induction session, simply using the term *hypnosis* can alter the effects. For example, Ghandi and Oakley (2005) found that hypnosis produced less of an effect when it was described as relaxation. They performed a standard induction on two groups of participants. One group were told that their suggestibility was going to be tested whilst in hypnosis; the other group were told that their suggestibility was going to be tested whilst being relaxed. Apart from their use of the key words 'hypnosis' and 'relaxed', the inductions remained identical. Before and after the induction process participants performed a range of standard suggestibility tests and Ghandi and Oakley found that those given the hypnotic induction showed greater compliance to suggestions than participants told it was simply a relaxation procedure. Thus, some of the effect may be dependent on the label 'hypnosis'. Indeed, Ghandi and Oakley go so far as to suggest that the label used to describe the induction process is the *most* significant component.

Related to this is the type of information made available concerning hypnosis and its effects on those participating in hypnotic studies. For example, there is a widespread belief that hypnosis has the ability to enhance memory, which may encourage those participating in hypermnesia studies to misinterpret thoughts and fantasies as possible memories. This could account for the increase seen in errors and the misguided levels of confidence participants report in them. If so, informing participants prior to the induction that hypnosis can lead to an increase in false recall may lead them to be more cautious and stem the flow of such inaccurate memories. This is precisely what Burgess and Kirsch (1999) did, when they compared the effects of hypnosis on the memory performance of two groups to that of a third non-hypnosis control group. Crucially, one of the hypnosis groups was told that hypnosis enhances memory, whilst the other was warned that hypnosis can lead to false recall. They found that those told that hypnosis improves memory produced more inaccurate information than controls, whilst those given the warning did not. These results are consistent with the idea that hypnosis is strongly influenced by participant expectation and as such it would seem prudent to ascertain participants' level of understanding regarding hypnosis and its effects prior to the induction process.

The timing of the hypnotic induction may also be an important factor in eliciting an effect. For example, if a person completes a hypnotic induction which includes suggestions that he will perform better on a task, and then immediately completes the task, performance may be enhanced. However, if, as is the case with many of the memory tasks, the individual is required to encode the information and only after this undergo a hypnotic induction to improve his recall, its effects may be less than if he were to receive the induction prior to the encoding episode.

Finally, the particular type of suggestions offered during the induction process may also influence the outcome. For example, relaxation hypnosis, which involves suggestions of calming restfulness, is thought to encourage participants to feel more relaxed and sleepy, producing low levels of activity. Active-alert hypnosis, in contrast, invariably involves providing suggestions of alertness and energy to encourage a heightened attention span, along with feelings of excitement. Liebert *et al.* (1965) found that participants undergoing an active-alert hypnotic induction were more accurate when learning nonsensical word associations than participants receiving relaxation hypnosis. In contrast, De Vos and Louw (2006) found no difference in the efficacy of these two hypnotic approaches when examining academic performance. The different pattern of findings from the two studies may to some extent be due to the type of tasks used. Nevertheless, the specific nature of the suggestions used should be monitored and reported to ascertain whether they do interact with the outcome or not.

Task

It may seem obvious that the effectiveness of hypnosis on enhancing performance may in part be due to the nature of the task, yet there is very little research that directly addresses this issue. A number of researchers have shown that hypnotic suggestions to improve memory recall only produce a beneficial effect when the task involves recalling meaningful information (DePiano and Salzberg 1981; Shields and Knox 1986). It is possible that all tasks deemed to have meaning would exhibit beneficial effects from an intervention using hypnosis, with those tasks identified as showing more meaning eliciting greater effects than less meaningful tasks. Such possibilities are speculative and would need to provide some sort of criterion for assigning meaning to a task in order to denote which tasks are meaningful and which are not.

Arousal level

The level of arousal experienced by the person undergoing hypnosis may also influence the outcome. Early suggestions by Rosenthal (1944) were that material which elicits high levels of emotional arousal during the hypnotic process may facilitate learning because this helps to stimulate the individual. However, a more recent examination of the effect of distinct levels of arousal on hypnotically induced hypermnesia found greater levels of recall for material associated with low levels of arousal (DePiano and Salzberg 1981).

DePiano and Salzberg (ibid.) manipulated participants' levels of arousal by showing films of varying emotional content containing traumatic, sexual or low-arousal images. They found that the various film clips were able to induce changes in level of arousal, with those exposed to the low-arousal clips showing low physiological arousal and low measures of self-reported arousal compared to those viewing the traumatic film clip. In addition, they found that the level of recall was higher in the low-arousal condition and decreased as the level of arousal increased (see Figure 2.13).

This would suggest that hypnotic induction procedures encouraging low levels of arousal may be more successful in eliciting a positive outcome.

Overview

Hypnosis as a technique has its roots in mesmerism but it wasn't until the early part of the nineteenth century that it began to be taken more seriously by clinicians, which in turn led to the development of various societies promoting and organising training in hypnosis both as a clinical intervention and, more recently, to enhance the performance of healthy individuals. Despite the lack of consensus regarding what hypnosis is, many would agree that it involves the individual setting aside his critical judgement and becoming absorbed by the hypnotic suggestions. Such absorption may bring about a greater degree of cognitive flexibility, but it doesn't mean giving up one's free will.

The hypnotic process is invariably a three-stage procedure, beginning with an assessment of the hypnotic susceptibility of the individual. This can be achieved by using one of a variety of standardised scales and results in a classification of either high or low susceptibility. This is followed by the induction process, which often, although not always, includes suggestions to

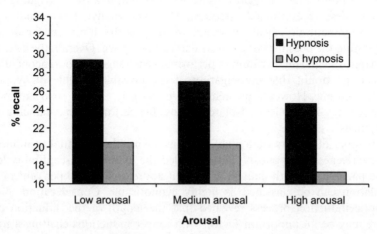

Figure 2.13 Mean recall under low, medium and high arousal conditions for hypnosis and control groups.

(Adapted from DePiano and Salzberg 1981)

relax, encouraging a focused and dissociated state of consciousness. The final stage is the suggestion stage, with the hypnotist making specific suggestions regarding particular aspects of behaviour.

Theoretical accounts of hypnosis have traditionally been divided into either a non-state or a state approach. The non-state approach maintains that hypnosis is not an altered state of consciousness but relies more on individual belief and a motivation to comply with the suggestions of authority figures. In contrast, the state approach maintains that hypnosis represents a state that is distinct from everyday waking consciousness. Certainly the evidence from brain imaging studies showing distinct patterns of cortical activity associated with hypnosis would concur with state theory in suggesting that it produces an altered state of consciousness. However, few would contend with the view that social and motivational factors can also play a part in the outcome. Thus, it may be that a more comprehensive account lies with the multi-level approach, which attempts to incorporate both non-state and state views to produce a more detailed understanding of hypnosis.

In terms of the use of hypnosis to enhance performance, the results are often mixed and ambiguous. Hypnotic hypermnesia, for example, may occur for deeply processed meaningful material encoded by highly susceptible participants, but at the same time it produces a worrying increase in the number of errors reported, which often carry an alarmingly high level of false confidence. With regard to academic performance, there is only limited evidence to suggest that schemes incorporating the use of hypnosis benefit student learning. However, due to such schemes adopting a multi-technique approach, it remains unclear precisely what, if any, role hypnosis *alone* plays in this. The evidence from motor tasks suggests that hypnosis is of little benefit and may in fact impair performance due to relaxation-based suggestions slowing down motor responses. With regard to sport, the findings are intriguing and certainly deserve continued attention. However, many of the studies are plagued by methodological weaknesses restricting the interpretation of data and limiting the possible conclusions that can be drawn. Overall, the evidence that hypnosis can enhance human performance is suggestive but inconclusive. There is no doubt that investigation of the possible benefits of hypnosis should continue. However, as mentioned previously, a more stringent methodology is needed to clearly isolate the possible performance-enhancing role of hypnosis.

A number of factors were highlighted as having the potential to influence the effectiveness of hypnosis. This included the hypnotic susceptibility level of the participant, with data showing that approximately 10 per cent of the population can be classified as highly hypnotisable. Consideration of the hypnotic induction process revealed that the length of the induction procedure may be an important factor, with longer inductions eliciting a more robust effect on behaviour. In addition, it was shown that simply using the term 'hypnosis' can lead to greater levels of compliance in participants than when the word 'relaxation' is used. Furthermore, warning participants of the possible effect that hypnosis may have on producing false memories was found to mitigate this, showing how information provided as part of the induction process could influence its outcome. Examination of the type of task which may benefit from hypnosis led to some speculative suggestions that meaningful tasks and tasks containing meaningful material would benefit more from such training. Finally, the influence of hypnosis was shown to interact with the level of individual arousal, with low levels of arousal associated with greater benefits.

3 Sleep learning

To achieve the impossible dream, try going to sleep.

(Joan Klempner)

Imagine someone retiring to bed for the night. However, just before they switch out the light they select *Polish language lesson one* on their audio player, insert their earphones and press play. Throughout the night as they sleep, a gentle voice can be heard in the background pronouncing a variety of Polish words and their English counterparts:

Dzien dobry – Good day
Jak sie masz? – How are you?
Jestem bardzo dobrze – I am very well

When the sleeper awakes the following day she is now able to recall and utilise a range of new Polish words and phrases. This scenario outlines the idea behind sleep learning: that it is possible for an individual to learn new information while she sleeps, which can subsequently aid her behaviour when awake. Thus, this chapter examines whether information presented to a sleeping person can subsequently aid learning and enhance performance.

The chapter begins by establishing what sleep learning is and how it emerged. Given the premise that learning occurs during sleep, the chapter provides a brief outline of the nature of sleep and its various stages. This is followed by a summary of the sleep learning procedure and the rationale underpinning the notion that learning can occur during sleep. The chapter then examines whether it is possible for an individual to perceive a stimulus during sleep which can be recalled later when awake. Following this, the chapter examines evidence suggesting that information given to a sleeping person can enhance some aspect of her later waking behaviour. The chapter then explores some of the factors that have been shown to influence the effectiveness of sleep learning, including the suggestibility of the individual as well as the level of exposure to material to be learnt. The chapter then examines the potential negative effects of sleep learning and finally highlights how use of the term *sleep learning* to describe what takes place may in itself act as a form of constraint.

Sleep learning

Definitions of sleep learning, or hypnopaedia, range from 'teaching during sleep' to the 'process of introducing information into the brain while asleep' to the more specific 'sleep assisted instruction' (Aarons 1976). The key point is that it represents a techniqe whereby information is presented to a sleeping person in an effort to enhance their processing and/or recall of it. The *promise* of sleep learning is that it will enhance performance in a relatively effortless manner. This is based upon a number of assumptions. The first is that people are capable of processing information while asleep, even if they remain unaware of it. Second is the notion that such information is retained for later use when awake. Advocates of sleep learning argue that it can provide a wide range of benefits, including facilitating foreign language learning, improving memory and enhancing confidence. The practical implications of being able to learn during sleep are considerable, particularly as most of us spend quite a proportion of our lives asleep (see Box 3.1).

The history of sleep learning is vague, making it difficult to pin down with any degree of precision exactly where the idea came from. Some have suggested that science fiction writers were among the first to extol the possible virtues of learning whilst asleep. For example, Hugo Gernsback produced a magazine article at the turn of the twentieth century describing a machine called the *hypnobioscope*, which transmitted information directly into the

---

Box 3.1   Summary of the average amount of time a person spends sleeping

Ever get the feeling you're sleeping your life away?

People generally spend a large chunk of their lives sleeping. For example, if the average woman were to sleep for eight hours each day of her life and live for the allotted three score years and ten, she would spend approximately **204,400** hours sleeping.

To put this into context, this would equate to approximately just over 8000 days, or a little over **20 years!**

Such figures can make most people feel that they are indeed sleeping a large part of their lives away.

brain of a sleeping person (1911). Aldous Huxley's novel, *Brave New World* (1932), was another publication that suggested the possible uses of audio learning while sleeping to condition attitudes. These ideas have continued to pervade public consciousness and pique public interest.

A central assumption made by proponents of sleep learning is that sleep itself represents lost or wasted time, or, at the very least, time that is not used productively. It is beyond the scope of this chapter to provide a comprehensive summary of the nature of sleep. However, given such assumptions, it would be useful to briefly examine the nature of sleep in an attempt to try and gain some understanding of what happens to a person when they are sleeping.

Sleep as the thief of time

Sleep is far from a uniform state that a person enters shortly after retiring to bed and then exits upon awakening. The type of sleep can range from a light doze to a deep sound sleep and these differences can be observed in the sleeper's brain activity as measured by the electroencephalogram (EEG). The human EEG has traditionally been separated into a number of distinct bandwidths, each associated with a specific brain wave pattern and particular aspects of thought or behaviour (see Table 3.1).

The EEG of a sleeping person highlights a number of distinct stages of sleep, with differing patterns of EEG activity occurring in each. For instance, stage 1 sleep is the lightest level of sleep and occurs as the person drifts off to sleep. Here, the EEG shows irregular brain waves of relatively low amplitude. Stage 2 represents a deeper level of sleep and is identified by the appearance of very rapid brain waves known as *sleep spindles*. As sleep deepens, the number of slow brain waves in the EEG increases, leading to stages 3 and 4, which are sometimes referred to as regions of slow wave sleep (SWS). Stage 3 marks a transition from relatively light to a deeper sleep and here the EEG begins to show more low-frequency high-amplitude waves known as delta waves. Stage 4 is the deepest level of sleep and corresponds with the appearance of delta waves in the EEG.

These changes in EEG show that a sleeping person moves from a relatively shallow sleep in stage 1 to a deeper sleep in stage 4. Whilst these stages may suggest a simple ordered set of events, periodically throughout the night,

Table 3.1 Electroencephalographic rhythms

Rhythm	Range	Meaning
Delta	0.5–4 Hz	Deep sleep (non-dreaming)
Theta	4–8 Hz	Drowsiness
Alpha	8–12 Hz	Relaxed, aware with eyes closed
Beta	13–35 Hz	Awake, alert, intense mental activity
Gamma	+35 Hz	Cognitive and motor functions

the EEG patterns of the sleeping person shift from the deep levels of stage 4 back up to stage 1. Other changes occurring alongside this include alterations in breathing, heart rate and blood pressure. In addition, the sleeper's eyes may begin to move rapidly back and forth under her closed eyelids, denoting what is commonly referred to as *rapideye movement*, or REM, sleep, which is associated with dreaming. In contrast, all other states of sleep became known as non-REM, or NREM. Thus sleep consists of two distinct states, NREM sleep, which contains four stages, ranging from light to deep sleep, and REM sleep, which occurs periodically throughout the night.

Such changes highlight the fact that a typical night's sleep is marked by a series of descents and ascents through the stages of sleep, punctuated by ever-longer periods of REM sleep. The deeper slow wave sleep occurs during the first half of the night, with most of the REM sleep occurring in the second half of the night. Given the heterogeneous nature of sleep, Mollen (1998) suggests that if sleep learning were a reality, it is unlikely to occur evenly across all the different stages.

With the distinction between REM and NREM sleep, as well as between the various stages of NREM sleep, it should come as no surprise that a number of theories have been put forward to account for what happens during sleep. These range from energy conservation, biological adaptation and body restoration to memory consolidation (see, e.g., Hobson 1989; Peigneux *et al.* 2001). Thus it seems that sleep is a complex process containing various stages and states that may provide the sleeper with some benefits. This is difficult to reconcile with the assumption made by advocates of sleep learning that sleep simply represents lost or wasted time. If sleep really were a waste of time, sleep deprivation would be expected to have little or no effect on behaviour. However, this is not the case, as research has shown that deprivation of sleep can impair both cognitive and motor skills (Kuo 2001).

Sleep-learning procedure

The sleep-learning procedure may seem intuitively obvious: information is simply presented to the individual as she sleeps. However, there are two aspects of this procedure that deserve consideration. The first relates to how sleep is defined and operationalised and the second involves how the to-be-learnt information is presented.

It is important to ascertain whether the person receiving the information is sleeping or not, partly because this has implications for the notion that learning occurs *during* sleep, but also because sleep thresholds vary between individuals. For instance, the criteria by which a person is considered to be asleep have traditionally been based on behavioural evidence. This includes the appearance of the sleeping person, including physical relaxation, lack of communication and lack of response to external stimuli. However, monitoring EEG allows for a more precise, detailed and objective measure of sleep. According to Druckman and Bjork (1991), an ideal demonstration of sleep learning should adhere to the following guidelines. Prior to sleep, the individual should not be informed of the procedures to be employed during sleep learning. The material to be learnt should *only* be presented during sleep, not before. To ensure that the person is asleep, strict physiological measures, including EEG and EMG, should be taken. For example, the presence of alpha (8–12 Hz) EEG activity, which may be seen during the early stages of sleep, has been taken to indicate higher levels of conscious arousal and, as such, the absence of alpha is thought to represent a conservative estimate of deeper sleep (Evans *et al.* 1970). Consequently, a conservative approach may be to present the information to be learnt during sleep when alpha activity is absent from the EEG.

Once some agreement has been reached regarding how to identify whether the person is asleep or not, the next issue is how to present the information. Given the nature of sleep, most agree that presenting auditory information seems to be the best way of making contact with the sleeper, while safeguarding the sleep process itself. Traditionally, presenting auditory information to the would-be sleep learner was classified as using either an *air-conduction* or a *bone-conduction* method (Eich 1988). Air conduction refers to the use of a loudspeaker and bone conduction to the use of a speaker placed inside the pillow of the sleeper. Some have suggested that a combination of these methods may prove to be more effective, incorporating the simultaneous transmission of information using a speaker placed in the pillow as well as loudspeakers placed around the room (Zukhar *et al.* 1965). It is interesting to note that, while sleeping, the focus of the sleeper is turned inwards, to their own internal dialogue. As such, a potentially useful technique that to some extent could mimic this internal voice, and possibly improve the effect of sleep learning, would be the use of personal earphones, similar to those worn by many as they listen to music on personal audio players.

Thus, a laboratory-based sleep-learning procedure invariably consists of ensuring that the participant is asleep and then presenting information to be learnt in an auditory manner. However, the particular criteria used to identify sleep and the specific thresholds of the auditory stimuli are not always consistent amongst researchers, which may to some extent account for their disparate findings. Indeed, Bierman and Winter (1989) suggest that the negative results often seen within sleep learning may be due to inadequate levels of auditory stimulation.

Rationale for sleep learning

Unfortunately, there is no clear theory stating how or why learning should occur during sleep. None of those conducting research on the phenomenon of sleep learning have, as yet, put forward a theory that would account for the possibility of learning during sleep. In general, the assumption conveyed by many is that the simple repetition of information acts as a *prime*, which is sufficient to ensure the information is encoded and possibly recalled at a later stage. For example, Tilley (1979) suggested that the presentation of material during sleep can aid awake learning by *reinforcing* or *reactivating* memory processes. This in turn may aid the consolidation process, leading to improved retention. It is not clear at this stage whether the presentation of material during sleep would merely act to reinforce awake learning of the same material or could be utilised to learn new things. Nevertheless, this idea stems from a broad empirical base of findings within mainstream memory research showing that, if a person is presented with a stimulus more than once, her response will differ compared to someone who sees the stimulus only once (see, e.g., Roediger and McDermott 1993). For example, if a person is shown a list of words and asked to read them aloud and, unbeknown to her, hidden in amongst the list are words that are repeated, she will invariably be faster and more accurate when responding to the repeated words. The person's memory for these words is *primed*, allowing her to process them in less time. Importantly, this priming doesn't require conscious effort; it is implicit or automatic. At an intuitive level, it's easy to see how the concept of priming may relate to sleep learning. For example, if a list of words is presented to a person whilst sleeping, she may automatically encode them. Later, when awake, and the same words are re-presented, along with a list of new words, her response to the repeated words will differ. Thus, the presentation of words during sleep may act as a prime, so that, when they are encountered again, they will be processed more efficiently. Of course, this idea is based upon the assumption that it is possible to perceive and encode information whilst asleep.

Perception during sleep

There are anecdotal accounts of mothers sleeping through high levels of ambient noise yet awakening to the soft cry of their newborn baby, something which has been called *mother's cry phenomenon*. There is also evidence showing that, if a person's name is called when they are sleeping, it elicits a measurable psychophysiological response (Oswald *et al.* 1960). Others have also found that it is possible for individuals to perceive information whilst sleeping and produce a behavioural response (Cobb *et al.* 1965; Lasaga and Lasaga 1973).

For instance, Lasaga and Lasaga (1973) tested the sleep perception of a group of participants who were played a recording containing a range of numbers as they slept. Shortly after the end of the recording each participant was woken up and asked if they had heard anything. They found that participants' memory for the numbers was significantly better than would be expected by chance (see Figure 3.1). Lasaga and Lasaga argued that this showed that participants are capable of perceiving verbal information while asleep.

However, others have suggested that, whilst it is possible to perceive information during sleep, it may be forgotten when the person wakes and as a consequence has little impact on waking behaviour (Evans *et al.* 1966). For example, Evans *et al.* (ibid.) *cued* sleepers to move specified parts of their body when they entered stage 1 sleep by repeating the suggestion, 'Whenever I

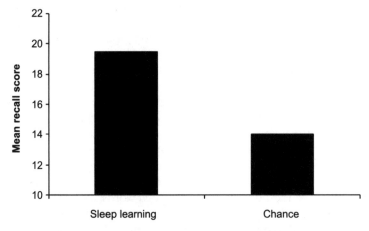

Figure 3.1 The mean recall score of those undergoing sleep learning compared to chance.

(Adapted from Lasaga and Lasaga 1973)

say the word "leg" your left leg will feel extremely cramped and uncomfort-able until you move it' (p. 666). Following this suggestion, the cue word 'leg' was given aloud and participants' responses monitored. If participants moved their leg, this was classified as a successful trial. Later, when the stu-dents were woken up, they were questioned concerning any memory of the suggestion presented during sleep. On a second night, each participant was given only the cue word (i.e. leg) during stage 1 sleep to see if this would elicit any behaviour. When they awoke the following day, they were again ques-tioned concerning any memory of the cue words presented during sleep.

Evans *et al.* (1966) found that on the first night, 61 per cent of participants produced a behavioural response to match the suggested cue given while they slept. However, when questioned the following day concerning any memory of either the suggestion or cue, 73 per cent were unable to recall any details of either. On the second night, the number of participants responding to the cue alone dropped to 39 per cent, but again none of them had any waking memory of its being presented to them while they slept. Similar findings were reported in a follow-up study using different cues, which were presented during alpha-free stage 1 sleep (Evans *et al.* 1970).

This shows that it is possible for people to respond physically to suggestions presented during stage 1 sleep without being aware of either the suggestion or the cue. Interestingly, this occurred against a backdrop of what Evans *et al.* (ibid.) called *waking amnesia*, where the sleeping person remained unable to recall the experiences when awake. They used the term 'amnesia' and not *forgetting* because on the second night, following a day during which partici-pants failed to recall information about the suggestions or cues, a cue could still evoke a response for some during sleep. Evans *et al.* (ibid.) suggest that, while it may be possible for a sleeping person to encode and respond to suggestions during sleep, the material learnt may only be useful *during* sleep itself because the sleeper is unable to recall the information presented when awoken.

Enhancing performance

Given that it's possible to perceive information whilst sleeping, a key question to ask is whether there is any evidence to suggest that such a technique can alter or enhance performance that is of practical use when awake. Only a limited number of studies have focused on sleep learning as a way of enhancing performance and these can be grouped under the headings of behaviour adaptation, verbal learning and general knowledge learning.

Behaviour adaptation

One of the earliest studies to utilise sleep learning to modify behaviour was by LeShan (1942). He was particularly interested in the potential conditioning effects of suggestions given during sleep which could subsequently influence waking behaviour. This involved him in putting together a recording that repeated the sentence 'My fingernails taste terribly bitter' and then playing this to a group of sleeping boys identified as nail biters 16,200 times, over a period of 54 nights. The specific procedure involved asking the boys whether they were awake before turning on the audio message. If they appeared restless, the audio recording was turned off until the child returned to a former level of calm restfulness. The aim was to see whether this record-ing could lead the boys to stop biting their fingernails. Interestingly, LeShan (ibid.) did not inform the children that they were involved in a sleep study. To assess the effects of the message, he compared the fingernails of boys receiving the audio message every two weeks to those of a nail-biting control group who received no message. This revealed a 40 per cent decrease in the number of boys biting their nails among those receiving the audio message in comparison to controls, who showed no change (see Figure 3.2).

These findings led LeShan (ibid.) to propose that suggestions given during sleep have the ability to modify waking behaviour. It is particularly interest-ing, as a separate report by Wechsler (1931), examining the incidence rate of nail biting in children aged between eight and 14 years, indicated that in fact one would expect to see a small but steady increase in the number of children biting their nails during this time period. However, the study has been criti-cised for failing to control for the volume of the audio message and to iden-tify an objective sleep criterion (Lewis 1968). For instance, the volume of the audio message was merely turned down if one of the boys exhibited restless behaviour; it was not turned off. This meant that the suggestion could have been heard by boys who were not completely asleep. Still, it is intriguing that, whilst the findings may be limited, there has been no attempt to replicate them.

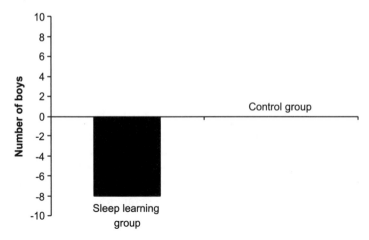

Figure 3.2 The change in the number of boys biting their nails among those receiving an audio message during sleep and the no-message controls.

(Adapted from LeShan 1942)

Verbal learning

By far the most popular area of sleep learning research is in the acquisition of new verbal information. In part, this may be due to the nature of the stimulus, the spoken word, which can easily be incorporated within a sleep learning paradigm. However the results are mixed, with some showing evidence of learning as a result of information presented during sleep (Cooper and Hoskovec 1972; Fox and Robbins 1952; Leuba and Bateman 1952; Tilley 1979), whilst others have failed to elicit any learning effects (Bruce 1970; Emmons and Simon 1956, Tani and Yoshi 1970).

Both Fox and Robbins (1952) and Cooper and Hoskovec (1972) focused on presenting word pairs, with one of the words in English and the other in a foreign language. For example, Fox and Robbins played different audio recordings to three groups of participants as they slept. The first group were presented with English–Chinese word pairs matched for meaning, the second group were given English–Chinese word pairs that had different meanings, and the third group, acting as controls, were played a recording of music. None of the sleepers were directly monitored but all were played the recordings via a pillow speaker system which came on automatically between the hours of 2.30 and 3.00 a.m. Following the night's audio presentation, participants from each group were required to learn the correct English–Chinese pairings. This involved playing the participants a recording of the correct English–Chinese word pairs, followed by the Chinese words alone and then asking them to recall the correct English words. Fox and Robbins (ibid.) found that those who were presented with the correct English–Chinese pairings whilst they slept learnt the list in fewer trials than those given the incorrect pairings or those presented with music (see Figure 3.3).

Interestingly, those who were presented with the incorrect English–Chinese pairings while they slept took longer than controls, suggesting that the incorrect pairings may have interfered with their learning. Fox and Robbins (ibid.) argued that this showed clear evidence that learning during sleep can occur and is detectable using what they called a 'savings in learning' method.

However, the study was limited by the fact that all audio presentations took place in the individual's own home, and therefore no one was able to observe whether they were actually asleep or not. Fox and Robbins (ibid.) admit that this could weaken their argument but suggest that if anyone were to awaken during the night, without reporting it, it is probable that the numbers would be equally distributed across each of the groups, and as such wouldn't alter the pattern of results. Nevertheless, Bruce *et al.* (1970) have expressed doubts about this notion and remain unconvinced that some learning did not occur when participants were partially awake.

Others have attempted to produce a more robust effect by combining sleep learning with hypnosis (Cooper and Hoskovec 1972). Initially this involved selecting individuals identified as highly susceptible to hypnosis and having them sleep in a lab for two consecutive nights, the first of which served as an adaptation night. Following the first night's sleep, they were given positive affirmations stating that they would easily remember everything that was said to them and then they were given a list of English–Russian word pairs to learn, which provided a baseline measure of learning whilst awake.

On the second night, prior to sleeping, each learner underwent a hypnotic induction and was instructed to remember everything that was said to them during the night. While they slept their EEG was monitored to identify stage 1 sleep, and they could press a button at any time throughout the night to

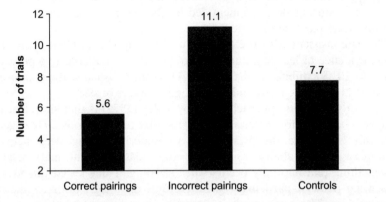

Figure 3.3 Mean number of trials taken to learn English–Chinese word pairings for those receiving the correct pairings during sleep, incorrect pairings and controls.

(Adapted from Fox and Robbins 1952)

inform the researchers that they had awoken. This helped to provide a clear measure of when the participants were asleep. When stage 1 REM sleep was identified using the EEG, positive affirmations concerning memory were again given to each of the sleepers, along with a different list of English–Russian word pairs. Immediately after presentation of the word list the sleepers were awoken and asked to complete a series of memory tests for the word pairs.

Performance on the memory tests did show some evidence of learning, but this was only about one-third of that seen when the same people were tested while awake. Cooper and Hoskovec (1972) pointed out that, whilst learning during sleep may be *possible*, given its reduced impact compared to awake-learning, it may not be *practical*. It may be that a direct comparison between sleep learning and learning while awake is unhelpful, given that the former is unlikely to be as effective as the latter. It also indicates that sleep learning, if used at all, could represent a useful *supplement* to awake learning rather than a replacement. However, apart from the lack of a control group, the study also confounds interventions by combining sleep learning with hypnosis, making it impossible to tease apart the individual effect these two factors may elicit. Any positive learning effects could result from either of these interventions, or a combination of the two.

Emmons and Simon (1956) adopted a more stringent sleep criterion when presenting information to sleeping participants. They suggested that the existence of alpha (8–12 Hz) activity in the EEG indicates an awake but relaxed state with eyes closed. This led them to present material to sleeping participants repeatedly but only when alpha activity was absent from the EEG. On waking, the participants were required to select target words from a list provided and their choices were compared to the mean frequency of selection from an untrained awake group. Unfortunately, performance of the training group was no better than controls, indicating that when information is presented during sleep, as identified by the absence of alpha activity, no learning takes place (see Figure 3.4).

This is consistent with the findings of Tani and Yoshi (1970), who also found evidence of learning during sleep, but only if material was presented when the EEG exhibited alpha activity. This may be because the presence of alpha EEG activity corresponds to the lighter stages of sleep.

A slightly different approach taken by Tilley (1979) is that sleep learning may only be useful for material already familiar to the learners. He suggests that this is because the presentation of material during sleep helps to reinforce a person's ability to process or consolidate such information, which is something that naturally occurs when sleeping. Tilley tested this idea by presenting pairs of participants with pictures of objects prior to allowing them to sleep. Then, as they slept, their EEG was recorded and some of the names of the objects relating to a subset of the pictures were played as one of the pair entered stage 2 sleep and the other exhibited REM sleep. The following morning both participants were woken and their memory of the pictures

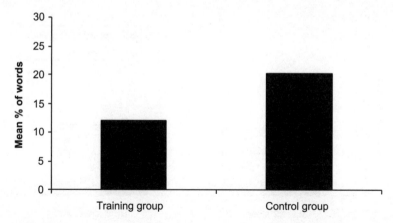

Figure 3.4 Percentage of target words selected by sleep learning and control groups. (Adapted from Emmons and Simon 1956)

tested. Tilley found that recall was significantly better for pictures that had their names repeated during the night, but only for those who received the audio presentation during NREM stage 2 sleep (see Figure 3.5). There was no improvement for those receiving the information during REM sleep. Therefore, repetition of material during NREM stage 2 sleep significantly reinforced pre-sleep learning.

There are a number of points worthy of note regarding this study which set it apart from the less rigorously controlled ones. First, irrelevant speech was played in the background from the start of the sleeping session to allow participants to become accustomed to the sound of speech during the night. This is a useful idea because it shows that any learning throughout the night is unlikely to be the result of changes in arousal levels of the sleeper due to changes in background noise levels. Secondly, and perhaps most importantly, sleep was defined using the EEG and, in addition to this, material was presented during both REM sleep and NREM sleep. Furthermore, Tilley (ibid.) found a clear effect of sleep learning occurring specifically in stage 2 NREM sleep. This implies that presentation of information during stage 2 sleep enhances the sleeper's ability to learn it, provided that she has encountered it previously when awake. In addition, this indicates that sleep learning may provide a useful complement to awake learning and that, combined, they may exceed the learning effects of either approach alone.

Not all those utilising sleep learning to enhance verbal processing have done so using simple word pairs or object names. For example, Leuba and Bateman (1952) attempted to use sleep learning as an approach to teach individuals the lyrics to songs they'd never heard before. This involved playing the words of three songs to a sleeping person five times a night for three successive nights. However, as the person slept, no observations were made as to whether she awoke during the night and no measures were taken of her

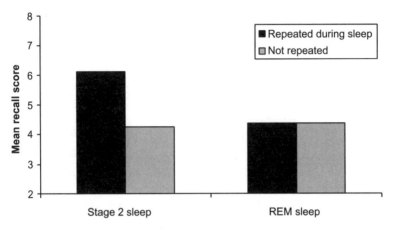

Figure 3.5 Mean recall score for repeated and non-repeated items played during stage 2 NREM sleep and REM sleep.

(Adapted from Tilley 1979)

EEG to identify distinct levels of sleep. Following the sleep learning period, when given the three song titles and asked to write down what she thought the lyrics to each song were, according to Leuba and Bateman, she was able to write the lyrics for two of the songs without any errors and the remaining song with only minor errors. This led them to claim that sleep learning of musical lyrics was successful.

Such an interpretation, while interesting, may be a little over-enthusiastic. It's important to keep in mind that the study was conducted on a single person, it contained no control condition, no criterion was used to identify sleep, and the participant's behaviour throughout the night went unobserved. Whilst it suggests some interesting possibilities that could be explored by future researchers, the methodological limitations mean that the findings should be interpreted with a degree of caution.

General knowledge learning

Simon and Emmons (1956) examined whether it is possible to learn more complex material while sleeping. In this instance, they used a range of general knowledge questions and answers played to sleeping participants; an example can be seen in Box 3.2.

Consistent with previous research, they presented the questions and answers via a loudspeaker when the participants were identified as sleeping using an EEG-based criterion. The following day, when the sleepers were awakened, it was found that they had no memory of the information presented to them as they slept. Whilst this may suggest that learning during sleep cannot take place, it is important to keep in mind the type of material presented. It may be that the presentation of questions and answers, which

Box 3.2   An example of a question and answer given to participants as they slept

Question: In what kind of store did Ulysses S. Grant work before the war?

Answer: A hardware store

(Source: Simon and Emmons 1956)

represents more complex information than simple word lists or object names, is beyond the limits of what an individual is capable of processing while asleep.

This highlights the notion that the effectiveness of sleep learning may be influenced by a number of factors, some of which are explored in more detail in the following section.

Factors affecting sleep learning

Researchers have identified a number of factors that are thought to influence the effectiveness of sleep learning. These include the suggestibility of participants, as well as their age and ability to learn, the level and duration of exposure to the material and the amount of sleep learning practice provided.

Suggestibility

Hoskovec and Cooper (1969) put forward the idea that a person's level of hypnotic susceptibility may be related to the possible success of sleep learning. When they examined the effects of sleep learning Russian–English word pairs, they recruited only highly hypnotically susceptible people to take part and reported some positive effects (see Cooper and Hoskovec 1972). Methodological limitations aside (see above), the findings led them to propose that highly suggestible participants may be better able to perceive and remember suggestions given during sleep. This led them to suggest that sleep learning studies may be more effective and elicit more robust effects if the participants are screened to include only highly suggestible individuals. However, Aarons (1976) points out that this shouldn't be taken to mean that in order to produce an effect *only* highly susceptible people should be used in sleep learning studies, because, whilst a high level of suggestibility may help, it need not be essential for sleep learning to occur.

Age and ability to learn

It has long been known that children and young adults are able to demonstrate a greater degree of cognitive flexibility when learning new material than their more mature counterparts. With this in mind, Aarons (1976) proposed that children and young adults may be able to develop and exhibit sleep learning abilities more readily than older adults.

Consistent with this is the idea put forward by Simon and Emmons (1956) that sleep learning may be more effective for individuals with high IQs or high learning capabilities whilst awake. The argument, here, is that those who exhibit the capacity to learn effectively when awake may be more likely to demonstrate a change in behaviour as a result of sleep learning. Thus, if a person is classified as a 'good learner' when awake, the chances are that sleep learning may be more beneficial for them than for someone less capable of learning.

The points made about age and intelligence and learning ability are speculative and, as yet, have received no direct empirical support. Nevertheless, it would seem plausible that a greater level of cognitive flexibility and an ability to learn when awake could be beneficial for attempting to learn during sleep.

Exposure to material

Level of exposure to the material to be learnt is also thought to influence the effectiveness of sleep learning. This can range from a single exposure during one night (e.g. Lasaga and Lasaga 1973) to thousands of exposures across multiple nights (e.g. LeShan 1942). Indeed, Aarons (1976) has suggested that distinct levels of exposure may influence ability to learn and possibly account for the contrary findings of researchers from the West compared to those from the East. Aarons points out that research conducted in the West invariably involves presenting material to the learner for a single episode only, during EEG-defined sleep, with the sleeping person kept blind as to what will be presented. In contrast, eastern researchers generally present material at the beginning and at the end of the sleep cycle, and this material is coordinated with material presented pre- and post-sleep, which may continue for several weeks.

Tani and Yoshi (1970) directly compared the effects of stimulus repetition on sleep learning using three groups of learners. All three groups were presented with a list of word pairs once during the night to provide a baseline measure of learning and this was compared to the effects obtained from a second target list presented multiple times during the night. For the first group, this target list was repeated between one and five times, for the second group, it was presented 8–13 times and the third group heard the list in excess of 15 times throughout the night. A clear effect emerged showing that those presented with the target list more than eight times per night recalled significantly more words than those hearing the list between only one and five times per night (see Figure 3.6). Such a pattern would imply that repeating the material to be learnt is an essential prerequisite of sleep learning.

In contrast, when Emmons and Simon (1956) used a simple list of words repeated 'as many times as possible' (p. 79) throughout the night, they found no evidence for sleep learning. This led them to argue that there is no clear relationship between the number of stimulus repetitions and the effectiveness of sleep learning.

It is not entirely clear why such differential effects emerged. One possibility is that the influence of stimulus repetition was mediated by the participant's level of arousal. For instance, Tani and Yoshi (1970) noted that presentation of material to a sleeping person often led to the production of alpha activity in the EEG, which is associated with higher levels of arousal and shallower stages of sleep. In contrast, Emmons and Simon (1956) used a very strict sleep criterion, which involved the presentation of material only when alpha activity was absent from the EEG. Thus, it is possible that the findings can be reconciled around the notion of the presence or absence of alpha activity in the EEG, implying distinct levels of conscious awareness that could be differentially influenced by the level of stimulus repetition.

Practice

Levy *et al.* (1972) suggest that the process of sleep learning may *itself* require time to learn. The idea here is that practice at learning while asleep may be necessary for any effective learning to occur. To test this idea, Levy *et al.* recruited a group of participants and had them acclimatise themselves to the lab and then spend five consecutive nights undergoing sleep learning training. During the training, the sleepers were allowed to sleep for eight

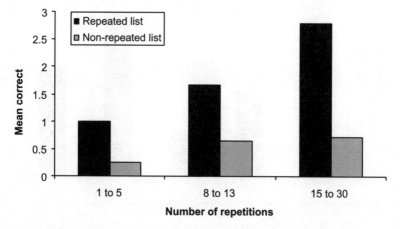

Figure 3.6 Mean number of words correctly recalled for each of the three sleep learning groups hearing the information repeated a number of times.

(Adapted from Tani and Yoshi 1970).

hours whilst audio recordings of Russian–English word pairs were played. When awakened, they were questioned about their sleep and given a variety of memory tests to measure their recall and recognition of the word pairs. Levy *et al.* found that participants' mean recognition scores for the word pairs were significantly greater than zero, which they claimed was evidence of sleep learning. Furthermore, participants showed a reliable improvement in recognition over time (see Figure 3.7). This, they argued, clearly shows that the ability to learn material while asleep improves with practice. As such, practice at learning while asleep may be essential in order to elicit evidence of learning.

Nevertheless, Mollen (1998) has expressed doubts concerning the findings from Levy *et al.* (1972). In particular, he argued that they illegitimately take zero as representing the chance level of recognition performance, against which they compared the scores for those undergoing sleep learning. In fact, Mollen calculated the chance level to be much higher and, when he re-computed the scores from the participants reported by Levy *et al.* (1972), he found little evidence of sleep learning per se, or of any improvement over time. As such, the results suggesting that sleep learning may improve with practice are at best ambiguous.

Negative effects

Imagine a person waking up after a night's sleep which was continuously disturbed by a noisy neighbour's party. Throughout the following day she complains of feeling 'a bit groggy' and is less awake, less focused and less productive than usual. The term *sleep inertia* is often used to describe the

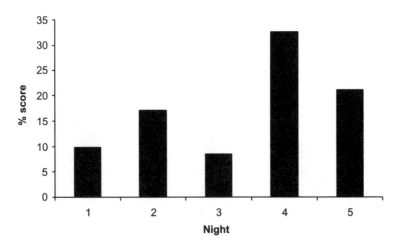

Figure 3.7 Mean percentage recognition scores for sleep learning participants across five nights of training.

(Adapted from Levy *et al.* 1972)

feelings of sluggishness and mental dullness commonly reported immediately after awakening. Such *inertia* may be exacerbated by a disturbed night's sleep. This raises some important questions. For instance, would playing a stream of sounds during the night disturb an individual's normal sleeping pattern? In addition, would the potential gain experienced by complementing awake learning with sleep learning be offset by any damage to the quality and duration of sleep, which in turn may have a negative effect upon waking behaviour?

Evans *et al.* (1970) have tentatively suggested that attempting to encourage sleep learning may interrupt or disturb the normal pattern of sleep; while Lasaga and Lasaga (1973) point out that presentation of auditory information to a sleeping person leads to increased arousal levels. These peaks of *micro-arousal* could disturb the normal sleeping pattern of a person and have detrimental carry-over effects on waking performance, particularly as Wyatt and Bootzin (1994) argue that regular and restorative sleep is essential for optimal cognitive performance.

Research focusing on this issue is sketchy and based predominantly on self-reports with little or no examination of physiological indices of health. For instance, some have reported a range of negative side effects resulting from attempts to utilise sleep learning, including nightmares, increased fatigue and diffuse headaches (Balkhashov 1965). Others have suggested that presenting material during the night to a sleeping person interferes with their ability to dream (Cooper and Hoskovec 1972) or impairs later learning when awake (Kugler and Kaumann 1967). However, as mentioned above, Tilley (1979) showed that presenting material to someone while they were in REM sleep, a stage typically associated with dreaming, had no negative side effects. Others have suggested that the quality of sleep may be influenced by the intensity of the training programme rather than whether the information to be learnt is presented during sleep or not (Khil'chenko *et al.* 1965). Furthermore, Evans *et al.* (1970) reported a negative correlation between the number of cues presented during sleep learning and the number of times this resulted in participants waking up. This would suggest that, as cues are continuously presented throughout the night, the individual habituates to them and they have less impact on the quality of sleep.

Overall, the evidence suggesting that presenting auditory information to a sleeping individual can have a negative effect on their quality of sleep is minimal and inconclusive. Nevertheless, it is an important factor that needs to be kept in mind and explored more fully for potential health hazards.

Naming difficulties

Scientific opinion, it seems, is mixed as to whether or not sleep learning is truly effective at enhancing performance. Many of the difficulties revolve around potentially flawed methodologies, with perhaps the most damning criticism based upon the use of specific terminology, in this instance the word *sleep*. A great deal of criticism has been levelled at many of the studies in terms of how they monitor sleep and/or whether they are able to clearly define a sleep criterion. The main issue seems to be identifying whether a person is asleep or not. This is important as it directly influences the level of confidence one may have in conclusions stating that learning *during sleep* may be possible. In some cases researchers simply observed those sleeping, while in others they asked whether the individual was asleep or not. There is some agreement that one of the more effective methods is to examine the EEG, which can help identify the specific stage of sleep. Of course, it's possible that the most effective way of ascertaining whether an individual is asleep or not may be one that uses multiple criteria. Nevertheless, a key contention is that, if any learning occurs, it needs to be clearly identified whether the person was asleep or not when it took place and during which stage of sleep it occurred.

It is important to recognise the usefulness of scientific procedures that require terms to be clearly defined, providing a more comprehensive understanding of the process under consideration. However, it may be that, within the field of sleep learning, researchers have become so entrenched in their attempts to define what constitutes sleep learning, in particular the criteria used to identify whether someone is asleep or not, that research into the possible beneficial effects of simply presenting information during the night is constrained. For example, given that sleep learning may only occur when a message is played while an individual is in stage 2 NREM sleep, it is unlikely that those who purchase sleep-learning products are going to set them up to play only during this stage of sleep. Invariably what does happen is that an individual purchases a sleep-learning recording and simply repeatedly plays this throughout the night. Of course, this might not constitute *sleep learning* per se, and this raises an interesting point. Perhaps the term 'sleep learning' doesn't represent a useful definition for what is actually going on when people use sleep learning recordings. Perhaps, in order to capture the full range of potential possibilities that match more closely what a potential *sleep learner* may do, it should be called something else. Tani and Yoshi (1970) have suggested that it should more accurately be called *sleep-bed-learning*, whilst Aarons (1976) has proposed *sleep-assisted learning*. Or one could do away with the notion that it relies on sleep and simply call it *night learning*.

The point is that, while it's important to try and understand what, if any, information can be processed during sleep, this may represent only part of the story. In this instance, there may be a divergence between the pure goals of science on the one hand and the pragmatics of using sleep-learning products on the other. While empirically based research is essential to understand how something may work, it is important not to lose sight of the possible beneficial effects that the repetition of material played throughout the night could have on learning, particularly as this is what most people will do.

Overview

Sleep learning, or hypnopaedia, refers to the ability to learn new and/or additional material presented during sleep. While the idea of sleep learning may have its roots in science fiction, advocates of this technique have proposed that it has a wide range of beneficial applications. A central assumption made by such supporters is that no other important cognitive processes are taking place during sleep, and that it is possible to perceive information while asleep. However, research focusing on the nature of sleep has shown it to incorporate a number of distinct stages, each with its own psychophysiological index. Furthermore, there is an emerging consensus among those who have examined the nature of sleep that, far from representing idle 'down time', during which the individual is in a state of cognitive hibernation, a number of important processes may occur, including the consolidation of memories encoded throughout the waking day.

There is little consistency regarding the nature of the sleep-learning procedure itself beyond that of an audio message played while the individual sleeps. Nevertheless, the use of strict physiological measures, such as EEG and EMG, to identify the level and stage of sleep has become more common. Unfortunately, there is no theoretical rationale for sleep learning beyond that offered by a simple priming effect resulting from the repetition of material. Nevertheless, the evidence does indicate that it's possible for a sleeping person to perceive and respond to suggestions given during sleep.

The effects of sleep learning have been explored in relation to behaviour adaptation and improving verbal and general knowledge learning. In terms of behaviour adaptation, the evidence, while suggestive, is both limited and methodologically flawed. In contrast, the effects of sleep learning on verbal learning are more encouraging. Although many studies still exhibit methodological flaws, there is some evidence that sleep learning may provide a useful adjunct to awake learning, acting as a supplement for familiar material rather than a replacement for awake learning. However, the effects of sleep learning in this instance may be influenced by the stage of sleep; in particular, information presented during the shallow stages of sleep that exhibit alpha activity may be more effective. The idea that sleep learning can enhance the acquisition of general knowledge information has no empirical support, although to some extent this may be influenced by the complexity of such information.

A number of factors have been identified as potentially influencing the outcome of sleep-learning studies. This includes the degree to which an individual is amenable to suggestions, with highly suggestible people potentially exhibiting greater sleep-learning effects. There are also some speculative proposals that sleep learning may be more effective for children and young adults because of their inherent neural flexibility and provide greater benefits for those identified as good learners when awake. The level of exposure to the target material has also been highlighted as a possible mitigating factor, with higher stimulus repetitions producing more positive effects. However, the evidence for this is inconclusive. It has also been suggested that the sleeping person should be given the opportunity to learn how to learn during sleep. Whilst the proposal that sleep learning may occur, or improve, with practice sounds appealing, there is, as yet, little empirical support for this.

Inherent within the notion of sleep learning is the idea that sleep represents wasted or lost time. However, as seen earlier in the chapter, this simply is not the case. It is important to realise that the presentation of messages played during the night could impair the individual's quality of sleep, which in turn may influence subsequent waking behaviour. Nevertheless, evidence suggesting that presentation of material during the night can have a negative effect on waking behaviour is equivocal; indeed, there is some evidence that people habituate to repeated sounds, although this too has implications for sleep learning that have yet to be fully explored.

Finally, it was noted that 'sleep learning' may not represent the most useful term to describe what happens when people use sleep-learning products. In addition, it was proposed that such a term may constrain the focus of research. Alternatives offered include sleep-bed-learning, sleep-assisted learning and night learning.

4   Subliminal training

> We know the brain responds to subliminal messages, we just don't know
> whether that response is automatic.
>
> (Bahador Bahrami 2007)

There is a wide range of subliminal products available and they are easy to
use. All the individual needs to do is sit back and relax, switch on the relevant
device (e.g. audio cassette/CD/DVD) and he will be presented with a variety
of relaxing sounds and/or images. However, according to the distributors of
such products, hidden behind these relaxing platitudes are messages aimed
at stimulating the individual to change his behaviour. Advocates of these
products claim that the hidden or *subliminal* messages have the power to
modify a range of behaviours, including stopping smoking and stress reduction, as well as improving such abilities as reading comprehension, exam
performance, memory, and even psychic abilities, to name but a few.

Such claims would suggest that subliminal training may represent a
valuable technique that could help people to reach their full potential. This
chapter examines the effectiveness of subliminal messages and asks whether
they are capable of enhancing human performance. The chapter begins by
clarifying the term 'subliminal' and provides a brief history of the development of subliminal training. It then focuses on whether it is possible to
perceive a stimulus without becoming consciously aware of it and whether
the influence of a subliminal message is more effective than its supraliminal
counterpart. The main section of the chapter deals with empirical evidence
from studies assessing subliminal training using audio and visual messages to
enhance performance. Finally, the potential long-term benefits of subliminal
training are explored.

Subliminal training

The term *subliminal* has gained widespread use, particularly with reference
to the notion of subliminal perception. The word itself means 'below the
threshold', which in this case refers to the threshold of conscious perception

(see Figure 4.1); *supraliminal* is used to denote processing of consciously perceived information occurring above the threshold.

The idea is that a subliminal message suggesting a positive change is presented so quickly or at such a low level of stimulus intensity that it fails to breach the threshold of conscious awareness (Druckman and Bjork 1991). Nevertheless, the presentation of such a message is thought to be able to influence subsequent behaviour. Although the term used here is 'subliminal perception', other terms used to describe similar effects include subliminal persuasion (Natale 1988), unconscious processing (Merikle 1988), subthreshold learning (Brosgole and Contino 1973), preconscious perception (Ledford *et al.* 1988) and subception (Cook 1985).

However, the idea that subliminal refers to a level of stimulation below a fixed threshold of conscious awareness is problematic, in that it is bound to an outdated concept of a well-defined sensory threshold, a concept made obsolete by the introduction of signal detection theory (Green and Swets 1966). The notion of a sensory threshold suggests that the sensory system operates around a simple dividing line, which serves as an 'all or none' limit to what can or cannot be perceived (see Figure 4.2A). However, there is no fixed threshold separating the detectable from the undetectable; instead, it varies as a function of stimulus strength and individual situational factors (see Figure 4.2B).

Thus, the notion of a threshold would be better represented as a continuum as opposed to a dichotomy, and it would be more accurate to think of this as a range of floating cut-off points rather than an immovable threshold. This means that the ability of a person to perceive a message may vary as a function of his level of motivation and various situational factors.

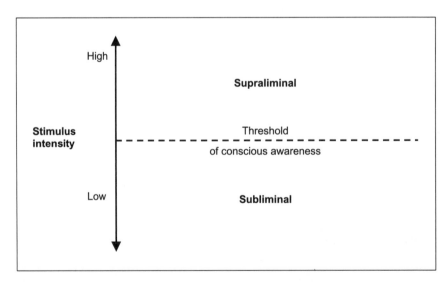

Figure 4.1 The threshold of conscious awareness separating subliminal from supraliminal perception as a function of stimulus intensity.

A

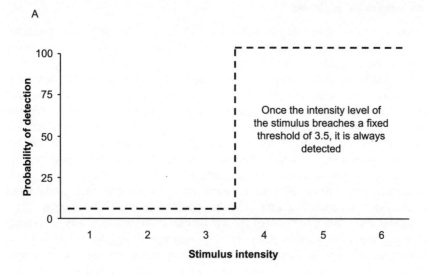

B

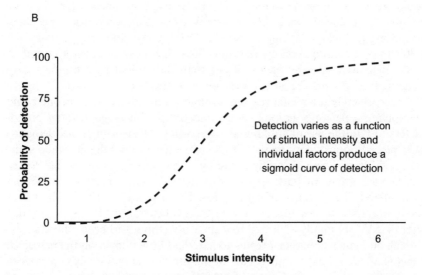

Figure 4.2 A hypothetical relationship between stimulus strength and probability of detection with a fixed threshold set at an intensity level of 3.5 (A) and a variable threshold, showing a more typical relationship between stimulus strength and probability of detection (B).

Therefore, what is subliminal for one person may be supraliminal for another. Given these difficulties, one suggestion has been to adopt a more concise definition such as 'perception in the absence of subjective confidence' (Merikle 1988: 360), which refers to perception of a stimulus when the perceiver is confident that in fact no stimulus was perceived.

An 'auspicious' beginning

There are two events worth noting in the history of subliminal training. The first represents the work of Otto Poetzl and the other is the infamous fraud perpetrated by James Vicary.

Interest in subliminal influence goes back to the work of sensory physiologist Otto Poetzl, who studied the effect of rapidly flashed pictures on dreams (Poetzl 1960). As part of his research, Poetzl speculated that pictures flashed at an ultra-short duration (10 msec) would stay in the nervous system in a hidden and inactive form, only reaching consciousness during dreaming. In his experiments he found evidence to suggest that dream imagery may contain elements of subliminal pictures. However, his results were largely anecdotal and proved difficult to replicate. Nevertheless, this marked the beginning of an enduring interest in the effects of subliminal messages.

In the 1950s the invention of the tachistoscope provided a way of rapidly flashing images to people in an effort to examine their effect and, in 1957, James Vicary argued that such an instrument could be used to influence people's choice of food and drink. He reasoned that if an individual's brain could process an image presented below the perception threshold, it might be possible to influence their behaviour by presenting very brief messages. According to Vicary, flashing the words 'Drink Coke' and 'Eat popcorn' for 1/3000th of a second every five seconds on a cinema screen over a period of weeks increased sales by up to 58 per cent. Subliminal perception, Vicary suggested, represents the most powerful marketing tool yet known.

Unsurprisingly the media reacted strongly to the idea that someone could manipulate a person's actions via an undetectable message, leading broadcasters to ban the use of subliminal advertising. At the same time, demands were placed upon Vicary to show that such effects were reliable, while some attempted to replicate his original findings (Sharp 1959). For example, Sharp presented a group of participants with the subliminal message 'beef' and then offered them a range of sandwiches. Unfortunately, he found that beef was not chosen to any greater degree than other fillings. It was some time later that Vicary finally admitted that the whole thing had been a hoax.

Such an inauspicious start seems to have had little impact on the perceived benefits of subliminal training. Part of the problem is that many commercial organisations selling subliminal products still use the defunct claims of Vicary as evidence that their product works, leading to a general acceptance of subliminal products and their alleged benefits.

Popular

Public belief in subliminal products seems extensive, with research showing that 81 per cent of people surveyed were familiar with the term 'subliminal advertising', and, of these, 68 per cent believed it to be effective (Pratkanis 1992). The plethora of commercial organisations provides a wide range of subliminal products, with one survey showing over 400 audio cassette titles available (Spangenberg *et al.* 1992). This combination of public confidence and availability has led to a booming industry in subliminal products, with American consumers alone spending more than $1 billion per year (Lofflin 1988).

Subliminal training procedure

While there is no standardised procedure for subliminal training, there are a number of general features that form the basis of most training paradigms. They involve the presentation of a message of some form that is assumed to bypass conscious awareness and impact directly on the unconscious, producing a subsequent change in behaviour. For example, such training may require an individual to listen to an audio-recording which has a supraliminal component and a subliminal component. The supraliminal component clearly identifies the message, which is also presented subliminally, hidden behind subdued music intended to lull the individual into a state of relaxation. In addition to audio messages, visual information can also be presented using a video/DVD/computer to flash a message on screen so quickly that an individual fails to notice it consciously.

Irrespective of the mode of delivery, subliminal techniques work on the assumption that a message can be masked by other sounds/pictures or presented so briefly that the individual fails to note it consciously. For instance, according to the claims of one manufacturer, 'subliminal messages bypass the conscious mind, and imprint directly on the subconscious mind, where they create the basis for the new kind of life you want' (Pratkanis 1992: 269). All that the listener perceives are background sounds aimed at producing a relaxing atmosphere. However, this approach raises a number of issues. First, there is an assumed distinction between a conscious mind and an unconscious mind; second, that it is possible to perceive a stimulus without becoming consciously aware of it; and, third, that a subliminal message may be more effective than its supraliminal counterpart.

Conscious versus unconscious mind

Supporters of subliminal products often make reference to the idea that subliminal messages directly access the unconscious mind, or are capable of influencing behaviour by recruiting the power of the unconscious. For example:

> To gain control, it is necessary to speak to the
> unconscious mind in a language that it comprehends –
> we have to speak to it *subliminally*.

****

There are subliminally embedded messages at work. You
won't be able to hear them consciously. But your
unconscious will. And it *will* obey.

These examples illustrate a number of confused assumptions made by advocates of subliminal products. First, there is the assumption that subliminal messages represent the *lingua franca* for communicating with the unconscious. Second, they assume a need to bypass the conscious critical mind and that, irrespective of what an individual may consciously feel or think, his subconscious will obey the commands of the subliminal message. Third, that there is a clear distinction between the conscious mind and the unconscious mind.

These assumptions highlight the fact that proponents of subliminal products are confusing the cognitive notion of unconscious processing with the psychodynamic notion of an unconscious mind. For cognitive psychologists, unconscious processing, often referred to as implicit, may refer to a process or effect of which the individual has no conscious awareness (Roediger and McDermott 1993). How a person remains balanced when riding a bicycle or knows the correct grammatical rules of his native language are both examples of what cognitive psychologists refer to as unconscious/implicit learning. This is distinct from the term *unconscious* employed within the realm of psychodynamic therapy, where it is used in an all-embracing fashion to denote a hidden reservoir containing complex motives, desires and preferences. The point is that, while psychologists may agree that unconscious or implicit processes can influence behaviour and may do so in a way that is distinct from conscious explicit processing, the notion that an individual has a conscious mind that is distinct from an unconscious mind remains contentious.

Perception without awareness

A central assumption of subliminal training is that a person can perceive a stimulus without becoming consciously aware of it. The research literature provides two observations to support this idea. First, material presented for brief durations or masked in such a way that the individual fails to perceive it consciously can still influence behaviour (see, e.g., Abrams *et al.* 2002; Marcel 1983). Second, information presented below the level of conscious awareness can produce a different effect on behaviour from when the individual is made consciously aware of it (Merikle and Daneman 1998; Murphy and Zajonc 1993).

For example, Cheesman and Merikle (1986) presented a colour word (e.g. the word 'blue') on a screen for three different durations: 300 milliseconds (msec), 56 msec and 30 msec. When the colour word was presented for 300 msec, participants reported that they could clearly see the word and this led to 100 per cent accuracy on a recognition task. When the colour word was presented for only 30 msec, not only did participants fail to see it but their recognition performance deteriorated to that of chance. However, when the word was presented for 56 msec, despite participants stating that they couldn't see it, their scores on the recognition task were significantly greater than chance (66 per cent). This shows that, even though participants remained subjectively unaware of the presentation of the word, it was able to influence their subsequent performance.

Such findings have led researchers to attempt to distinguish between subjective and objective thresholds of perceptual awareness (Merikle and Daneman 1998). A subjective threshold is identified by the failure of an individual to report conscious awareness of a stimulus that can still produce an effect on behaviour. An objective threshold is identified by an individual's inability to make accurate forced-choice decisions about the presence or absence of a stimulus (i.e. guess at an above-chance level whether there is a stimulus or not).

In addition, researchers have shown that, rather than unconscious perception merely representing a weak form of conscious perception, the two are capable of producing different effects on behaviour. For example, Murphy and Zajonc (1993) showed two groups of non-Chinese-speaking participants a range of Chinese ideographs and asked them whether they thought the characters represented 'good' or 'bad' concepts. The interesting twist is that, just prior to presenting the Chinese characters, a picture of a human face was shown, expressing either happiness or anger. For one group this face was presented long enough for them to be capable of identifying it (e.g. 1000 msec), whilst for the other group it was presented so briefly (4 msec) that none noticed it. They found that the emotional expression of the face had no effect on whether participants rated the Chinese characters as good or bad when it was clearly visible. However, those who were consciously unaware of the face were more likely to rate the various characters as representing a good concept when they followed a happy face, and a bad concept when they followed an angry face. Thus, those who were consciously aware of the face were able to ignore its influence, whereas those who were not conscious of its presence showed a clear behavioural effect. These findings provide compelling support for the idea that subliminal perception represents a valid phenomenon.

However, such findings are based on experimental research using clearly legible stimuli that have simply been masked or presented for very brief durations. It is worth noting that commercially available subliminal products often combine a message with other information, or manufacturers may accelerate or compress the message to such a degree that it remains unintelligible, even if played at a supraliminal level. The point is that subliminal audio tapes and CDs often present a subliminal message hidden alongside much louder audible sounds or tunes. This alters the question of whether it is simply possible to perceive a stimulus without being consciously aware of it to whether such perception is still possible when a subliminal message is competing against a much louder supraliminal stimulus.

The power of a subliminal message

Given that it's possible to perceive a stimulus without becoming consciously aware of it, and that this can influence behaviour, the question then becomes: how effective is a subliminal message in comparison to a supraliminal one?

Contrary to what may be expected, it seems that subliminal presentation of a message may in fact produce a *greater* effect than its supraliminal counterpart. For instance, research based on the *mere exposure effect*, which has been shown to enhance affect towards a repeated stimulus, indicates that the degree of attitude enhancement elicited by mere exposure to subliminal stimuli can exceed that produced by exposure to consciously recognisable stimuli (Bornstein 1989; Mandler *et al.* 1987). A review and meta-analysis of the mere exposure effect by Bornstein (1989) revealed that exposure to subliminal stimuli resulted in attitude changes that were greater than those produced by stimuli that were consciously perceivable. Psychodynamic activation studies using subliminal messages to encourage feelings of closeness with a mother figure have also produced stronger effects on behaviour than the same message exposed at supraliminal levels (Silverman 1983).

That a subliminal message may have a greater influence than a message that is clearly recognisable may seem counterintuitive. Nevertheless, a number of researchers have attempted to account for this by suggesting that perception of a supraliminal message naturally engages a greater number of cognitive processes, which may be involved in the critical analysis of stimulus content, which may work to counteract the influence of the message (Bornstein 1989). In contrast, a subliminal message will activate implicit knowledge, which Kihlstrom (1987) argues is not subject to such 'conscious countercontrol' (p. 1448). The result is that a subliminal message may be capable of eliciting effects of greater magnitude. Nevertheless, while such findings highlight the potential effect a specifically constructed subliminal message may have, a degree of caution should be used when extrapolating such findings to commercially available products.

Enhancing performance

This section focuses on the use of audio and visual subliminal messages to enhance a particular aspect of behaviour.

Audio messages

Many commercially available audio cassettes contain subliminal messages aimed at improving self-esteem and memory (Greenwald *et al.* 1991; Pratkanis *et al.* 1994; Spangenberg *et al.* 1992), as well as attempting to enhance academic performance (Russell *et al.* 1991).

One of the most rigorous assessments of the effectiveness of subliminal self-help audio tapes to improve self-esteem and enhance memory was carried out by Pratkanis *et al.* (1994). For this, they used two different mass-marketed audio tapes, one containing a subliminal message to enhance self-esteem – 'I have high self-worth and high self-esteem' – and the other aimed at improving memory containing the message, 'My ability to remember and recall are increasing daily'. In both cases, the subliminal messages were masked by classical music. To test the effectiveness of these products, they recruited a group of volunteers, who completed a variety of measures of self-esteem and memory. The volunteers were then given a tape to play at home. However, there was an interesting twist added to the experiment, in that Pratkanis *et al.* (ibid.) swapped the labels of half the tapes, so that some of the self-esteem tapes were mislabelled as containing a subliminal message aimed at enhancing memory and vice versa. The volunteers were separated into four groups and each group was encouraged to listen to a set tape for five weeks, a period suggested by the manufacturer to be sufficient to elicit positive effects. After the five-week 'training phase', each of the volunteers returned to the lab and once again completed a range of tests measuring self-esteem and memory. In addition, they were asked to indicate whether they felt that the tapes had been effective.

Pratkanis *et al.* (ibid.) found that the subliminal tapes produced no change in either level of self-esteem or memory performance (see Figure 4.3). Nevertheless, when asked to rate the effectiveness of the tapes, the volunteers rated them as effective, *believing* that they had influenced their behaviour. Thus, those who listened to the tape labelled 'self-esteem' were more convinced that their self-esteem had improved, regardless of whether it was correctly labelled or not. The same pattern emerged when participants were asked whether the tape marked 'memory' improved their memory performance.

These findings are consistent with earlier research showing that subliminal audio tapes have no discernible effect on either self-esteem or memory, yet those using them continue to exhibit a belief that such tapes produce a benefit consistent with the assigned label (Greenwald *et al.* 1991; Spangenberg *et al.* 1992). Such findings have led Greenwald and colleagues to suggest that the effect of the tape label on perceived changes in behaviour is nothing more than an illusory placebo effect, so called because there is no actual improvement in the targeted behaviour, even though participants believe there is.

A further study examining the effect of subliminal audio tapes on academic achievement produced similar negative findings (Russell *et al.* 1991). In this instance, the tapes contained positive subliminal affirmations to help improve study habits and facilitate exam performance. Those participating in the study were required to listen to the tapes for ten hours a week over a period of ten weeks, a period of time in excess of that recommended by the manufacturer. However, this had no effect on students' final examination scores, or their grade point average (see Figure 4.4).

Although such commercially available audio tapes are ubiquitous, there is little empirical evidence that subliminal audio messages aimed at enhancing performance can influence behaviour. Nevertheless, it seems that using

A

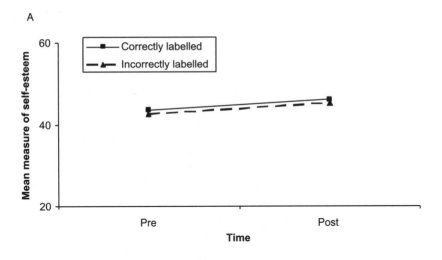

B

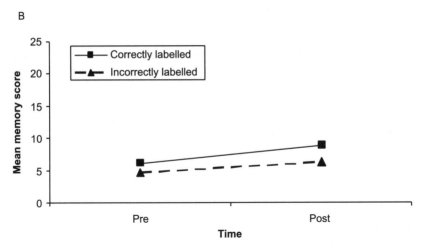

Figure 4.3 Pre versus post scores on measures of self-esteem (panel A) and memory
(panel B) for those receiving correctly labelled subliminal audiotapes and
those receiving the mislabelled tape.

(Adapted from Pratkanis *et al.* 1994)

subliminal audio tapes does produce an illusory placebo effect, where the
individual listening to an alleged message *believes* that his behaviour has
improved. This is consistent with the idea that it is not the subliminal message
per se that may be affecting the individual, but a belief in the power of
subliminal messages (Spangenberg *et al.* 1992). The argument put forward by
Greenwald and colleagues is that the illusory effects resulting from the use
of subliminal materials may be better explained in terms of a self-fulfilling

A

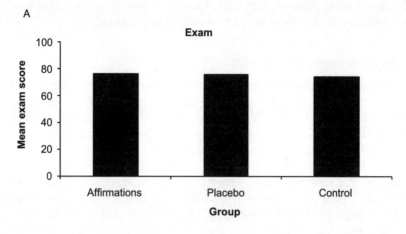

B

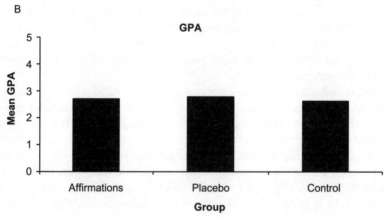

Figure 4.4 The mean exam score (panel A) and term grade point average (panel B) of three groups. The first group were given subliminal tapes with positive affirmations masked by sounds of the ocean, the second group received a placebo tape which duplicated the sound of the ocean waves but had no subliminal message. The third group acted as non-contingent controls.

(Adapted from Russell *et al.* 1991)

prophecy, consumer expectancies or a placebo effect. Greenwald *et al.* (1991) also point out that the effectiveness of subliminal audio tapes may be based on consumer expectancies. In the same way that 'brand image' rather than actual composition can influence a person's choice of clothes or beer, the *belief* that subliminal messages can aid learning creates an expectation that learning will occur.

Overall, the studies outlined above failed to produce any evidence consistent with the claims made by those who supply subliminal audio tapes. Such failures to document effects for the use of subliminal audio messages support Moore's (1995) conclusion that subliminal audio messages are incapable of influencing motivation or complex behaviour. A possible explanation for this may reside in the nature of the alleged subliminal message.

A case of the emperor's new clothes

Those who use a subliminal audio product will be aware of the fact that they cannot consciously hear the subliminal message, but nonetheless assume it is there. The layperson, of course, has no means of evaluating the content of subliminal products and this therefore requires a degree of faith in the supplier. Such faith, however, may be misplaced.

According to Merikle (1988), while subliminal perception is a valid phenomenon, for subliminal audio messages to have an effect on behaviour it is necessary to show, at the very least, the presence of a detectable message. If no message is detected, it seems obvious that no effect would be expected on behaviour. Two approaches were used by Merikle to examine whether commercially available subliminal audio cassettes contained a detectable message. The first involved submitting commercially available tapes to a spectrographic analysis. The second involved a study designed to see whether listeners could distinguish between audio tapes, some of which contained a message and some didn't.

Spectrographic analysis is a research technique used to study the construction of sound waves, and in particular the identification of human speech. The spectrograph works by recording a sound wave, which is then filtered and separated according to pre-selected frequency bands. Such an instrument is capable of producing a visual representation of a given set of sounds, incorporating the parameters of time, amplitude and frequency of the sound waves. For example, Figure 4.5 shows a spectrogram of the word *phonetician*.

In this way, a spectrogram is able to provide an accurate picture of the various components that make up a particular sound.

However, when Merikle (ibid.) conducted a spectrographic analysis on a range of commercially available subliminal audio tapes, they failed to show

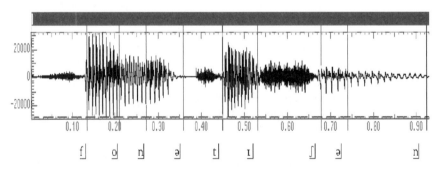

Figure 4.5 A spectrogram of the word *phonetician*.

(Adapted from an on-line tutorial available at: http://www.ling.lu.se/research/speechtutorial/ tutorial.html)

any evidence of human speech embedded within the background sounds. This suggests that subliminal audio tapes, or at least the ones examined by Merikle, do not contain embedded messages and it raises the question of whether any subliminal audio tapes contain a detectable message.

Participants have also been shown to perform at levels no better than chance when attempting to discriminate between audio tapes that contain a subliminal message and those that don't (Moore 1995). Such discriminative difficulties led Moore (1992, 1995) to propose a four-stage model of subliminal perception (see Figure 4.6). According to this model, for subliminal audio tapes to influence behaviour they need to contain a signal that is capable of triggering sensory activity in the listener. This message then needs to be internally represented in order for the person to know what the message is saying. Following this, there needs to be a motivational change, i.e. the person becomes more motivated to comply with the suggestions contained within the subliminal message, and, finally, the individual needs to change his behaviour in the desired way.

Moore (1995) points out that it is both logical and necessary that success at all four stages is needed for a subliminal message to influence behaviour, and that success at later stages is reliant upon the success of earlier stages. He tested this idea by asking a group of participants whether they could discriminate between the messages from two different audio tapes. Unfortunately none of the participants was able to discriminate between the two tapes at better than chance. Moore (ibid.) points out that, given the chance performance of participants to identify the message content, it is reasonable to infer that such messages did *not* trigger any perceptual activity or internal representation and therefore would be unable to produce a motivational change or elicit any change in behaviour. Nevertheless, Merikle (1988) notes that 'it is probably safe to predict that the present evidence will be

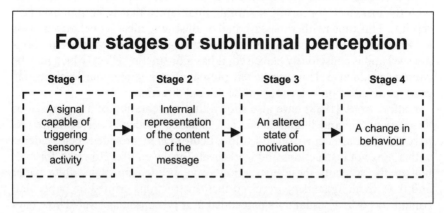

Figure 4.6 The four stages of processing necessary for successful subliminal training to elicit a change in behaviour.

(Adapted from Moore 1995)

completely ignored by everyone who wishes to continue to believe in the mystical nature of subliminal perception' (p. 371).

Visual messages

In contrast to the studies focusing on commercially available audio subliminal products, research examining the effects of visually presented subliminal messages has focused on messages created in the laboratory. The effect of presenting visual subliminal messages has been examined with reference to writing behaviour (Zuckerman 1960), academic performance (Ariam and Siller 1982; Cook 1985; Ledford *et al.* 1988; Parker 1982) and maths performance (Hudesman *et al.* 1992).

One of the earliest studies to examine the effects of subliminal visual messages found a positive effect on verbal behaviour (Zuckerman 1960). Zuckerman performed two experiments to examine the effects of both a subliminal and a supraliminal message on verbal productivity. During both studies he presented two groups of participants with three different picture cards for very brief exposure durations. Each time they were required to write a story describing the picture card. The first presentation allowed him to obtain a baseline measure of participants' word output from both groups. During presentation of the second picture card one of the groups was also presented with the subliminal message 'Write more' and during the third presentation the same group were given the subliminal message 'Don't write'. For those presented with the subliminal messages, he found that presentation of the message 'Write more' led to the production of more words, whilst the subsequent message 'Don't write' led to a slight decrease in the number of words, compared to the steady increase shown by controls who were given no subliminal messages (see Figure 4.7).

In a second experiment, Zuckerman (ibid.) repeated this procedure but with the messages appearing at supraliminal levels, that is, consciously perceptible. This time neither message had a consistent effect on behaviour. This led Zuckerman to suggest that, when the message is presented at a supraliminal level and is consciously perceived, it has a distracting effect, which may be counter-productive. However, when presented at a subliminal level, it may produce an effect on behaviour in the desired direction.

Ledford *et al.* (1988) have also shown that presentation of a preconscious visual symbolic and linguistic cue can enhance academic performance. As part of a standard course on education, Ledford *et al.* provided their students with a range of instructions and worksheets for the course. However, for one-half of the students these instructions were printed on plain white paper and the remaining students received their instructions printed on paper that contained positive visual cues embedded at a preconscious level. These cues consisted of words such as 'succeed' and 'excel'. Analysis of academic performance prior to completing the course showed no differences between the two groups. However, by the end of the course they found that, for the males

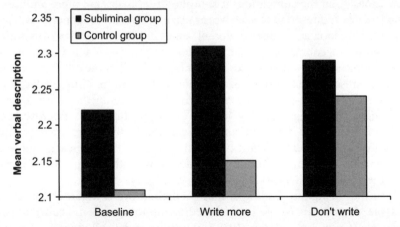

Figure 4.7 The mean number of words produced across three conditions: a baseline condition and presentation of the subliminal messages 'Write more' and 'Don't write' to the experimental group only.

(Adapted from Zuckerman 1960)

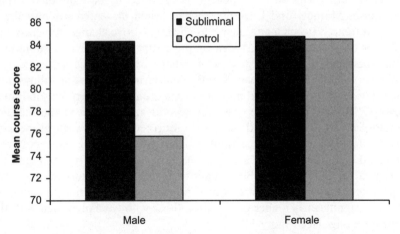

Figure 4.8 Mean course score for males and females receiving either subliminal materials or control materials.

(Adapted from Ledford *et al.* 1988)

only, those receiving their instructions on paper embedded with positive cues obtained significantly higher course scores than those who received their instructions on plain paper. In contrast, there was no difference in performance for the females (see Figure 4.8).

Ledford *et al.* (ibid.) suggested that this pattern of findings implied that gender could be a determining factor in the possible effects of subliminal messages. They argued that the reason only males showed an effect was because the words 'succeed' and 'excel' are more male oriented. However, this view is based on the contentious assumption that males are more ambitious than females and respond to such words in a more positive manner. Nevertheless, when we look at the distribution of scores in Figure 4.8 it is worth noting that the mean course scores for both female groups and the male group receiving the subliminal messages are similar, and in fact the difference comes about because of the low score of the male control group. Thus, the lack of a subliminal effect for the females may have been because they were already performing at ceiling, allowing little if any opportunity for improvement. Performance for the males, in contrast, was markedly lower, leaving ample room for improvement. Such a possibility would fit with research showing that females invariably obtain higher grades during their educational career than their male counterparts (Mau and Lynn 2001).

A further intriguing finding is that subliminal presentation of the visual message '*Mommy and I are one*' has led to improvements in academic performance (Cook 1985; Parker 1982), and more specifically increased scores in maths tests (Ariam and Siller 1982; Hudesman *et al.* 1992). Parker (1982) suggests that 'activating unconscious fantasies of symbiotic gratification or oneness with the good mother of infancy' (p. 19) can lead to positive effects on behaviour. The wish for 'oneness' is assumed to be embodied within the phrase 'Mommy and I are one', which when presented subliminally is sufficient to activate such a fantasy and elicit a positive change in behaviour.

Parker (ibid.) examined this idea by presenting three different subliminal visual messages to separate groups of college students. The students' academic performance was measured in the first term and this was followed by presentation of the subliminal messages. One group was given the subliminal message 'Mommy and I are one', the second group received the message 'My Prof and I are one', and the third group received the neutral message 'People are walking'. Using a double-blind procedure, the messages were presented eight times a week across a period of six weeks, with each message presented for only 4 msec. Subsequently, inspection of the students' final exam scores showed both groups receiving a message relating to 'oneness' obtained significantly higher grades than those who were presented with the neutral message (see Figure 4.9).

Parker (ibid.) suggested that the performance-enhancing effects of the message 'Mommy and I are one' are based upon its ability to reduce unconscious conflict and satisfy wish fulfilment for maternal warmth, leading to better resource allocation of tasks at hand. The fact that those receiving the message 'My Prof and I are one' also showed higher scores than controls may be because exposure to such a message encouraged a willingness on the part of the recipients to adopt the techniques and/or instructions of their professor more readily, leading to a more effective learning style and resulting in better grades.

Such findings are not only intriguing but have consistently been replicated by others in the field. For example, Cook (1985) found that participants receiving a subliminal version of the message 'Mommy and I are one' obtained

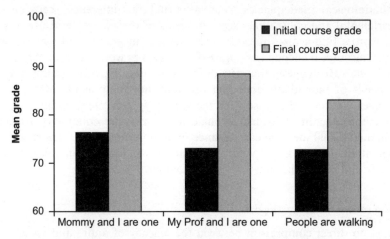

Figure 4.9 Mean initial and final course grades for the three groups receiving the positive subliminal messages 'Mommy and I are one', 'The Professor and I are one' or the control message 'People are walking'.

(Adapted from Parker 1982)

significantly higher grades than a group receiving the neutral message 'People are walking'. These findings have also been extended to other cultures, with the phrase 'Mommy and I are one' translated into Hebrew resulting in significant improvements in Israeli students' maths scores (Ariam and Siller 1982). Hudesman *et al.* (1992) also found that subliminal presentation of the message 'Mommy and I are one' before each session of a maths course led to improved performance for students during their final exam compared to those receiving the neutral message 'People are walking on the street'.

Such findings have led researchers to propose that 'the question no longer is whether subliminal stimuli affect behaviour, but rather how profound these effects are' (Mayer and Merckelback 1999: 574). Furthermore, the fact that this effect has been found across different cultures suggests that it may represent a general human phenomenon. However, it is not entirely clear how or why presentation of the subliminal message 'Mommy and I are one' produces a positive influence on behaviour. According to Parker (1982), the message affects the widely felt need for closeness with a mother figure, encouraging a sense of protection against separation from the mother, which in turn is thought to provide a reduction in anxiety and enhance a person's ability to adapt to a variety of psychological and behavioural tasks. Given that the alleged basis of the effect relates to a need for closeness with a mother figure, it would be intriguing to ascertain whether young children are more receptive to such messages, as one would expect their desire for closeness to be greater than that of adults.

Such findings, however, are not without their critics. For instance, Fudin (1993) has indicated that the effects may be a result of various methodological inadequacies, such as structural differences between the experimental and control messages, in terms of their length and use of specific words. Fudin also questions whether the meaning of the entire subliminal message is encoded as opposed to single key words, such as 'Mommy', 'I' or 'one'. He suggests that any differences found between groups may be the result of individuals encoding different sub-components of the given message. Whatever the reason for the seemingly consistent findings, at this moment in time they represent strong evidence that presentation of a specific subliminal visual message can enhance human performance. This represents a potentially fruitful area for future researchers to focus on in an attempt to identify and isolate the cause of such behavioural changes.

Audio versus visual messages

Whilst no direct comparison between the efficacy of audio and visual subliminal messages has been conducted, the evidence reviewed above indicates that visual messages have met with more success than their audio counterparts. It is not entirely clear why such a difference would emerge as a function of the communication mode. One possibility may be that the visual sensory system is more sensitive than the auditory sensory system. Although speculative, this is consistent with arguments that have been put forward intimating that visual stimuli presented subliminally have a higher probability of being processed than auditory stimuli (see Theus 1994). It may also be that subliminal audio messages are unsuccessful because they are presented alongside other audio sounds, such as the relaxing sound of ocean waves, whereas the subliminal visual messages are invariably presented in isolation. It should also be noted that the data from subliminal audio messages were based on commercially available materials, whilst the data from subliminal visual messages were based on specifically constructed and presented messages. On the one hand, this highlights the troubling question of whether commercially available materials contain a detectable message or not. On the other hand, it shows that a specifically constructed message presented in isolation from other distracting sources has the potential to enhance performance. Whatever the reason, the findings do not bode well for commercially available audio products claiming to enhance human performance. However, given the seeming success with the subliminal visual message 'Mommy and I are one', it would be interesting to see whether similar effects could be elicited when the message is presented in an auditory form.

Long-term effects

Given that visual subliminal messages can enhance some aspects of performance, it would be good to know how long such effects are expected to last. Unfortunately, there is a lack of data examining this issue and it is therefore difficult to know whether exposure to subliminal messages leads to relatively long-lasting effects or whether they have only a short-lived impact. A clear understanding of the long-term benefits of such training would seem essential if such a technique is to be of any lasting value.

Research does suggest that subliminal messages may have a short-term effect on the performance of relatively simple tasks, such as colour naming or lexical decisions under laboratory conditions. This is consistent with the proposal put forward by Greenwald *et al.* (1996) that effects of subliminal stimulation tend to be short lived, in the sense that they occur within a very short timeframe following initial exposure to the stimulus. Nevertheless, two further observations would suggest that the effects of exposure to a subliminal message may last for hours, if not weeks (Merikle 1988; Parker 1982). Merikle (1988) conducted a meta-analysis on studies investigating memory for specific information presented to patients during routine operations when they were anaesthetised. He found that patients exhibited clear evidence for memory of information presented during anaesthesia for up to 24 hours. Additional long-term effects have been reported by Parker (1982), resulting from the presentation of a subliminal message focusing on 'oneness' with the mother figure. As seen earlier, those exposed to this message achieved higher exam grades than controls. The important point here is that, after a four-week delay, he conducted a follow-up analysis and found that the difference in academic performance between the groups exposed to the different messages was maintained. However, when he analysed academic performance again after a delay of three months, this difference had all but disappeared. Such findings imply that unconsciously perceived information may have a relatively enduring impact, with effects lasting for up to four weeks, but deteriorating over longer periods of time.

Overview

Subliminal training refers to the presentation of a message, either audio or visual, below the threshold of conscious awareness, which is aimed specifically at influencing a particular aspect of behaviour. However, the idea that there is some form of fixed threshold of conscious awareness is problematic and outdated. A more accurate representation would be of a movable threshold of awareness that can be influenced by individual and situational factors. It is thus unclear how advocates of subliminal products can be sure that a subliminal message produced using a 'one threshold fits all approach' truly appears below each individual's level of conscious awareness.

The use of subliminal messages stems from the early part of the twentieth century and one of the most commonly cited claims is that based on the alleged Coke and popcorn study of Vicary. However, it has been known for some time that this was a sham and never actually took place. Nevertheless, this has not reduced the popularity of subliminal products: indeed, the data suggest that, if anything, public interest in subliminal products is increasing.

The subliminal training procedure involves the presentation of an audio or visual message that is either masked by other information or presented for a very brief period so that the individual remains consciously unaware of its presence. The general idea is that such messages work by gaining access to the unconscious mind. However, this highlights a number of confused assumptions concerning the nature of unconscious processing, which in turn draws attention to the lack of a clear theoretical approach explaining how subliminal messages are thought to influence complex behaviour. Nevertheless, it is certainly possible to perceive a stimulus without becoming consciously aware of it. Data from a wide range of studies using subliminal messages have demonstrated its viability in a number of different contexts. Furthermore, although limited, there is some indication that a subliminal message may be more effective at eliciting changes in behaviour than a message that is consciously recognised.

Unfortunately, despite the many and varied marketing claims, an examination of the evidence from commercially available subliminal audio tapes shows no evidence that these products can enhance human performance. Some have even questioned whether such products contain a subliminal message. However, while such findings have been known and available for some time, it seems that people are unwilling to give up on the possibility that such products may help and continue spending money on them. Thus, it would seem that the motivation for using subliminal audio tapes is more a matter of faith than a decision based upon empirical evidence, and such faith seems immune to the findings of science. In contrast, the data from visual subliminal messages, in particular the use of the phrase 'Mommy and I are one', has produced some consistently suggestive and intriguing results. This may represent the best opportunity for subliminal training to enhance performance. Nevertheless, more work is needed to identify the precise parameters of such an effect and the possible mechanisms involved in producing it.

Finally, in terms of the duration of effects such messages can produce, there is some evidence showing that exposure to a subliminal visual message may produce an effect that lasts for weeks, but not months, although further exploration of this is needed to be sure.

5   Audio-visual entrainment

The brain is a little saline pool that acts as a conductor, and it runs on electricity.

(Judith Hooper and Dick Teresi 1986)

Staring into the flickering flames of an open fire can often produce a calm state of reverie. Of course, this may be due in part to the feeling of warmth generated by the heat of the fire, but it may also be related to the flickering light of the flames. The idea that a flickering stimulus can influence behaviour is responsible for the warnings given out prior to certain television programmes, or films that incorporate flashing lights. Such warnings are given because these flashing lights can directly influence the electrocortical activity of the human brain, encouraging it to mimic, or repeat the pattern of, the flashes. For most people this doesn't pose a problem, but for those suffering from epilepsy it has the potential to induce a seizure. Knowing that an external stimulus, whether light or sound, can result in what's commonly referred to as an *entrainment effect* on the brain has led to the development of a variety of products aimed at inducing such effects to help stimulate certain behaviours. Advocates of audio-visual entrainment equipment suggest that it can produce a range of beneficial effects on behaviour, including reducing stress, boosting IQ, accelerating learning, enhancing creativity and improving memory.

Given such claims, this chapter, which is the last to focus on the use of a passive technique, explores the performance-enhancing effects of audio-visual entrainment (AVE). The chapter begins by defining entrainment and exploring some of the possible mechanisms by which entrainment of the brain is thought to influence behaviour. This is followed by an explanation of the three main forms of entrainment: audio, visual and combined audio-visual stimulation. The chapter then focuses on evidence to suggest that such methods of entrainment can enhance human performance. In addition, the potential long-term benefits of entrainment are examined and, finally, the chapter raises the issue of whether entrainment can produce any negative effects.

Entrainment

Entrainment refers to the tendency of two oscillating bodies to lock into phase, so that they vibrate in harmony (Regan 1989). A simple example is given in Figure 5.1, which shows three oscillating waveforms. Waves A and B are oscillating *in phase*, with the peaks and troughs of the waveform occurring at the same time. In contrast, waveform C is oscillating *out of phase* with waveforms A and B.

It is not just simple waveforms that can become entrained. An often cited example used to support the notion of entrainment is the idea that, when a group of women live together in the same household, they find their menstrual cycles begin to coincide (Weller *et al.* 1999). Of particular interest here is the idea that entrainment of the brain occurs via the repeated presentation of a stimulus, which in turn may affect behaviour.

Entraining the brain

Audio-visual entrainment (AVE) can be elicited by the repetitive presentation of a sound, a light or a combination of the two. When an auditory and/or visual stimulus is presented to an individual, this incoming sensory information is relayed to the various regions of the brain via the thalamus. Entrainment occurs when the electrocortical activity of the brain mirrors the frequency of the incoming stimuli. This notion of entrainment is based on the concept of a *frequency following response*. This represents the tendency of the electrocortical activity of the brain to entrain, or to resonate, at a frequency

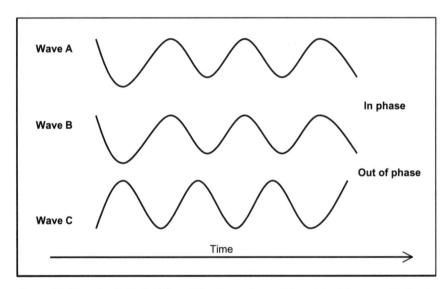

Figure 5.1 The phase relationship of three waveforms. Wave A and B are oscillating in phase, whereas wave B and C are not.

that 'follows' that of externally presented stimuli. Given such changes, it is possible that AVE can influence behaviour by directly affecting a number of physiological mechanisms, either individually or simultaneously. Candidate mechanisms include cerebral blood flow, growth and connectivity of brain cells and/or specific frequency components of electrocortical activity.

Cerebral blood flow

Visual stimulation has been shown to result in increased cerebral blood flow (Sappey-Marinier *et al.* 1992). For example, Fox and Raichle (1985) found that the stimulation resulting from visual entrainment produced a 28 per cent increase in regional cerebral blood flow (rCBF) in the striate cortex. Sappey-Marinier *et al.* (1992) suggested that such changes may be the result of increased brain activity stimulated by the flashing lights. However, it's not clear whether such changes in blood flow are sufficient to induce changes in behaviour, so that it remains unclear at this point whether modification of rCBF represents a causal factor influencing behavioural change, or simply reflects the effects of the stimulation itself.

Neural connectivity

The notion that AVE may influence the growth and connectivity of brain cells is based on research showing that electrical stimulation of the cortex can ameliorate motor dysfunction (Canavero and Bonicalzi 2002). In addition, researchers have shown that stimulation of a rat's cortex improves impaired forelimb function, which coincides with an increase in dendritic growth (Adkins-Muir and Jones 2003). These findings suggest that cortical stimulation via entrainment may promote cortical plasticity, which can subsequently affect how neural networks develop. A possible link between induced stimulation brought about by entrainment and neuronal plasticity is based on evidence showing that the electrical activity of the brain regulates the synthesis, secretion and action of neurotrophins which promote the formation of new connections between nerve cells (Schindler and Poo 2000). The notion that changes in the level of neuronal growth and connectivity, stimulated by entrainment, could lead to changes in behaviour is plausible but has yet to be fully established.

Frequency components of the brain

The idea that has received the most attention is that AVE influences behaviour by affecting specific frequency components of the electroencephalogram (EEG). This is supported by a number of studies showing entrainment of the EEG via audio, visual or combined audio-visual stimulation (Rosenfeld *et al.* 1997; Teplan and Stolc 2006; Uldo and Berg 2007). For instance, visual stimulation by repetitive flashes of light has been shown to elicit a clear entrainment of the alpha rhythm (8–12 Hz) in the EEG recordings of healthy participants (Schwab *et al.* 2006). However, Rosenfeld *et al.* (1997) have suggested that the effects of such entrainment may be mediated by individuals' baseline levels of EEG activity. Given that audio and/or visual stimulation can entrain the EEG, the notion that this can in turn influence behaviour is based upon two assumptions. First, that particular cognitive states, such as memory or attention, can be represented by distinct frequency components of the EEG (see, e.g., Klimesch 1999). In this way, entrainment provides a mechanism that enables the individual to alter her EEG, which in turn may allow her to access or enhance these desired cognitive states. The second is that the evoked or entrained EEG frequencies resulting from audio-visual stimulation involve the same pathways, mechanisms and overall physiology as the more natural, spontaneous EEG frequencies.

With regard to the assumption that the entrained EEG is similar to a healthy, normal EEG, very little direct work has focused on this issue. Nevertheless, some insight may be gained from the finding that effects on the EEG from AVE can outlast the period of stimulation itself (Rosenfeld *et al.* 1997). Although not conclusive, this does suggest that entrainment of the EEG can influence the subsequent spontaneous activity generated by the brain and as such may be similar in nature.

Auditory versus visual entrainment

Entrainment can be based on an audio signal, a visual stimulus or a combination of the two.

Audio entrainment

Auditory entrainment is generally achieved by using headphones through which a pre-set tone can be presented to both ears simultaneously. The assumption is that, after listening to this for some time, the brain of the listener responds by firing in synchrony with the rhythm of the signal. Thus, if an individual is presented with a rhythm that is sufficiently strong and consistent, the brain responds by synchronising its own electric cycles to the same rhythm. However, much of the focus within the field of entrainment has been on the slower cortical rhythms, between 10–20 Hz, which is problematic because the hearing range for a healthy human falls between 20 Hz and 20,000 Hz. Nevertheless, audio entrainment of lower frequencies can be accomplished using *binaural beats*.

Binaural beats

In 1839, the German experimenter H. W. Dove found that, when he presented a participant with two separate frequencies composed of different wavelengths, one to each ear, this produced the sensation of a third *phantom frequency* called a binaural beat in addition to the two *carrier frequencies* (Oster 1973). The difference between the two carrier signals waxes and wanes as the two distinct frequencies mesh in and out of phase with one another. These differences produce an amplitude-modulated standing wave, the binaural beat, which can be perceived. In this sense, the binaural beat is a fluctuating rhythm perceived as the frequency of the difference between the two auditory carrier signals. For example, if a 100 Hz tone is presented to the left ear and a 110 Hz tone is simultaneously presented to the right ear, the brain is capable of perceiving the difference in phase between the two signals as a distinct frequency component of 10 Hz. However, this binaural beat of 10 Hz is not 'heard' in the literal sense of the word, but, rather, the brain encodes it as an auditory beat, and as such it can be used to entrain the neural activity of the brain via the frequency-following response.

Clear evidence that a binaural beat can entrain the electrocortical activity of the brain comes from researchers who have found that binaural beats produce an auditory evoked response as measured with an electroencephalograph (Karino *et al.* 2006; Kennerly 2004; Schwarz and Taylor 2005). For example, Kennerly (2004) reported evidence of a frequency-following response occurring in the EEG for two groups of participants approximately five minutes after each participant was presented with two distinct tones to set up a binaural beat. The first group exhibited increased theta (4–8 Hz) and the second group increased delta (0.5–4 Hz) EEG activity, reflecting the virtual frequencies of the binaural beats. Karino *et al.* (2006) have also reported evidence of a frequency-following effect occurring after the presentation of a binaural beat within the theta (4–8 Hz) frequency range. Others, such as Schwarz and Taylor (2005), presented dual tones of 380 and 420 Hz in order to induce a higher frequency binaural beat of 40 Hz, and found that such audio stimulation evoked a steady and discernible response in the EEG, although it exhibited less power than a single tone of the same frequency played only to one ear. Furthermore, the frequency-following response evoked by the binaural beat was evident across frontal and central sites of the scalp, indicating that the electrocortical responses to binaural beat entrainment may be widespread.

However, a recent study examining the effects of 7 Hz binaural beat entrainment found no change in electrocortical activity after 30 minutes (Wahbeh *et al.* 2007). Furthermore, listening to the binaural beats was associated with a reduction in participants' immediate recall. Such a reduction in cognitive performance may be expected given that the aim was to entrain 7 Hz, which falls within the theta frequency range (4–8 Hz), and that theta is commonly associated with a relaxed, drowsy, hypnagogic state. Nevertheless, the fact that participants failed to exhibit any evidence of a frequency-following effect in their EEG raises some concerns about the effectiveness of such a technique. Wahbeh *et al.* (ibid.) suggest that one possible explanation for the lack of an effect on the EEG may be due to the frequency of the carrier tones used to create the binaural beat. They used two pure tones of 133 Hz and 140 Hz to create a binaural beat of 7 Hz, which may be too low to achieve an entrainment effect. This would be consistent with the suggestion that carrier tones in the range of 450–500 Hz are more effective at inducing cortical changes than tones of 100 Hz or less (see, e.g., Oster 1973; Perrrott and Nelson 1969). Nevertheless, such a finding highlights the need for additional research to elucidate the optimal range and effectiveness of the carrier tone frequencies.

Visual

Visual, or photic, stimulation is invariably achieved by flashing lights into the eyes of the individual using specially made glasses that contain light-emitting diodes (LED) on the inside. Given the intensity of the lights, it is invariably the case that an individual keeps their eyes closed during the process, allowing the light to penetrate their closed eyelids. The glasses themselves may be attached to a small portable unit that acts as both a power supply and a control centre. The LEDs then flash out a pre-set frequency pattern entraining the brain via the optic nerve, where it has been shown to induce the EEG of the brain to match the frequency of the flickering lights. This is based on early research showing that rhythmic electrical potential changes can be recorded from the occipital region of the scalp when an individual is required to look at a flickering light field and that the elicited waves are of the same order of magnitude and rhythm as the flickering field (Adrian and Matthews 1934). Over time, this finding stimulated researchers to examine what happens to the electrocortical activity of the brain when an individual is exposed to flickering lights (see, e.g., Herrmann 2001; Lansing and Barlow 1972; Toman 1941). For instance, when Toman (1941) recorded the EEG of people exposed to a flickering light, he found that they exhibited *flicker-following potentials* in both the occipital and central regions of the scalp. These potentials represent a frequency-following response to visual stimuli. Since then a number of researchers have shown that visual stimulation at a specific frequency is sufficient to produce a frequency-following response, particularly in the visual cortex, leading to an increase in power of the same frequency within the EEG (Frederick *et al.* 1999; Rosenfeld *et al.* 1997; Schwab *et al.* 2006).

Although the EEG has traditionally been divided into a number of components with generally agreed-upon frequency ranges (see Table 3.1), there is increasing evidence that the frequency range of a specific component can vary between individuals (e.g. Klimesch 1999). Klimesch has suggested that, instead of using a generic frequency range for everyone, each person's EEG should be identified individually using the peak of their EEG activity as an anchor point. In this way, rather than alpha simply representing a fixed frequency range of 8–12 Hz, it would represent a 2 Hz window to either side of an individual's peak frequency. This has been referred to as the individual alpha frequency (IAF) range. The idea that EEG frequency ranges can vary between individuals has led some to suggest that visual entrainment may be more effective at driving the EEG when the stimulus frequency matches the individual's peak alpha frequency than using the midpoint of a traditional bandwidth (Frederick *et al.* 2004). Furthermore, although visual entrainment engages predominantly with the primary visual cortex, research has shown that it is capable of eliciting changes in cortical activity that are widely distributed across the cortex (Timmerman *et al.* 1999).

These findings confirm the notion that a visual stimulus presented at a specific frequency rate can elicit a change in the amplitude of the responding frequency within the EEG. Furthermore, the effects of such entrainment may spread beyond the localised regions of the visual cortex, although its effectiveness at entraining a particular frequency component of the EEG may depend on the individual's resting baseline activity.

Audio versus visual

Given the distinction between auditory and visual stimulation, an obvious question is whether one or other of these modalities is more successful at eliciting changes in the brain, or whether a combined audio-visual approach is more effective.

One study directly addressing this issue was conducted by Frederick *et al.* (1999), and compared the effectiveness of a variety of entrainment methods. These included auditory stimulation, when the recipient had her eyes both open and closed, visual stimulation with eyes closed, and combined audio-visual stimulation with eyes closed. Keep in mind that visual stimulation paradigms invariably occur using an eyes-closed procedure, as a flashing light perceived through closed eyelids is still sufficient to elicit an entrainment effect and maintaining an eyes-closed position is often more comfortable for the participant. The entrainment procedure involved a single seven-minute period during which the participant was stimulated at a frequency of 18.5 Hz. Post-training examination of the EEG revealed a significant increase in the amplitude of each person's EEG at 18.5 Hz for all types of stimulation. This is consistent with previous research and confirms that audio and/or visual entrainment can produce a frequency-following effect in the brain. Importantly, additional analysis comparing the different modalities of entrainment showed that the auditory eyes-closed condition produced the most effective change in EEG. Thus, the most effective entrainment paradigm may be one utilising audio entrainment, with the participant sitting with eyes closed. It may seem counter-intuitive that the combined audio-visual entrainment did not produce more of an effect on the EEG than either audio or visual conditions alone. However, Frederick *et al.* (ibid.) account for this by suggesting that simultaneous stimulation in both the auditory and visual domains interferes with, rather than reinforces, the entrainment effect.

Overall, data resulting from a direct comparison of the effectiveness of audio to visual entrainment is limited and therefore any conclusions reached at this stage are necessarily tentative. Nevertheless, the results would suggest that entrainment via the audio domain may be the most effective means to elicit entrainment effects in the brain.

Enhancing performance

Entrainment has been shown to be an effective mechanism at producing frequency-following effects in the EEG. However, there has been only a limited amount of research focusing on the application of this technique to enhance human performance. Given that entrainment may occur using auditory, visual or a combined audio-visual approach, this section examines the evidence from each of these approaches in turn.

Audio

To date, all of the research examining the potential benefits of audio entrainment has focused on the use of binaural beats. This has produced some encouraging findings in terms of benefits for memory performance (Kennerly 1996), creativity (Hiew 1995), as well as for mood and attention (Lane *et al.* 1998).

Kennerly (1996) found that playing beta frequency binaural beats to a group of students helped improve their memory performance. This involved presenting one group with a music tape that contained binaural beats within the beta (15–35 Hz) frequency range played in the background and another group with a tape containing the same music but no binaural beats. Initially, both groups were simply required to listen to the tapes. However, after a period of 15 minutes the groups were given a range of memory tasks to complete, including free recall, recognition and digit span, whilst they continued to listen to the tapes. The results showed that those listening to the tape containing the binaural beats performed significantly better on three out of four memory tasks compared to those who listened to music only (see Figure 5.2).

The results led Kennerly (ibid.) to suggest that binaural beats represent a mechanism for facilitating memory and that such a technique can function as a stand-alone form of brain wave entrainment. However, the findings are restricted by the fact that Kennerly failed to identify the precise frequency of audio beats used. This makes it difficult, if not impossible, to replicate such findings and fails to identify whether it is a particular frequency component of the beta range that is producing the effect, or whether it is necessary to entrain the full frequency range.

Similar difficulties are evident in the report by Hiew (1995), who attempted to enhance creativity using a commercialised product called Hemi-Sync, which contains binaural beats. Hiew recruited two groups of participants and had them listen to different audio tapes. For one group the tapes contained Hemi-Sync tones designed to produce an entrainment effect, whilst for the remaining control group the tape simply contained relaxation instructions and the sounds of ocean waves. After listening to the tapes participants from

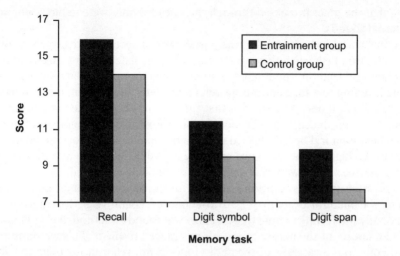

Figure 5.2 Performance on three memory tasks: free recall, digit symbol and digit span, for those exposed to binaural beats and controls.

(Adapted from Kennerly 1996)

both groups completed measures assessing creativity, which required them to name as many alternative uses for common everyday objects as they could (e.g. alternative uses for a house brick). Hiew found that those who listened to the tape with the Hemi-Sync tones generated more uses for objects when completing the creativity task and exhibited a greater level of creative flexibility as represented by a shift in the use of categories for each object. These findings led to the proposal that listening to Hemi-Sync tones can enhance creativity by encouraging thinking that is more divergent and flexible. Here again, however, the methodology lacks sufficient information concerning the precise nature of the auditory tones used to produce the entrainment effect.

A somewhat different approach was adopted by Lane *et al.* (1998) to examine the effects of binaural beat entrainment on mood and attention. They used a three-stage procedure which required participants initially to complete a range of questionnaires, which included measuring mood, followed by a task measuring attention, and then a second set of questionnaires which again measured mood. The participants completed this procedure three times, listening to different audio tapes during performance of the attention task each time. During the first session they listened to a tape containing only pink noise. This was used to obtain baseline levels of mood and cognition. During the second session they were presented with an audio tape containing binaural beats of 1.5 Hz and 4 Hz, aimed at entraining delta and low theta activity. In the third session the audio tape contained binaural beats of 16 and 24 Hz and was aimed at entraining beta activity. The presentation order of the tapes was counterbalanced across the group and, interestingly, the participants didn't know that they were listening to auditory binaural beats: they were simply told that the tones presented through their headphones were to block out any external sounds.

Lane *et al.* (ibid.) found that the participants detected more targets during the attention task when they were simultaneously listening to a tape containing binaural beats entraining beta and produced more false alarms when they were listening to a tape entraining delta and theta. In addition, measurement of changes in mood state showed that the binaural beats aimed at entraining delta/theta produced a greater increase in task-related confusion and fatigue than beta binaural beats. This led them to propose that auditory entrainment within the beta frequency range can have a positive effect on attention, even when people are unaware that such signals are being presented.

This study provides additional support for the notion that auditory entrainment via binaural beats may lead to enhanced cognitive performance. It is especially interesting to note that an effect was found even though participants were unaware of the nature of the sounds played to them. This would imply that conscious awareness of the audio tones is not relevant for them to elicit an effect on cortical activity and, in turn, influence behaviour. However, once again, the study suffers from the methodological problem of failing to clearly identify which frequency component is producing the desired effect. By combining two frequencies to entrain beta they make it impossible to identify whether the effect is the result of frequency component alone or the result of a combined effect.

Visual

The use of visual stimulation to entrain the EEG has been shown to impact on the psychological status of a person and affect imagery ability as well as arousal levels (Richardson and McAndrew 1990; von Gizycki *et al.* 1997, 1998). For instance, Richardson and McAndrew (1990) proposed that visual entrainment may be one of the easiest methods to bring about a *hypnogogic state* and facilitate the emergence into conscious awareness of visual imagination images. A hypnogogic state refers to the dreamlike experience that often represents the state between being fully awake and falling asleep, which may be accompanied by physical immobility and lucid visual and auditory hallucinations. To test this idea, they examined the visual entrainment effect of three different frequencies (6 Hz, 10 Hz and 18 Hz) on the imagery ability of a group of female students. They found that entrainment of the lower frequency ranges of 6 and 10 Hz led participants to produce more complex images than when a higher frequency of 18 Hz was used. Von Gizycki *et al.* (1997) attempted to extend these results by examining the effects of visual entrainment on imagery across five different frequencies (5, 10, 15, 20 and 25Hz). They found that such visual stimulation induced a range of complex imagery phenomena similar to the images perceived during sleep onset and dreaming.

The work of Richardson and McAndrew (1990) is encouraging, although more needs to be done to explore possible differential effects resulting from entrainment of a 6 Hz frequency compared to one of 10 Hz. Unfortunately, the work of von Gizycki and colleagues is less robust and as such its results are more ambiguous. For instance, their procedure involves the visual entrainment of five distinct frequencies. Yet it remains unclear what the rationale was for using such a wide range of frequencies and, in addition to this, they fail to identify which of the five frequencies, or combinations, was responsible for eliciting the effect on imagery. They also failed to include any controls and it is therefore difficult to attribute the alleged effects on enhanced imagery to visual entrainment.

An alternative approach, adopted by Williams (2001), involves the use of a *flicker training paradigm* to induce visual entrainment and influence cognition. Rather than having a repeatedly flashing light in her eyes, a participant is presented with a flickering stimulus on a computer screen, such as a rectangle that changes colour from grey to white, which is set to change colour, or flicker, at a specific frequency. Williams used this paradigm to induce a visual entrainment effect using a flickering stimulus at one of three distinct frequencies (8.7 Hz, 10 Hz and 11.7 Hz). Each time the flickering stimulus was shown it was immediately followed by the brief presentation of a three-letter trigram forming either a nonsense word (e.g. TEF) or a real word (e.g. BID) and participants were asked to classify the trigram as either nonsense or real as quickly as they could (see Figure 5.3).

The fact that a target immediately followed a flickering stimulus may make

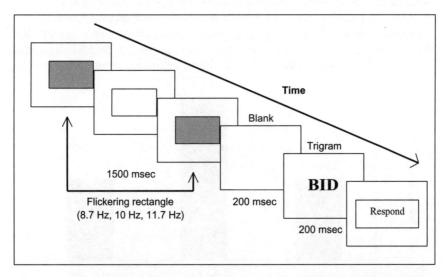

Figure 5.3 The flicker paradigm. A flickering stimulus (e.g., a rectangle which changes its colour from grey to white a pre-set number of times every second) is presented for a short period followed by a blank screen for 200 msec and then a trigram for 200 msec. The participant then needs to respond by classifying the trigram as either a real word or not as quickly as possible.

(Adapted from Williams 2001)

this paradigm more sensitive to the subtle changes in cortical activity brought about by visual entrainment, particularly if they fade over time. The different frequencies of the flickering stimulus were found to have no effect on the speed of participants' responses with regard to whether a trigram was classified as nonsense or real. However, in a follow-up memory task, participants were required to recognise which were the 'old' trigrams they had seen during the classification task when presented with a randomly mixed group of old and new trigrams. Williams (ibid.) found that participants recognised significantly more of the trigrams that followed the 10 Hz flicker than those that followed either the 8.7 Hz or the 11.7 Hz flicker (see Figure 5.4).

In addition, Williams (ibid.) was also able to show that the flickering stimulus was capable of entraining EEG activity, with each of the entrainment frequencies showing an increase in amplitude following presentation of the flickering stimulus. These findings show that a 10 Hz flicker is sufficient to elicit changes in cortical activity and that such changes are capable of improving recognition memory. This is consistent with research showing that better memory performance is associated with greater amplitude in the alpha (8–12 Hz) frequency range of the EEG (Doppelmayr *et al.* 2005).

More recently, Williams *et al.* (2006) used a similar visual flicker entrainment paradigm to show that frequencies close to 10 Hz can improve the recognition of elderly participants aged between 67 and 92 years. This led them to propose that visual entrainment can selectively facilitate the neural mechanisms of the brain, as evidenced by changes in EEG, and that such changes in cortical activity can directly influence psychological states.

Overall, use of the flicker paradigm provides compelling evidence that visual stimulation at 10 Hz can produce clear changes in the EEG and lead to enhanced memory performance. Furthermore, the fact that such a finding

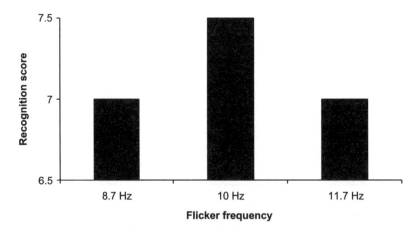

Figure 5.4 Mean recognition scores for trigrams following encoding with visual flicker entrainment at 8.7, 10 and 11.7 Hz.

(Adapted from Williams 2001)

has been shown to be stable across different age groups suggests that it may produce a general effect on cognition.

Combined audio-visual

Researchers have also combined audio and visual signals to help improve academic performance (Budzynski and Budzynski 2000; Budzynski *et al.* 1999). For example, Budzynski and Tang (1998) used a device called the 'Biolight', which is a combined audio-visual stimulation and electrodermal response (EDR) feedback device, in an attempt to see whether AVE could increase students' academic performance. The EDR reflects the electrical activity generated by the sweat glands of the skin, usually measured on the hand. It is also referred to as electrodermal activity or EDA and is thought to provide a measure of physiological arousal (see Andreassi 2000). According to some previous work, the Biolight is capable of eliciting changes in the amplitude or power of various frequency components of the EEG, as well as being able to increase peak alpha frequencies (Budzynski and Tang 1998).

To examine the effects of AVE, Budzynski *et al.* (1999) recruited a number of students, some of whom underwent an entrainment procedure whilst the remainder acted as non-contingent controls. Visual entrainment involved flashing amber lights to both eyes at frequencies that cycled between 14 Hz and 22 Hz. Auditory stimulation occurred in the form of a tone, the frequency of which was proportional to the participant's EDR level, with the frequency decreasing as the individual was able to relax and lower her EDR. This training was repeated each day for five days a week, for a total of six weeks. Thus, those undergoing entrainment completed a total of 30 sessions, or seven and a half hours of entrainment.

Analysis of participants' EEGs at the end of the training showed that those who took part in the entrainment exhibited an increase in their overall alpha frequency at left and right frontal regions (see Figure 5.5), as well as an increase in high alpha ratios (i.e. 11–13Hz/9–11Hz) in the right frontal region and an increase in their beta frequency at the right frontal region.

In addition to this, they found that those in the entrainment group showed a significant improvement in their academic performance as measured by their grade point average (GPA), whilst those in the non-training control group showed a small decrease in their GPA over time (see Figure 5.6).

Thus, AVE seems to have speeded up each individual's dominant alpha frequency and subsequently facilitated learning, resulting in improved grades. Budzynski *et al.* (1999) conclude that AVE results in an 'improvement in academic performance by changing certain EEG parameters to a more optimal level' (p. 20).

These findings are encouraging, suggesting a clear link between changes in the EEG via AVE and improved academic performance. However, once again, there is the confounding methodological issue of presenting multiple

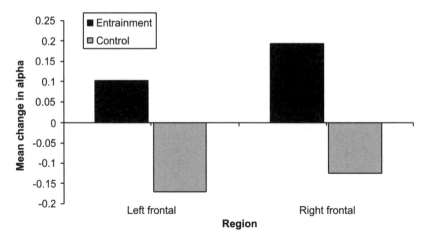

Figure 5.5 Mean changes in the alpha frequency following the training for the entrainment and control group at left frontal (F7) and right frontal (F8) regions.

(Adapted from Budzynski *et al.* 1998)

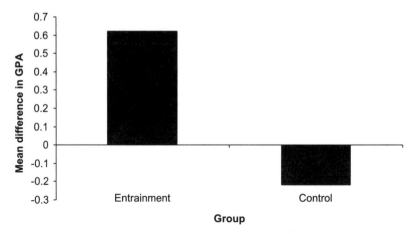

Figure 5.6 Changes in academic performance as measured by mean difference in grade point average for entrainment and control groups.

(Adapted from Budzynski *et al.* 1998)

frequencies (14 and 22 Hz), as well as the difficulties inherent in attempting to tease apart the individual effects of visual and audio stimulation when using a combined AVE paradigm. Given that the changes recorded in the EEG were found within the alpha frequency range (8–12 Hz), it may be the case that entrainment of the 14 Hz component was predominantly responsible for such effects. However, a direct comparison between the two frequency components is needed to clarify this issue.

Lasting effects of entrainment

Given that AVE can affect the amplitude and/or frequency of the electrocortical activity of the brain, which in turn may enhance an individual's ability to perform certain tasks, an important point to consider is the duration of such effects. Are such changes enduring or does such training elicit only short-term benefits?

Rosenfeld *et al.* (1997) examined what effect an eight-minute period of visual entrainment within both the alpha (10 Hz) and beta frequency (22 Hz) ranges would have on participants' EEGs. They found that stimulation within the alpha frequency produced only a transient enhancement and was moderated by an individual's baseline activity. However, entrainment of the beta frequency component produced more prolonged changes in the EEG that were maintained for up to 24 minutes. Thus, a single session of entrainment can generate changes in the EEG that can last beyond the end of the stimulation period itself, albeit for a limited amount of time. This would suggest that the entrainment of a specific frequency component may affect the brain's natural ability to produce that frequency and, in so doing, facilitate its production beyond that of the entrainment period. Moreover, Rosenfeld *et al.* (ibid.) point out that more robust entrainment effects may be elicited if individual differences in baseline EEG activity are taken into account.

Nevertheless, Frederick *et al.* (2004) found that changes in electrocortical activity as a result of entrainment failed to last for very long. They examined the effects of AVE on EEG and found that a single 20-minute session, where those taking part were either stimulated at their dominant alpha frequency or at twice their dominant alpha frequency, exhibited a significant change in their EEG in the desired direction. However, EEG recordings taken 30 minutes after the entrainment ended showed little evidence of these effects persisting.

Taken together, these results would suggest that a single period of entrainment is capable of producing changes in the EEG in the desired frequency range, and that such changes may last for up to 24 minutes, but not beyond. Such results, while limited, are encouraging. If a single entrainment session is capable of producing changes in the EEG that last beyond the stimulation itself, it seems probable that a more persistent effect may be obtained with a greater number of sessions. More research is needed that not only takes into account individual differences in baseline EEG activity but also compares the effectiveness of the various entrainment methods to ascertain which is the most effective at producing long-term effects and why.

Negative effects

There have been a range of studies utilising AVE for clinical populations. Indeed research has shown, *inter alia*, that such entrainment techniques can lead to improvements in the academic performance of children exhibiting learning difficulties (Olmstead 2005), decrease the symptoms and improve the problem behaviours of children with attentional disorders (Joyce and Siever 2000) and reduce the effects of chronic pain (Boersma and Gagnon 1992). Such findings have led to the suggestion that entrainment technology 'has the potential to greatly enhance cognitive abilities and quality of life for the learning-disabled individual' (Olmstead 2005: 49).

In spite of this, it is also widely recognised by those in the field that there are certain populations that should be cautious in their use of such equipment. These include those with a history, or family history, of seizures or epilepsy. Furthermore, anyone using a pacemaker, or suffering from cardiac arrhythmia or other heart disorders, and anyone taking stimulants, psychoactive drugs or tranquillisers should be wary of using AVE equipment. Such groups are urged to be cautious because entrainment could potentially have a negative effect on their behaviour. For example, use of such equipment by those suffering from epilepsy could provoke a seizure.

Even if an individual doesn't fall into any of the categories outlined above, it may pay to remain cautious, particularly when using visual entrainment devices. One reported case study has shown that a product marketed as a brainwave synchroniser induced epileptic seizures in an otherwise healthy person (Ruuskanen-Utoi and Salmi 1994). In general, most epileptic seizures occur unexpectedly and in a spontaneous fashion. However, it is possible for an epileptic seizure to occur in response to a specific environmental stimulus or event. These are often referred to as reflex seizures. Ruuskanen-Utoi and Salmi (ibid.) reported on a woman with no history of suffering from epileptic seizures, or neurological disease, who experienced such a seizure while using a brainwave synchroniser that presented intermittent flashing lights against a background of tones. This happened the first time the woman used the device and resulted in her losing consciousness for approximately 30 minutes. A follow-up examination ten months later showed no further evidence of seizures or symptoms. However, unsurprisingly, the woman had refrained from using the device any further.

Such a finding may give cause for concern over the use of entrainment devices, particularly those emitting a visual signal. Indeed, some have suggested that the use of photic stimulation equipment should be monitored for possible health risks (Striano *et al.* 1992). However, it is important to keep in mind that this finding represents the only published report of a visual entrainment device producing a negative effect on someone's health and should be cautiously interpreted against the backdrop of a large number of users, none of whom have reported any ill effects from such training. In addition, there is no evidence as yet that audio entrainment techniques can produce such negative effects.

Thus, while many consumers often adopt a pragmatic approach when using such devices, it may be worth noting that there are some who may not benefit from AVE.

Overview

Entrainment refers to the synchronising of two or more rhythms or frequencies in such a way that they begin to oscillate or resonate in harmony. For instance, the continuous presentation of a visual or auditory stimulus can produce an entrainment effect on the electrical activity of the brain. This effect is most clearly seen in the human EEG and is often referred to as a frequency-following effect, because after a sufficient amount of time the frequency of the EEG begins to follow that of the presented stimulus.

A number of physiological mechanisms have been proposed to be influenced by entrainment, which in turn may affect behaviour. They include the idea that entrainment may stimulate blood flow in the brain, leading to increases in blood flow in certain areas as a result of such stimulation. However, it is not clear as yet whether such changes are sufficient to induce behavioural changes. There is also research suggesting that cortical stimulation resulting from entrainment may encourage greater connectivity between neurons, although more work is needed to establish this point. The most prominent candidate mechanism is represented by the various electrocortical frequency components of the brain. A great deal of research has been undertaken to examine the spectral components of the human EEG with a view to relating specific components to particular aspects of behaviour. If, as suspected, such components play a causal role in behaviour, then attempting to modify them via audio-visual entrainment would be expected to produce behavioural changes. However, it has yet to be established whether cortical activity induced via entrainment involves the same pathways and physiology as naturally occurring rhythms.

Cortical entrainment can be induced using auditory, visual or a combination of audio-visual stimuli. Audio entrainment may be the result of a single audio signal presented to both ears simultaneously or of two distinct audio frequencies presented simultaneously, one to each ear, creating a binaural beat. Visual entrainment, in contrast, invariably involves flashing lights at a pre-set frequency range into the eyes of the recipient. Both audio and visual stimulation have been shown to be capable of eliciting a frequency-following response in the EEG and thus exhibit the potential to alter behaviour. Nevertheless, a direct comparison between the effectiveness of audio and visual signals suggests that audio entrainment may be the more effective of the two modalities.

In terms of enhancing performance, audio entrainment using binaural beats has produced some encouraging findings, suggesting that such a technique may be capable of facilitating memory, creativity and attention. Unfortunately, the research is often plagued by a variety of methodological problems, restricting the interpretation of the data. In contrast, the findings from visual entrainment studies, in particular those using a flicker paradigm, have shown more robust effects indicating that visual entrainment of a 10 Hz frequency can enhance memory. In addition, combined audio-visual entrainment has produced some encouraging effects on improving the academic performance of students. However, this also exhibited a number of methodological short-comings. Overall, the results from audio and combined audio-visual entrainment studies are suggestive but not conclusive. By far and away the best results have come from studies using only visual entrainment. However, a cautionary note should be added here because the use of visual entrainment has been shown to induce a seizure in an otherwise healthy individual, although this is the only reported case to date. Finally, although there is only limited evidence, the effects of a single entrainment session may be only short lived.

Thus, the data from studies focusing on the use of entrainment to enhance human performance are encouraging and suggestive. Nevertheless, more needs to be done to fully explore the potential applications such technology may offer for the entrainment of electrocortical activity and its subsequent benefits for behaviour.

Part II
Active techniques

6　Meditation

The function of meditation is to take one beyond the limits of the mind.
(Meher Baba)

This chapter marks a shift in focus from passive techniques, requiring little or no effort, to more active techniques that require the individual to undergo a regime of training in order to enhance performance and/or learn new ways of behaving. One active technique that is long-established and in particular cultures represents a very traditional method of improving behaviour is that of meditation. According to Davidson *et al.* (2003) the use of meditation to improve health and performance is not only widespread but also growing in popularity. Thus, this chapter focuses on the potential performance-enhancing effects of meditation.

The chapter begins by outlining what meditation is and identifies some of the key components contained within the meditative process. It then explores some of the available meditative techniques, highlighting two key aspects that are shared by many approaches: mindfulness and concentration. Following this, the chapter examines the psychophysiological changes that can occur as a result of meditation, each of which provides a plausible mechanism for altering or enhancing behaviour. The main section of the chapter deals with the question of whether meditation can enhance human performance. The chapter also highlights some of the factors that have been shown to influence the effectiveness of meditation. It ends by reviewing recent discussions concerning the notion that meditation may predispose a person to exhibit epileptic-like behaviours.

Meditation

The practice of meditation may have existed for many centuries but there is little agreement as to what the term 'meditation' specifically refers to. Nevertheless, there is some consensus that meditation refers to an *approach* rather than a specific technique. According to Fisher (2006), meditation originally referred to all types of physical and cognitive exercise and only later came to signify the contemplative and philosophical thinking that is often associated with it today.

A key component of meditation is its seeming ability to elicit changes in consciousness. According to Cahn and Polich (2006), it represents a way of self-regulating the mind and body and as such is capable of influencing cognitive processing. The regulation or control of attention forms a central component of many of the different meditative approaches. For example, it may involve a systematic narrowing of attention with a focus on breathing and relaxation. Meditation is also portrayed as a self-regulatory process designed to help the individual bring his mental processes under greater voluntary control.

While the various meditative approaches may differ, the procedure itself invariably involves a person sitting or lying quietly, focusing inward on their breathing, adopting a positive attitude, and may or may not involve the repetition of a mantra or positive affirmations. In addition, the individual may utilise various tools to help focus attention and establish a meditative state. These can include the use of a visual image, or mandala (see Figure 6.1),

Figure 6.1 A mandala image which may be used as part of meditative practice.

rosaries or prayer wheels. Such tools are thought to aid the individual in his attempts to reach a meditative state by reducing rumination and encouraging a focused yet relaxed state of awareness.

Over time, meditation has been associated with a range of religious and/or spiritual approaches and, whilst this is not thought to be an essential component, research by Wachholtz and Pargament (2005) indicates that spiritual meditation may be more effective at eliciting behavioural changes than secular meditation. For example, they examined some of the differences between secular and spiritual meditation and found that those practising meditation that included a spiritual component exhibited a greater reduction in levels of anxiety, an improved mood, and were able to tolerate pain for longer than their non-spiritual counterparts.

Meditative techniques

As noted above, 'meditation' tends to be used as an umbrella term to denote a variety of different techniques. For instance, there is transcendental meditation, Vipassana meditation, Buddhist meditation, yoga mantra meditation and Zen meditation, to name but a few. To provide some idea of what these techniques involve, this section provides a brief outline of transcendental and Vipassana meditation, highlighting some of the key components thought to be shared by these and many other approaches.

Transcendental meditation represents a technique developed by Maharishi Mahesh Yogi, which formed the central component of a popular movement during the 1960s, particularly in America, and whilst it has links with one of the orthodox systems of Indian philosophy (e.g. Vedanta), it is not strictly connected to any religious tradition. According to Goleman (1972), the transcendental approach includes three major steps. The first involves the mental repetition of a mantra to still the activity of the mind of the practitioner, encouraging a deeper level of consciousness. The second step aims to infuse the state of transcendental consciousness experienced during the first stage into normal waking states. The third and final step is thought to involve devotion to a particular object and can also include initiating others into transcendental meditation.

In contrast, in Vipassana meditation the individual begins by learning how to focus or stabilise his concentration on a particular target, such as his breathing. He then slowly begins to broaden his focus, whilst simultaneously cultivating what is referred to as a non-reactive form of sensory awareness or 'bare' attention. This form of attention is non-reactive in the sense that the individual does not become caught up in making judgements about sensory events.

Goleman (ibid.) found that, whilst there are many different types of meditation, they often share two core components: *mindfulness* and *concentration*. Mindfulness, which is sometimes also referred to as opening-up meditation, refers to the maintenance of a particular attentional stance towards all objects of awareness. It is thought to represent a specific non-judgemental awareness of present-moment stimuli without cognitive elaboration. The aim is to allow thoughts and feelings to rise to the surface whilst maintaining a thoughtful and yet unattached awareness of the process. Zen, Vipassana and westernised mindfulness meditation all incorporate this dimension (Kabat-Zinn 2003; Shapiro and Walsh 1984). In contrast, concentration requires a focusing of attention upon a specific target or activity, a repeated sound, a visual image or a physiological sensation such as the rate and depth of breathing. According to Goleman (1972), the goal is for the mind of the individual to merge with the target object and a frequently reported effect of concentrative meditation is a reported decrease in awareness and reactivity to external environmental stimuli. Davidson and Goleman (1977) suggest that this may be because during meditation environmental stimuli are attenuated and therefore produce less of an impact on levels of cortical arousal. Examples of concentrative meditation are the many forms of yoga and the Buddhist Samatha approach which focuses on breathing.

Mindfulness and concentration need not be distinct components of the meditative process but can be integrated in an interactive manner, with concentration used to enhance the effects of mindfulness (Goleman 1972). A particular meditative technique may thus include either or both of these different elements, but place a particular emphasis on one aspect.

However, differences in the particular meditative approach adopted or the emphasis placed on various components can have a number of implications. For example, it may be that the different approaches to meditation lead to the development of distinct skills and abilities. Thus, the effects of one particular approach may be different from those of another, as each has highly specific procedures and goals. What may be true for one approach may not be true for another and what one adopts another may shun. This can make comparing meditative approaches problematic and limits the possibility of revealing generic insights into the meditative process.

Meditation and the brain

Meditation has been shown to elicit a number of changes within the brain, any of which may constitute a mechanism for altering behaviour. These include changes in brain structure, cerebral blood flow and electrocortical activity (see Cahn and Polich 2006).

Brain structure

The first study to show structural changes associated with meditation was conducted by Lazar *et al.* (2005). This involved taking a number of brain scans from a group of people who meditated for an average of 40 minutes per day and comparing them to non-meditators. Lazar *et al.* found that specific areas of the cortex were thicker in the participants who practised meditation.

These areas included the right anterior insula, known to be involved in monitoring bodily functions, and parts of the prefrontal cortex involved in attention and sensory processing. In addition, the extent of the thickening correlated with meditation experience, with long-term meditators showing greater levels of cortical thickening. It is not clear as yet whether such cortical changes are simply the result of participating in meditative practice or are mediated by behavioural changes emerging as a consequence of engaging in meditation. Nevertheless, Lazar *et al.* (ibid.) suggest that changes in cortical thickness associated with meditation may support increased neural functioning as well as offer some level of protection against possible age-related neuronal loss.

Cerebral blood flow

Others have reported changes in the level of cerebral blood flow, which is thought to provide an index of cortical activity, as a function of meditative practice (Jevning *et al.* 1996). Jevning *et al.* found that meditators exhibit increased levels of blood flow to the frontal and occipital regions during meditation compared to resting controls. Such changes are thought to index the increase in attentional demands of the meditation procedure, as well as highlight possible alterations in visual experience. Jevning *et al.* note that such alterations in the level of cerebral blood flow may be indicative of improved executive attentional focus, as clear associations have been found between increased frontal activity and performance on executive attention tasks (see e.g. Benham *et al.* 1998).

Electrocortical activity

Meditation has also been shown to influence the different components of electrocortical activity (see Table 3.1), as well as activity occurring in specific cortical regions. For instance, Davidson *et al.* (2003) found that those who took part in an eight-week meditation programme exhibited a significant increase in cortical activity within the left anterior region of the brain, compared to non-meditating controls. Davidson (2005) has argued that activation of this region of the brain is associated with positive emotional states, emotional well-being and happiness. He has suggested that meditation may provide a mechanism for training positive emotional states and improving levels of happiness.

There have also been a number of reported changes in the activity levels of specific frequency components of EEG activity. For example, adept meditative practitioners exhibit profound changes in gamma (30 + Hz) activity compared to novices (Lutz *et al.* 2004). Lutz *et al.* suggest that, given the role gamma plays in the integration of distributed neuronal processes, meditation may encourage large-scale brain coordination, leading to a more stable and coherent mental experience, which in turn could positively influence attention, working memory and learning.

Others have found that advanced practitioners, with over 10,000 hours of meditative practice, exhibit elevated levels of alpha (8–12 Hz) activity compared to non-meditating controls (Aftanas and Golocheikine 2005; Herbert and Tan 2004), though it remains unclear as yet whether such changes reflect the greater levels of relaxation achieved by experienced meditators or an increased level of internally directed attention. Furthermore, Aftanas and Golocheikine (2003) found an association between meditation and enhanced levels of theta (4–7 Hz) activity, with more proficient practitioners exhibiting greater levels of theta. Such a pattern may indicate that increases in theta power during meditation may be due to the developmental level or stage of the individual, with the more advanced practitioners exhibiting greater changes. Moreover, increases in the level of theta activity have been reported during tasks requiring sustained attention (Gevins *et al.* 1997), which has led to the suggestion that the enhanced levels of theta seen during meditation may represent a cortical signature of enhanced concentration (Pan *et al.* 1994).

The above findings show that meditation can influence the brain in a number of different ways. Such changes in cortical functioning provide a plausible mechanism for modifying behaviour. The variety of effects may be influenced by a number of factors, including the individual's skill and experience as a meditator, the particular technique adopted, a combination of the technique and the subjective experience of the individual, or methodological differences with regard to the recording set-up and environment. Furthermore, it should be noted that such changes associated with meditative practice do not necessarily mean that the meditative process per se is the *causal* factor. It may be that meditation causes such changes or it may be that they are a by-product of the meditation process itself. For example, meditation may lead to changes in behaviour and/or lifestyle, which in turn could lead to changes in brain activity.

Enhancing performance

Enhancing performance via meditation has invariably focused on attentional processing as well as various cognitive and academic skills.

Attentional performance

Attention is known to be a limited resource, which can influence and possibly restrict the level and amount of information made available to the individual. Given that a key component of many meditative techniques is that the individual spends time learning how to focus on a specific thought, image, sound or feeling, it should come as no surprise that the practice of meditation is associated with improved attentional performance. Specifically, meditation has been shown to benefit the allocation of attentional resources (Slagter *et al.* 2007; Tang *et al.* 2007), help sustain attention over time (Davidson 2005;

Valentine and Sweet 1999), improve speed of processing (Jha *et al.* 2007) and aid executive attentional performance (Chan and Woollacott 2007).

Slagter *et al.* (2007) compared the attentional performance of expert meditative practitioners to that of novices using an attentional blink paradigm. This paradigm involves presenting two targets that occur in close proximity embedded within a larger stream of events (see Figure 6.2). The two targets are thought to compete for attention and, as a consequence, what often happens is that participants identify the first target but fail to identify the second.

Despite this, Slagter *et al.* (ibid.) found that expert meditative practitioners showed higher detection rates for the often missed second target than did novices. In addition, the experts exhibited a reduced cortical potential response to the first target, which Slagter *et al.* suggest indicates a decrease in the level of attentional resources allocated to that target. This reduction in the level of attention given to the first target was thought to provide expert practitioners with more resources, enabling them to deal more effectively with the second target.

Such findings indicate that meditation may lead to increased control over the allocation and distribution of limited attentional resources, which in turn leads to enhanced attentional processing. Alternatively, it may be that meditation, which often requires an individual practitioner to work hard in order to gain some control over the direction and content of their attention, decreases the impact of possible distractors such as intruding thoughts or other stimuli and thereby aids attentional focus. This latter view is consistent with the findings of Tang *et al.* (2007), who found that individuals with no previous experience of meditation exhibited improved conflict scores after completing

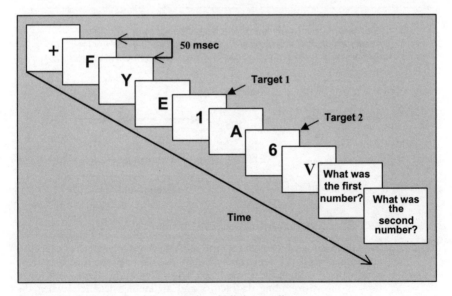

Figure 6.2 A schematic of the attentional blink paradigm.

a five-day course of integrative mind–body meditation. A conflict score represents the difference in response times between a congruent and an incongruent trial (see Figure 6.3). The better (i.e. lower) the conflict score, the less
the participant is thought to be influenced by surrounding cues.

Meditation has also been shown to help maintain attentional vigilance and
sustained attention. Vigilance is a component of attention that involves
remaining attentive to a stimulus over long periods of time. For instance, a
person may complete a task that requires him to watch a computer screen, on
which a letter appears every 30 seconds, and to press a button as quickly as
possible, but only if the letter on screen is an 'X'. Research has shown that
over time the speed of an individual's response will deteriorate as his attention wavers. However, Davidson (2005) found that with continued meditation
practice this slowing of response times doesn't happen. This led Davidson to
suggest that meditation may be responsible for enhancing attentional
vigilance.

In a similar vein, Valentine and Sweet (1999) have shown that meditators
demonstrate superior performance on sustained attention tasks. For instance,
when they compared the performance of a non-meditating control group to
that of a group of meditators on a task requiring both groups to count the
number of auditory tones presented across a number of trials, they found
that the meditators were more accurate in identifying the correct number of
tones compared to the non-meditating controls (see Figure 6.4).

Chan and Woollacott (2007) have also found that individuals who meditate
make fewer errors when completing the Stroop test than did non-
meditating controls. The Stroop test is a classic task utilising focused attention

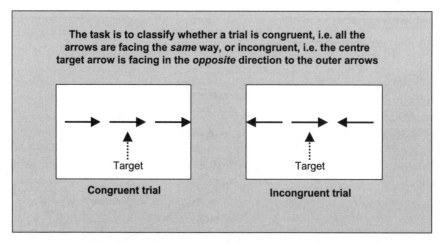

Figure 6.3 A conflict score, which is thought to indicate the involvement of executive
attentional networks, represents the difference in response time between a
congruent trial when the centre target arrow is pointing in the same direction as the surrounding distractors and an incongruent trial when the
target arrow faces in the opposite direction.

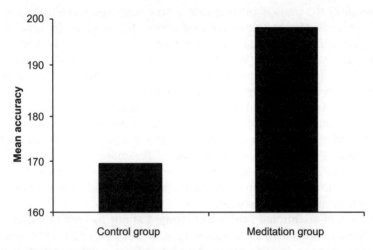

Figure 6.4 Mean number of audio tones correctly identified by control and meditation groups.

(Adapted from Valentine and Sweet 1999)

and involves presenting each participant with a number of different words, each in a different colour of ink. The participant is then required to name the colour of the ink the word appears in while ignoring the actual word itself. This proves to be increasingly difficult when the word is also a colour name printed in non-matching ink (e.g. the word yellow printed in red ink). The fact that meditative practitioners make fewer errors when completing such a task led Chan and Woollacott (2007) to suggest that meditation improves the efficiency of executive attentional networks used during the Stroop test, which enables a more efficient and effective processing of the target stimulus.

These findings highlight a general consensus within the literature that practising meditation leads to enhanced levels of attentional performance and improved concentration. This may be because meditators are better able to ignore intrusive and distracting thoughts and focus on the task at hand.

Cognitive performance

Beyond the positive effects reported on attention, meditation has also been suggested to elicit improvements in perceptual sensitivity (Fergusson 1993; Gelderloos *et al.* 1987; Pelletier 1974), memory (Jangid *et al.* 1988; Wagstaff *et al.* 2004) and the cognitive flexibility of elderly adults (Alexander *et al.* 1989). However, not all have found that meditation leads to improved levels of cognition (Carsello and Creaser 1978; King and Coney 2006; Yuille and Sereda 1980).

Fergusson (1993) compared the ability of students practising meditation to that of non-meditating controls to locate a number of target designs hidden within the Group Embedded Figures Test. This is a perceptual test that requires the participant to locate a previously seen target-figure which has been embedded within a larger complex figure so as to obscure the sought-after target. The test is thought to provide a measure of both cognitive and analytical ability (Witkin *et al.* 1971). Fergusson (1993) found that those who practised meditation were able to identify more of the embedded figures than non-meditating controls (see Figure 6.5).

This improved perceptual sensitivity is consistent with previously reported data by Pelletier (1974), who found that after three months' instruction in transcendental meditation techniques, participants were able to identify hidden targets within the Embedded Figures Test more quickly than controls. Pelletier has suggested that such improvements may, amongst other things, be related to the ability of an individual practising meditation to direct and control their attentional resources.

Changes in attentional processing brought about by meditation are also likely to influence individual experience; as James (1890) points out, 'each of us literally *chooses*, by his ways of attending to things, what sort of universe he shall appear to himself to inhabit' (p. 424). Such a notion is consistent with research showing that individuals practising meditation identify with more positive personality characteristics than non-meditators and find it easier to recognise positively valued words (Gelderloos *et al.* 1987). For instance, Gelderloos *et al.* found that participants practising transcendental meditation identified positively valued words in less time than negatively valued words, compared to controls, who exhibited no difference when asked to identify both types of word (see Figure 6.6).

Gelderloos *et al.* (ibid.) point out that the enhanced positive attitude evident within meditators may be the result of a cognitive bias, with such

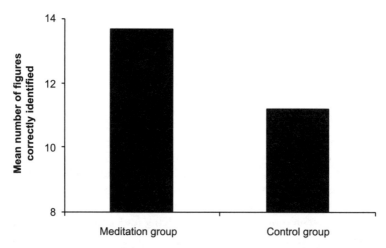

Figure 6.5 Mean number of figures correctly identified by meditation and control groups when completing the Embedded Figures Test.

(Adapted from Fergusson 1993)

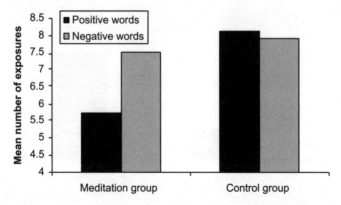

Figure 6.6 Mean number of exposures required before positive and negative words were identified by meditative practitioners and non-meditating controls.

(Adapted from Gelderloos *et al.* 1987)

individuals orienting their own personal schemas towards positive values. This, in turn, may lead to a perceptual bias enabling meditators to recognise positively valued words at lower thresholds compared to non-meditating controls. Thus, meditation may influence an individual's perceptual set towards more positive values, which in turn leads to enhanced perception of positively valued words.

Meditation has also been shown to enhance memory performance (Jangid *et al.* 1988; Wagstaff *et al.* 2004). For example, Jangid *et al.* (1988) examined the effect of a six-week training course in meditation on memory, anxiety and electrocortical activity. They found that a group of normal healthy adults who completed the six-week course showed significant improvements in memory performance, along with decreased levels of anxiety (see Figure 6.7). This led them to suggest that meditation leads to an enhanced ability to organise thoughts, resulting in improved processing skills. Furthermore, they indicate that such a pattern of findings highlights the possibility that meditation may lead to better mental health. Unfortunately, their failure to include a control group means that such findings should be interpreted with a degree of caution.

The issue of adequate controls is one that arises frequently within the field of optimal performance training and represents a recurring theme throughout this book. It is particularly relevant to the literature examining the effects of meditation. In some cases the researchers fail to include a control group (e.g. Jangid *et al.* 1988), suggesting that by taking measures pre- and post-meditation training the participants act as their own controls. In other cases researchers may include a non-meditating control group and then compare their performance to that of a group receiving training in a particular meditative technique (e.g. Fergusson 1993; Gelderloos *et al.* 1987). However, in both these cases the methodology may be inadequate to delineate clearly the

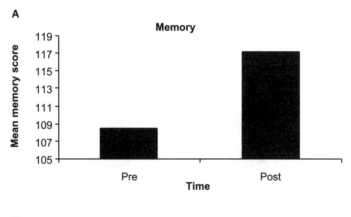

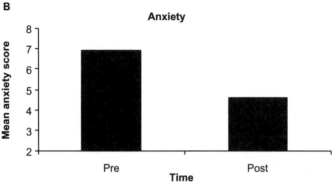

Figure 6.7 Mean memory performance (panel A) and anxiety levels (panel B) before and after the meditation training.

(Adapted from Jangid *et al.* 1988)

possible effects of meditation. For example, the findings of a study which fails to include a control group can more easily be accounted for in terms of practice effects. Any improvements noted in memory and anxiety levels observed following meditation training may simply be the result of familiarity and practice with the test and a more familiar setting, reducing possible arousal levels. In addition, inclusion of a non-meditating control group that doesn't receive equal contact with the experimenter highlights another potential confound. For example, it may be that the increased exposure and interaction with the experimenter of the group completing the meditation training encourages the participants to become more motivated, working harder to produce an effect.

King and Coney (2006) attempted to address some of these issues by comparing the effects of meditation on cognition utilising an equal-contact, relaxation-only control group. Participants from both groups initially completed a number of cognitive tests followed by a 20-minute period during which the meditation group meditated and the control group sat with eyes closed and simply relaxed. After this, both groups again completed the same range of cognitive tests. Whilst both groups showed some evidence of practice effects on two of the seven tests, King and Coney found no difference in performance between the two groups on any of the tests. This implies that the short-term effects of meditation are no different from those of relaxation. Indeed, King and Coney argue that such results clearly show that 'meditation does not produce a short-term improvement in cognitive performance' (p. 209).

However, before such a conclusion can be accepted, it is important to note that this study was not without its own methodological difficulties. First, King and Coney (2006) allow only a 20-minute period for meditation and relaxation. It may be that such a short period of time is insufficient for any potentially beneficial effects of meditation to emerge. To their credit, King and Coney (ibid.) acknowledge this point and indicate that additional research is needed to identify an optimum time period for the effects of meditation to emerge. Second, it may be that the particular meditation conducted, which in this instance was a mindfulness approach, is not sufficient to engender improved cognition. Given the various types of meditation, it may be that some techniques and approaches are more beneficial for some behaviours than others. Such a possibility is consistent with the findings of Valentine and Sweet (1999), who report distinct behavioural effects for concentrative relative to mindfulness meditation. Third, whilst King and Coney (2006) found no difference in cognitive performance between the meditating and relaxation groups, it should be noted that the average age of the meditators was much higher (mean of 42.2 years) than that of the control group (mean of 25.4 years). Given this age difference and the similar levels of cognitive performance, an alternative explanation could be that meditation helped a more mature group match their cognitive performance to that of a much younger group. These points highlight some of the difficulties and issues that should be kept in mind when interpreting such results.

Academic performance

Hall (1999) examined the effect of meditation on academic performance by recruiting a number of student participants and randomly allocating them to either receive meditation training or become part of a non-meditating control group. At the beginning of the academic year measurements taken showed no difference in academic performance as measured by grade point averages (GPA) between the two groups. After completing the relevant training for a term, which for the meditation group involved breathing techniques and attentional focusing techniques, and for the controls involved extra study time, Hall (1999) found that those in the meditation group exhibited significantly higher grade point averages than controls (see Figure 6.8).

Hall (ibid.) suggested that the improved academic performance seen for those completing the meditation training indicates that such training may

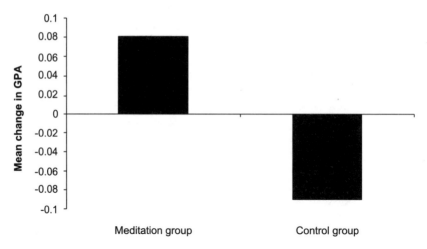

Figure 6.8 Mean change in grade point average (GPA) for the meditation and control groups.

(Adapted from Hall 1999)

help to reduce possible stress levels and facilitate improvements in academic performance. However, as can be seen from Figure 6.8, it's not simply that those completing the meditation training improved their academic grades, but also that performance of the control group deteriorated over time. This may reflect the better coping skills of the meditation group. It may not, then, be the case that meditation *improves* academic performance per se; rather, it helps the individual cope with the challenges of an academic regime and rise to meet such challenges more effectively. Nevertheless, such findings led Hall (ibid.) to suggest that meditation, made available as part of an academic regime, may be beneficial, particularly in reducing the possible anxiety students may feel when undergoing assessment. Others have echoed such a sentiment by proposing that meditation be taught to children in school as part of their education (e.g. Fisher 2006).

However, not all have found that meditation is a useful technique for facilitating academic performance. For example, Carsello and Creaser (1978) compared the academic grades of a group of students completing a transcendental meditation initiation programme to that of non-meditating controls matched for gender, academic level and grade. Following the meditation training, a comparison of academic grades between the groups failed to reveal any differences (see Figure 6.9). In fact, as can be seen in Figure 6.9, there was a small but insignificant decrease in grades over time for both groups. Thus, meditation training, in this instance, produced no positive effects on academic performance. Carsello and Creaser (ibid.) point out that studies which have shown a positive association between meditation training and academic performance may have done so because they selected biased

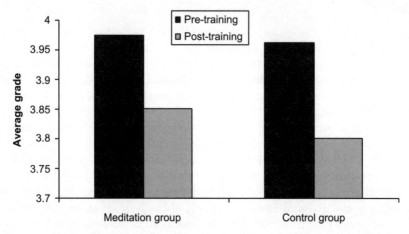

Figure 6.9 Mean academic grade pre- and post-training for meditation and control
groups.

(Adapted from Carsello and Creaser 1978)

samples of participants, namely, individuals who exhibit some level of
enthusiasm for meditation. In an attempt to control for such a possible bias,
they note that many of the participants who took part in their meditation
training 'never became enthusiastic about TM' (p. 645). Of course, by
attempting to eliminate the possible effects of enthusiasm it may be that
they biased their sample in favour of not finding an effect, due to the
antipathy of their participants towards meditation. Such a possibility would
imply that participants *need* to be motivated *and* interested in order to maintain the rigorous training procedure. Carsello and Creaser (ibid.) acknowledge this point, suggesting that transcendental meditation may not produce
universal effects, but may interact with the specific personality and goals of
the individual.

Overall, these findings provide compelling evidence that meditation can
enhance attentional processing. In addition, there are some encouraging
reports suggesting that meditation may also improve memory and academic
performance. However, research has shown that a number of factors can
mediate the possible effectiveness of meditation; the following section
explores some of these.

Factors influencing meditation

It is possible that the outcome of meditation training may be influenced by
any number of factors. Unfortunately, only a limited number of these have
received any specific attention. These include the length and duration of the
individual's experience with meditation and the particular approach used.

Time

It may seem an obvious point to suggest that an individual's level of experience with meditation may influence the outcome; indeed, a number of researchers have noted increased effects as a function of the length of time an individual has practised meditation (Brown and Engler 1980; Davidson *et al.* 1976), although such associations are not necessarily linear (see, e.g., Chin-Yen *et al.* 2007). For example, Davidson *et al.* (1976) found that people who meditate show increased levels of absorption and decreased levels of anxiety. Absorption refers to a state in which the person is fully immersed, or absorbed, in what he is doing. Furthermore, Davidson *et al.* found that these effects are clearly related to the length of time an individual has been practising meditation, with long-term practitioners showing greater levels of absorption and reduced levels of anxiety than those of short-term practitioners. Such a pattern would imply that meditation not only produces some benefits but also that these benefits may accrue as the individual continues to practise over time.

Such suggestions are consistent with the findings of an intriguing analysis carried out by Valentine and Sweet (1999). They found that long-term meditators, who had been practising for over two years, exhibited superior attentional performance compared to short-term meditators, who had been meditating for less than two years (see Figure 6.10).

Thus, it seems that continued practice of meditation leads to additional improvements in attentional processing. Valentine and Sweet (ibid.) note that it is unlikely that such effects are the result of changes in brain structure, but

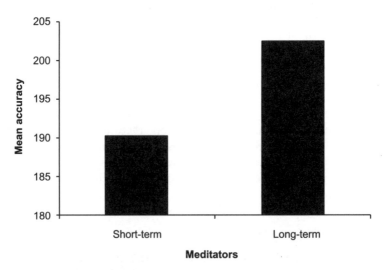

Figure 6.10 Mean accuracy levels on an auditory attentional task for short-term and long-term meditators.

(Adapted from Valentine and Sweet 1999)

are more likely to be the result of improvements in cognitive processing, in particular the distribution and allocation of attention. This is consistent with the proposal put forward by Jha *et al.* (2007), suggesting that the difference found over time within meditators may be due to the development of distinct attentional processes. For instance, meditation may initially lead to the development of a greater level of concentrative attention in the novice practitioner. This is because concentrated attention is thought to relate to an individual's ability to focus on a specific topic or task, such as his breathing. In contrast, over time, the more experienced meditator cultivates his level of receptive attention, which refers to an open and alert state without the need to orient or limit attention in any way.

Related to the length of time an individual has been practising meditation is the amount of time spent each day in meditation. Chan and Woollacott (2007) reported a positive association between the amount of time spent meditating each day and visual attentional performance. This could be due to a combination of enhanced visual-motor skills and greater ability to focus on the task, reducing the effect of possible distractors. Nevertheless, it would suggest that meditating for sessions that last for 60 minutes or more may have a greater benefit than shorter time periods.

Meditative approach

An additional issue that has received little attention is the possible behavioural effects that different types of meditation may bring about. Valentine and Sweet (1999) examined this issue by comparing the different attentional performance of concentrative versus mindfulness meditators using an auditory attentional task. They found that, when the stimulus was unexpected, that is, when there was a change in the frequency of the auditory tones to be attended to, those classified as mindfulness meditators performed better than those identified as concentrative meditators (see Figure 6.11).

Valentine and Sweet (ibid.) suggest that such differences in behavioural performance may be due to the particular style and focus of the specific meditative technique. For example, concentrative meditation requires the individual to focus on a single point or object, which may be expected to aid detection of a single expected target compared to an unexpected target. In contrast, mindfulness meditation supports a more receptive and open approach, encouraging the practitioner to expand his field of attention and thus may facilitate the processing of unexpected stimuli. Furthermore, these results support the notion that different meditative approaches may elicit distinct behavioural and cognitive effects.

Negative effects

There is an intriguing debate within the literature suggesting that meditation, in particular transcendental meditation, predisposes an individual to display

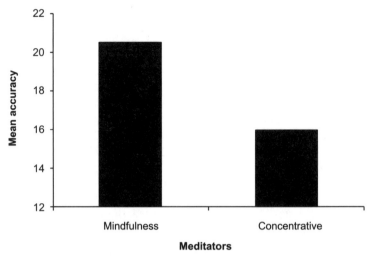

Figure 6.11 Mean accuracy levels on an auditory attention task for those classified as mindfulness meditators compared to concentrative meditators.

(Adapted from Valentine and Sweet 1999)

signs associated with epilepsy and may lead to epileptic seizures. This debate began when Persinger (1984, 1993) recorded the experiences of meditators using a personal inventory developed to measure unusual events such as haptic vibrations, hearing one's name, paranormal phenomena and religious phenomena, and compared them to those of non-meditators. Persinger (1993) found that meditators reported experiencing a greater number of such experiences than their non-meditating counterparts. Furthermore, because epileptic patients also report a wider range of such experiences, he interpreted this as suggesting that meditation, and in particular transcendental meditation, can elicit partial epileptic-like signs. Persinger (ibid.) went on to suggest that meditation may also promote what he called *cognitive kindling* and enhance the probability of epileptic-like signs. Cognitive kindling refers to the notion that a particular level of cortical stimulation may lead to increases in epileptic seizure susceptibility. Thus, the alterations in electrocortical activity resulting from practising meditation may result in a decrease in seizure thresholds, increasing the probability of such events occurring.

Jaseja (2005) agrees with such sentiments and points out that meditation is often associated with an increase in neuronal synchrony, particularly within the alpha frequency range. Jaseja (2006) also highlights the notion that meditation produces a progressive synchronisation in the EEG of the participant, which is similar to the patterns seen in NREM sleep, and that such patterns are associated with increased susceptibility to epilepsy. Jaseja (ibid.) suggests that similarities in the patterns of EEG activity, as well as changes in glutamate and serotonin, 'support the possibility of risk of epileptogenesis during meditation' (p. 1037). Furthermore, Jaseja (2005) notes that, when combined, these effects may pose a greater threat to normal healthy participants, rendering them epilepsy prone. Such findings would suggest, at the very least, that caution is needed 'over the practice of meditation in patients prone to epilepsy' (Jaseja 2005: 466).

However, not all agree, and some have voiced surprise at the seemingly speculative conclusions reached based only on a list of correlated subjective experiences (Fehr 2006; Orme-Johnson 2006). Fehr (2006), for example, points out that there is no evidence of an increase in epilepsy for those practising meditation. He also criticises Persinger for coming to the 'far fetched conclusion' (p. 1462) that religious beliefs represent an indicator for exhibiting epileptic symptoms. Furthermore, Fehr (2006) highlights a number of case studies which suggest that meditation, far from having a negative effect, is beneficial for those suffering from epilepsy. In addition, Fehr notes that, whilst a large number of epileptic patients have been prescribed meditation alongside their regular treatment, none have exhibited an increase in epileptic tendencies, which doesn't fit with Jaseja's view that meditation enhances the probability of epilepsy.

This sentiment is mirrored by Orme-Johnson (2006), who points out that there is no evidence that meditation leads to an increase in the predisposition to epilepsy, or causes epilepsy. He criticises Persinger's work as representing nothing more than 'baseless speculation' (p. 241). Orme-Johnson highlights a number of empirical points showing that practitioners of meditation exhibit fewer diseases of the nervous system compared to normative controls, markedly reduced hospital admissions and outpatient visits and no known cases of epilepsy. Furthermore, Orme-Johnson (ibid.) criticises Jaseja's work as both lacking in evidence and contradictory. He points out that the EEG patterns seen in epileptic patients and those elicited during meditation are distinct in frequency, amplitude and region of activation, and to use the term 'hypersynchrony' to describe them both is mere word play and does not mean that the two phenomena are the same. Orme-Johnson concludes by stating that there is no 'direct evidence that the transcendental meditation program, or any other kind of meditation, predisposes to epilepsy' (p. 245).

Nevertheless, Jaseja (2007) is, in turn, critical of Orme-Johnson, describing his work as empirically weak and contrary to scientific understanding and knowledge, and argues that it doesn't rule out the possibility that meditation leads to a predisposition to epilepsy. Indeed, St Louis and Lansky (2006) note a connection between meditation and epilepsy in their case study of an 18-year-old woman with no previous medical, psychological or psychiatric history, who had been practising transcendental meditation since childhood and exhibited epileptic spells. They note that such a case illustrates the 'onset of mesial temporal lobe epilepsy in a lifelong meditator who lacked known risk factors for epilepsy' (p. 248). However, they also point out that the patient has never experienced an epileptic spell during meditation and that she continues to practise. Furthermore, they note that there is insufficient evidence to link meditation conclusively to the emergence of such seizures. Nevertheless, Jaseja (2007) highlights this case and argues that, at the very least, 'meditation should be practiced with caution' (p. 917).

Without wishing to downplay the potential importance of the ideas put forward by Persinger (1993) and Jaseja (2005), it does seem that this debate has emerged from an over-interpretation of the associations between meditation and epileptic experiences; in particular, that a correlation between reported subjective experiences of meditators and some of the experiences reported by those suffering from epilepsy represents a case of cause and effect. Nevertheless, time will tell whether this debate can be resolved.

Overview

'Meditation' is a broad term used to denote a variety of techniques. It invariably describes a process rather than a specific technique and is thought to provide the practitioner with a means to learn self-control of physiological and psychological processes. The specific procedure used may differ according to the particular approach adopted and it need not be linked to religious and/or spiritual ideas.

Whilst meditation may involve a variety of specific techniques, many, if not all, include training in mindfulness and concentration. Mindfulness refers to the development of an open-minded attentional state which remains non-judgemental, whereas concentration requires the focusing of attention onto a specific target. In general, a specific meditative approach usually involves the development of either one or both of these skills.

In terms of psychophysiological effects, meditation has been shown to be capable of producing clear and measurable changes within the brain. These include a thickening of the cerebral cortex, improved cerebral blood flow and changes in the electrocortical activity of the brain, particularly within the gamma, alpha and theta frequency ranges. Any, or all, of these changes could support improved neural functioning and thereby provide plausible mechanisms for enhancing behaviour.

In terms of enhancing performance, there is convincing evidence that meditation can enhance attentional performance. Specifically, meditation has been associated with improved allocation of attentional resources, enhanced vigilance and speed of processing and superior executive processing. In addition, there are some suggestive findings indicating that meditation may improve memory and academic performance. However, due to a variety of methodological inadequacies, the data from these latter studies are less robust.

Despite the clear effects meditation has on attentional processing and the encouraging changes shown for memory and academic performance, a number of factors have been shown to influence the effectiveness of meditation. For instance, comparing the length and duration of an individual's experience in meditation has shown clear differences between long-term and short-term practitioners, with more pronounced effects emerging for those who have been meditating for longer. In addition, the amount of time an individual spends each day meditating has also been shown to influence behaviour, with those who meditate for longer periods exhibiting greater effects. As would be expected, research also supports the notion that different meditative techniques may elicit distinct behavioural effects. This also highlights the difficulty faced when an assumption is made that meditation represents a unitary construct.

Finally, concerns have been raised regarding the possible negative effects of meditation, in particular the idea that meditation may predispose a person to exhibit epileptic-like signs. At present, there is no evidence to show that meditation can cause such epileptic-like behaviours, although some have suggested that the possibility highlights a need for caution when practising. Despite the seeming over-interpretation of the available data, this debate looks set to continue.

7 Mnemonics

Memory is the mother of all wisdom.

(Aeschylus)

When learning musical scales students are often given the phrase, 'Every Good Boy Deserves Favour' to help them remember the position of various notes on a stave. The idea is that the first letter from each word relates to a position, or note, on the musical stave, reading from the bottom up (see Figure 7.1). In a similar way, when attempting to learn which colours go to make up the visible spectrum, often seen in rainbows, students are given the name ROY-G-BIV to help them remember the colours Red, Orange, Yellow, Green, Blue, Indigo and Violet. These are just two examples of a common method used to enhance learning and memory, called mnemonics. The use of mnemonics is both widespread and popular, with advocates suggesting they can help enhance learning and memory across a wide range of tasks. This chapter explores the use of mnemonics to enhance performance.

The chapter begins by defining what constitutes a mnemonic and provides a brief history of the development of mnemonic techniques. This is followed by an outline of some of the more commonly used mnemonic techniques. The chapter then deals with the notion that use of a mnemonic technique can enhance human performance on a range of different tasks, from improving memory to learning a new language. A number of factors are then identified which have been shown to influence the effectiveness of mnemonic training. The chapter also examines the notion of mnemonic transfer and ends by exploring the possibility that mnemonics can provide long-term benefits.

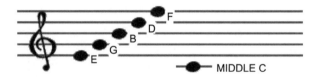

Figure 7.1 Notes on a musical stave.

Mnemonics

The term 'mnemonic' stems from the Greek word *mnēmonikos*, which means 'relating to memory'. More specifically, a mnemonic strategy refers to a particular technique used to help create associations with information to be remembered, making it easier to recall later. Mnemonics can take many different forms, such as a poem, a rhyme or a visual image, and are thought to help people learn and recall a variety of different types of information. They can also be useful in helping to organise information in a particular way, providing a framework that imposes an understandable order on an otherwise chaotic world.

The use of mnemonics to aid recall is certainly popular, particularly with students. One analysis found that, when given a simple word recall task, 94 per cent of participants used some form of mnemonic to help them memorise the words (Boltwood and Blick 1970). Others have also shown that, when given no specific instructions, people completing a memory task often enlist the use of a mnemonic to aid their recall (see, e.g., Camp *et al.* 1983; Carlson *et al.* 1976).

A brief history of mnemonics

Prior to the written word, only oral records of historical events and family histories existed. For example, individuals would have had to commit to memory their own family history, as well as the history of other leading and influential families to maintain a sense of community. Such requirements led to the development and utilisation of a variety of methods and techniques to assist memory. According to Higbee (1979), mnemonics originated with the Greeks and Romans and have been in use for over 2000 years. One of the earliest known references to the use of mnemonics was by Cicero in 55 BC, in his *De Oratore*, in which he relates the story of Simonides, the Greek poet of Cos, who identifies the guests of a dinner party by recalling their locations at the dinner table (Middleton 1885).

Over time the amount of information dealing with the topic of memory grew as more people published possible ways of enhancing memory using a variety of techniques. However, at the beginning of the twentieth century there was a drop in the level of interest and research focusing on the use and application of mnemonics. Higbee (1979) attributed this to the rising influence of behaviourism rather than a lack of interest in the area. According to Higbee, the upturn of interest and research into mnemonics which is evident in the latter part of the twentieth century is probably the result of the development of cognitive psychology and the implication that mental processes are once again an acceptable topic of enquiry.

Mnemonic techniques

There are a range of different mnemonic techniques available and what follows is a brief description of some of the more popular ones used to enhance performance. These include the peg system, the method of loci, the major system, the story method, the face–name method and the keyword method.

Peg system

For recalling information presented in a list and maintaining the target location, the *peg system*, also known as the *hook system*, is extremely useful. The peg system utilises both auditory and visual information. For instance, the *number–rhyme* peg system relies on the auditory skill of producing a rhyming word to match the numerical position of the target item (e.g. *one/bun, two/shoe, three/tree*; see Figure 7.2) and then forming a visual association between the rhyming word and the word on the list. For example, if the first target word on the list to be learnt is *tree*, this should be linked with the image of a bun. The individual links the two together using visual imagery, for instance with buns hanging like fruit from a tree.

In contrast, the *number–shape* peg system links the number to a visually similar shape. For instance, the number one may be represented by a pen, as both are long and thin. The number two shares visual similarities with the outline of a swan, three the indented curve on the top of a heart, and so on (see Figure 7.2).

If someone is given a list of words to learn, of which the first word is hat,

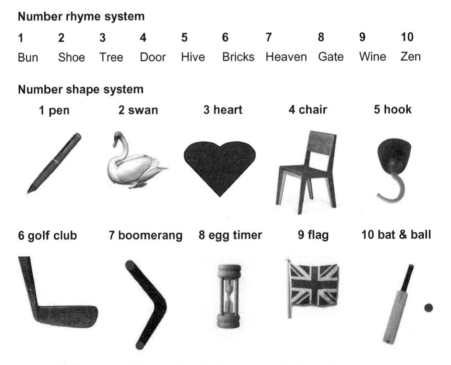

Number rhyme system

1	2	3	4	5	6	7	8	9	10
Bun	Shoe	Tree	Door	Hive	Bricks	Heaven	Gate	Wine	Zen

Number shape system

1 pen   2 swan   3 heart   4 chair   5 hook

6 golf club   7 boomerang   8 egg timer   9 flag   10 bat & ball

Figure 7.2 Examples of the number–rhyme system and the number–shape system.

and they use the number–shape system, then they need to associate hat with pen. For example, the person could imagine a large fat pen with skinny arms and legs walking along wearing a hat.

Both peg systems rely on the ability of the individual to pre-memorise either a list of words that rhyme with numbers or a range of objects that can be used to represent the numbers visually. However, rhyming peg lists can become ambiguous beyond the number ten, as 11 rhymes with seven. Number–shape peg lists can also become problematic as the numbers increase. Nevertheless, Buzan (1986) proposed that such limits may be overcome by introducing a secondary system. For example, for both types of peg system it is possible to associate targets with their relevant words and objects from the numbers one to ten. Then, from 11 to 20, the individual simply imagines the peg encased in ice, and from 21 to 30, engulfed in flames, and so on. Alternatively, it is possible to imagine each set of ten pegs represented by a different colour.

Method of loci

The *method of loci*, also referred to as the *journey method*, can be used to remember lists of items that need to be recalled in order. Interestingly, the method doesn't require the individual to learn any new component processes but merely to select existing processes and sequence them in a different way. There are two distinctive aspects to this method: the first is the location or place used and the second is the use of imagery to link the item to be remembered with that place. In addition, the various loci need to be arranged in a strict sequence with which the individual is familiar, such as a journey to work or a particular route taken around a familiar location. The to-be-remembered items can then be associated with the various locations along the journey, ensuring that each location is clear, set out in a particular order and spaced at moderate intervals apart. For example, a person may be given a long list of words to learn beginning with the word *tiger*. If they utilise the method of loci, incorporating locations on a well-known route to work, the first location could be the individual's front door as she leaves the house. This will require the individual to construct the image of a tiger associated with that of her front door. Later, when it is time to recall the items from the list she mentally revisits each landmark in turn, which acts as a prompt, bringing to mind the associated image and word.

The loci can be used to remember more than one set of things, with old images being replaced by new ones. In this way, the loci act as the wax tablets of memory, so to speak. An interesting and useful characteristic is that, once the individual is familiar with the various locations on the route, she can enter the journey at any point, it is not necessary to begin at the beginning, and it is possible to recall information in reverse order. In addition, Crovitz (1969) has shown that the locations need not be known a priori to the participant. For example, he found that a group of students were able to recall 85 per cent of a list of words in their correct order following a single trial when given an arbitrary selection of locations to use as a memory aid. Others have also shown that providing arbitrary locations can aid recall of information (Briggs *et al.* 1970). Thus, the locations need not be self-produced.

This method represents a useful strategy for learning lists of information but may be limited by a number of factors. First, each of the to-be-remembered words needs to be easily translatable into an image. In addition, the implementation of such a strategy takes time and, if information is presented too quickly for associations to be formed, it may be less effective.

The major system

The *major system*, or *phonetic number system*, can be used to replace numbers with words, which can then be turned into images, helping the individual to recall numerical information. More specifically, each number is related to a specific consonant or set of consonants. The code of the major system is summarised in Table 7.1.

The remaining consonants, w, h and y, are used as fillers. Once the relevant numbers have been converted into the associated consonants, the vowels are then added to make a word. One suggestion is that allocation of the vowels should ideally follow their alphabetical order (i.e. a-e-i-o-u), using the first vowel that makes an adequate memory word (Buzan 1986). It is important to note that the mapping of the consonants is *phonetic*, in the sense that it's the consonant sounds that matter, not their spelling. For example, the word *action* (pronounced ákshən) would translate into the number 762 and not 712. Similarly, double letters are generally disregarded.

Once the individual is familiar with the links between the various numbers and their associated codes, she can then incorporate visual imagery as an aid to learning a set or sequence of numbers. The complexity of this system necessitates a large investment of time and effort to learn all the relevant

Table 7.1 The code of the major system with the numbers zero to nine and associated consonants

Number	Associated code
0	s, z, soft c
1	d, t, th; both d and t have a single downstroke
2	n and ing; n has two downstrokes
3	m; three donwnstrokes
4	r; the letter r is the last letter in the word four
5	l; can be thought of as either the Roman numeral for 50, or a hand with five spread fingers – with the index finger and thumb forming an L-shape
6	j, sh, ch; a j looks like a mirror image of a 6
7	k, hard c, hard g, q; a capital K can be seen as two 7s
8	f, v; an f written in script has two loops similar to an 8
9	b, p; both letters have a single loop like a 9 and look like inverted mirror images of a 9

links, as well as a good facility for image creation. Nevertheless, once learnt, it is possible to use imagery to memorise a word, which represents a coded set of numbers, rather than the assumed to be more difficult task of remembering the numbers alone. Buzan (ibid.) has suggested that the more graphic and outlandish the image, the easier it should be to recall.

Such a system may seem overly complicated and take time to learn but, once mastered, it should be possible to commit to memory a range of numerical information, including important dates, times and phone numbers. Nevertheless, such a system may not be useful for everyone, as few people have sufficient need or desire to memorise long lists of numbers to make the initial cost of learning such a code effective.

Story method

Also referred to as the *narrative chaining* method, this is the verbal equivalent of the link method and involves chaining items together by linking them in a story. It requires the individual to construct a narrative story by linking, or chaining together, target items in the form of a story in the order in which they need to be recalled. The participant begins by placing the first item to be remembered in a particular setting and then adding items whilst linking them together with a theme. For example, if the task is to remember a list of words including *rucksack*, *diamond* and *bin*, the individual may begin by creating the image of a rucksack in their mind and then imagine themselves looking inside it to find their diamond, but, once found, realising that it is no longer useful so throwing it in the bin, and so on. A new story can be created for each list of items to be learnt, linking them together irrespective of whether they have an intrinsic connection (e.g. the kings and queens of England) or not. Such a method may also be used to memorise the key points of a speech.

The use of such a method may require additional time during encoding whilst the individual constructs a coherent narrative. Nevertheless, Bower and Clark (1969) found that the time taken to construct a story decreases with practice, suggesting that participants become more proficient over time.

Face–name association method

A commonly voiced complaint is that when one is meeting new people for the first time, particularly in busy social situations, it is often difficult to recall their name at a later date. McCarty (1980) proposed that use of a face–name mnemonic could help, so long as the strategy included all four key components as outlined in Box 7.1.

To remember the name at a later date the individual needs to identify and attend to the chosen feature, which is then used to help retrieve the interactive image from which the cue-word is derived and in turn leads to retrieval of the name. However, use of such an approach in a social situation requires a great deal of practice and there are a number of potential drawbacks. For instance,

---

Box 7.1   Key components of the face–name mnemonic

Encoding the name *Conrad* using a face–name mnemonic

Four key stages

1   Pay attention to the *name* and the *face*
2   Identify a distinctive feature of the face (e.g. nose)
3   Transform the name into a cue-word or words that are phonologic-
    ally similar (e.g. *Con* and *rat*)
4   Create an interactive image combining the cue-word and the target
    facial feature (e.g. a prison con riding a rat down a nose)

(Adapted from McCarty 1980)

---

it requires the individual to select a distinctive facial feature which is not
always easy or possible, particularly when the number of distractions is high
and time is limited.

The keyword mnemonic

The keyword method has been put forward as an especially useful strategy for
learning foreign vocabulary (see Atkinson 1975; Atkinson and Raugh 1975;
Pressley *et al.* 1982). This method consists of two stages, an auditory stage
and a visual stage. First, a foreign word is acoustically linked to an English
word that sounds like some part of the foreign word. For example, the
Polish word for thank you is *dziękuję*, the beginning of which sounds like
the English word *gin*. The keyword, i.e. gin, is then visually linked with the
English meaning of the foreign word by forming an interactive image. For
example, a person may visualise being very thankful for receiving a cool glass
of gin on a warm spring day. According to Atkinson and Raugh (1975), for
this mnemonic to be effective the keyword needs to sound as much like a part
or all of the target word, be easy to image and yet remain distinct from other
keywords to avoid confusion. It may also take time to learn and is unlikely to
help with pronunciation.

Enhancing performance

This section examines evidence that mnemonic strategies can enhance performance in a number of areas, including memory, linking faces and names,
learning new scientific facts, as well as learning a foreign language.

Memory

Mnemonic benefits, in terms of enhanced memory, have been found for the peg system (Krinsky and Krinsky 1996; Wood 1967), the method of loci (Briggs *et al.* 1970; Carlson *et al.* 1976; Hill *et al.* 1990) and the story method (Bower and Clark 1969; Hill *et al.* 1991).

For instance, Wood (1967) found that use of a peg mnemonic helped people to form images or create links between the peg word and the target word, leading to significantly greater recall compared to controls who were not given a mnemonic. Furthermore, Wood found that the order of recalled material was maintained more accurately when the mnemonic was used and that material in the middle of the list did not seem to be any more difficult to recall than material at either end of the list. Such a pattern is unusual, given that recall of material presented in a list is invariably more accurate for information appearing at the beginning and the end of the list, producing what is often referred to as a serial position curve of recall.

Bower and Clark (1969) reported similar benefits when using a story mnemonic. They found this helped one group recall over six times more information than controls (see Figure 7.3). Bower and Clark argued that this improvement in memory was the result of thematically organising material into a more meaningful, and consequently more memorable, context. Such a process is thought to involve the individual generating a meaningful sentence to help integrate the target words and relate each successive sentence around a particular theme, with different lists utilising distinct themes, thereby reducing possible interference effects. In this way, the first word acts as a cue to recall the theme and the individual is then able to reconstruct the story to identify the target words.

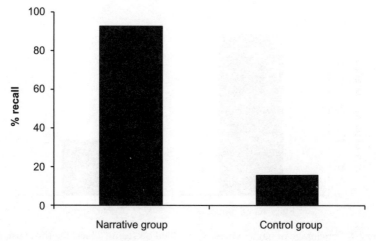

Figure 7.3 Median recall for the narrative story group compared to the control group. (Adapted from Bower and Clark 1969)

Favourable effects have also been found when using mnemonics to learn and recall words embedded within a passage of text (Dretzke and Levin 1996), as well as helping elderly people to learn and recall more information (Bottiroli *et al.* 2007; Hill *et al.* 1991). Thus, it would seem clear that use of mnemonics can enhance memory performance.

Faces and names

When Higbee (2001) conducted a survey asking people what aspects of memory they would most like to enhance, the majority stated that they would like to improve their memory of people's names. Such desires have led to the development of specific mnemonic strategies aimed at enhancing recall of a name when seeing a face. For example, McCarty (1980) found that use of a face–name mnemonic, similar to the one outlined above, significantly enhanced recall of names following presentation of a list of face–name pairs compared to controls who were given no specific instructions (see Figure 7.4).

Such a finding is consistent with data showing that use of a face–name mnemonic can aid recall of the names of strangers (Morris *et al.* 2005), as well as the names of famous artists (Carney and Levin 2000a, 2000b). Nevertheless, McCarty (1980) found that, if any one component of the face–name mnemonic was removed from the strategy, then the level of recall was no better than that of a non-mnemonic control group. Furthermore, McCarty reported a tendency for participants to confuse images for which the same prominent feature was chosen. Thus, the probability of retrieving a name for a face based on a prominent feature declined as use of that particular feature increased. In a similar vein, the more distinct a facial feature was judged to be, the more useful it could be as a cue. The use of a

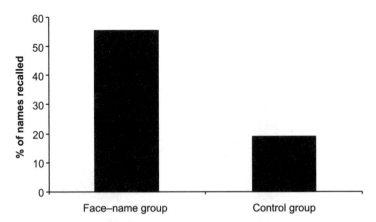

Figure 7.4 Percentage of names correctly recalled on seeing a face: for those using the face–name mnemonic and for the control group.

(Adapted from McCarty 1980)

face–name mnemonic can thus aid the recall of names but only when all components of the mnemonic are used and when the features used to distinguish between faces remain distinct.

However, Patton (1994) found that use of a face–name mnemonic during conversations did not aid recall. He suggests that the dual tasks of carrying on a conversation whilst simultaneously attempting to analyse and synthesise facial features represents a challenging task that may inhibit the subsequent recall of the person's name, unless the individual is highly skilled. Such a view is consistent with research comparing the effectiveness of the face–name mnemonic to that of expanding retrieval practice in a realistic social setting (Morris *et al.* 2005).

Expanding retrieval practice simply means attempting to retrieve the target information repeatedly with increasingly longer delay intervals. The idea here is that, when one is attempting to memorise the name of a person, the person's name should be recalled during the initial conversation, after a few minutes' delay and again later following a longer period. Morris *et al.* (2005) compared the effectiveness of the expanding retrieval practice technique to a face–name mnemonic in a realistic social setting which involved students meeting new people at a party and then attempting to recall their names after a delay of between 24 and 72 hours. They found that use of the retrieval practice technique led to significantly greater recall of names than both the face–name technique and a no-strategy control group. Moreover, those utilising the face–name strategy were no better at recalling names than controls were (see Figure 7.5).

Consistent with earlier indications from McCarty (1980), Morris *et al.* (2005) propose that the face–name mnemonic is a demanding and time-consuming process that requires a great deal of practice to ensure its fluent

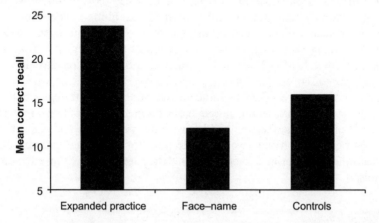

Figure 7.5 Mean number of names correctly recalled for those using the expanded practice technique, the face–name mnemonic and a no-strategy control group.

(Adapted from Morris *et al.* 2005)

and effective use. In contrast, Morris *et al.* (2005) point out that the expanding retrieval technique can enhance the recall of names, particularly within social settings, and that the simplicity of the technique means that long periods of practice are unnecessary.

It would seem that using the expanding retrieval technique represents a useful first strategy for attempting to learn names, particularly in a social situation, as it requires very little practice on the part of the learner and involves less effort than other techniques. Nevertheless, it may be that fluent learning of the face–name technique may be as good, if not better, in the long term, even though such an approach requires a more significant investment of time and effort.

Scientific facts

Researchers have also found that mnemonics can be useful when attempting to learn new factual information (Levin and Levin 1990; Levin *et al.* 1986). For instance, Levin *et al.* (1986) were interested in finding out whether a mnemonic would aid learning and memory for factual information contained within a passage of text. These text passages contained specific attributes of minerals which the students needed to learn. Levin *et al.* utilised an adapted version of the keyword method that consisted of the students initially recoding the mineral into a keyword which was then semantically related to various characteristics of the mineral. An example given was the mineral *corundum*, which is a hard dark mineral that may be used in the home. The keyword *car* was used to represent corundum due to the similarity in sound and it was linked to the mineral's properties of 'hard', 'dark' and 'used in the home' by specific images. In this instance, they were an old man (used to depict the term 'hard') driving a black (used to denote 'dark') car (corundum) in a living room (to identify that the mineral is used 'in the home'). They found that those using such a mnemonic outperformed two other groups, one of which used a summary strategy and the other acted as no-strategy controls, when tested immediately after learning the material and again three days later (see Figure 7.6).

Such findings were taken to indicate that mnemonic strategies could be useful for more than learning simple lists of items. They could also facilitate the recall of scientific facts embedded within a passage of text. Given these findings, Levin *et al.* (ibid.) were keen to point out the potentially beneficial implications for material delivered in booklets, particularly within educational settings.

Language learning

In terms of language learning, the keyword method has been shown to be an effective aid to learning Spanish (Raugh and Atkinson 1975; Wyra *et al.* 2007), Russian (Atkinson and Raugh 1975), Italian (Lawson and Hogben

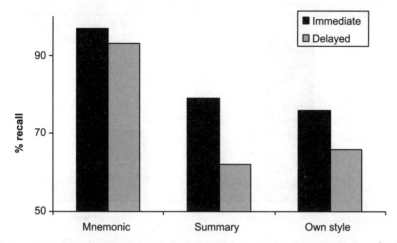

Figure 7.6 Mean recall immediately following the encoding session and after a three-day delay for three groups: one using an adapted keyword mnemonic, the second using a summary strategy and the third left to their own devices.

(Adapted from Levin *et al.* 1986)

1998) and Japanese (Taguchi 2006), as well as for learning new English vocabulary (McDaniel and Pressley 1984).

For instance, Atkinson and Raugh (1975) had two groups learn a list of Russian words. One group was instructed in the use of a keyword mnemonic and given the English translations for each word, whilst the remaining group was given only the English translations. When both groups were subsequently tested by being presented with Russian words and asked to identify the correct English translation, they found that those utilising the keyword method translated significantly more Russian words both at the initial testing session and at a subsequent session approximately 43 days later (see Figure 7.7).

Such findings have led to proposals suggesting that the keyword method can facilitate foreign language learning, because it is easily learnt and supports the direct learning needed to sustain performance over time (Pressley *et al.* 1982; Wyra *et al.* 2007). Pressley *et al.* (1982) have also proposed that the keyword method may be more effective than other vocabulary learning procedures. For instance, a comparison between the keyword method and a number of alternative procedures, including embedding words in meaningful sentences and requiring participants to generate their own meaningful sentences using the target words, revealed that the keyword method was most effective at facilitating recall of the target words (ibid.). Thus, according to Pressley *et al.* (ibid.), the evidence is overwhelming that 'use of the keyword method, as applied to recall of vocabulary definitions, greatly facilitates performance' (p. 70).

Nevertheless, Pressley and Levin (1978) note that it's not just the keyword

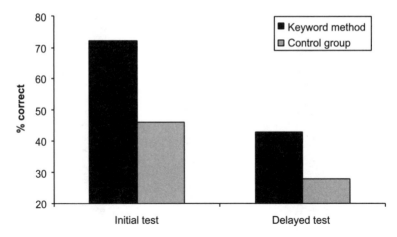

Figure 7.7 Percentage correct translations from Russian to English for those using the keyword method and a non-mnemonic control group.

(Adapted from Atkinson and Raugh 1975)

method itself that is essential to learning new vocabulary, it is also the use of an interactive image. For instance, they found that use of a keyword without an interactive image reduced performance to that of a non-mnemonic control group. In contrast, when a keyword was used alongside an interactive image, the mnemonic proved to be more effective at enhancing recall. Furthermore, Pressley *et al.* (1982) point out that, whilst the keyword method may be an effective technique for learning new words, particularly foreign language words, such learning is not influenced by the difficulty of the foreign language words involved.

However, not everyone has found that using a keyword mnemonic facilitates learning of foreign words. For instance, Willerman and Melvin (1979) found no difference in performance of a group of French students learning new French vocabulary when half of the group used a keyword mnemonic and the remainder used rote rehearsal. Indeed, some suggest that rote rehearsal may be more effective (Campos *et al.* 2003). For example, Campos *et al.* (ibid.) found that rote rehearsal of Latin words led to better recall than use of a mnemonic keyword method (see Figure 7.8).

To a great extent the different findings from the various studies may be attributable to their distinct methodologies. For example, some present material in a pre-determined, researcher-led manner (Atkinson and Raugh 1975), whilst others allow participants to pace themselves during the acquisition period (Campos *et al.* 2003). In addition, there may be differences in the amount of instruction participants have received in the relevant mnemonic technique (see Wang and Thomas 1995), as well as in the imageability of the target words used, the list length and whether the keyword is generated by the participant or provided by the experimenter (e.g., Campos *et al.* 2004).

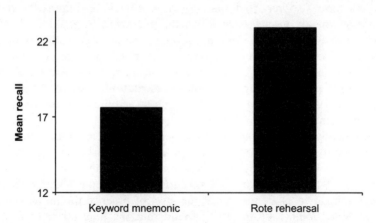

Figure 7.8 Mean number of words recalled for those using rote rehearsal and those using a keyword mnemonic.

(Adapted from Campos *et al.* 2003)

Furthermore, the keyword method has been shown to be more effective when taught individually rather than applied to whole groups (Levin *et al.* 1979).

The keyword method may thus prove to be useful, particularly during the early stages of foreign language learning and for those who struggle to learn new words. However, there may be a number of factors that can influence the outcome when learning with a mnemonic; some of the more common ones are explored in the following section.

Factors influencing learning with mnemonics

This section explores a number of factors that may influence the effectiveness of a mnemonic, including the amount of time given to study the material to be learnt as well as the time given to practise the particular mnemonic technique, the type of imagery used to construct a picture of the target material, as well as the specific mnemonic used. It also explores the assumptions made concerning the strategies, or assumed lack of them, of control groups.

Time

The use of a mnemonic strategy can aid learning and recall of information, but it may depend in part on the amount of time available. Wood (1967) tested this idea by presenting word pairs at differing time intervals to a group, half of which utilised a mnemonic. He found that those using the mnemonic recalled significantly more words than controls, but this difference was only evident for the word pairs presented at five-second intervals. When they were given only two seconds to form an image of the word pair, their recall was no better than controls.

Others have also reported that use of a mnemonic requires a certain amount of time in order for recall benefits to emerge. Bugelski *et al.* (1968) found that presentation rates of four and eight seconds were sufficient to elicit beneficial effects when using a peg mnemonic, but a faster presentation rate of two seconds reduced the effectiveness of the mnemonic technique. Pressley *et al.* (1982) have also suggested that presentation rates of greater than ten seconds may be needed for participants to acquire information using a keyword mnemonic.

It has also been shown that when participants use a mnemonic they often take longer to retrieve information. For example, Corbett (1977) reported slower retrieval times for those utilising a mnemonic compared to rote learners. However, the amount of time taken to execute a particular mnemonic strategy may alter as a function of the level of practice the individual has. For example, Wallace *et al.* (1957) found that the time taken to form an association between a peg and a target item to be recalled fell from 20 seconds to around three seconds over time. Others have also shown that providing additional training in the use of a mnemonic strategy can significantly increase recall of target material (Wang and Thomas 1995; Wyra *et al.* 2007). For instance, when Wang and Thomas (1995) examined the effects of three distinct levels of mnemonic practice on recall, they found a clear association between the level of recall and the number of practice sessions provided, those receiving more sessions exhibiting greater levels of recall (see Figure 7.9).

However, Bottiroli *et al.* (2007) have shown that, without continued practice, the benefits emerging from using a particular mnemonic can diminish and performance will tend to revert to its original level.

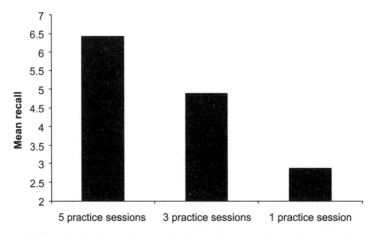

Figure 7.9 Mean level of recall as a function of the number of mnemonic practice sessions received.

(Adapted from Wang and Thomas 1995)

These findings show that the amount of time made available to utilise a mnemonic is a critical variable in determining how effective the mnemonic technique is. Initially more time may be needed to form images or links between targets and mnemonic pegs, to construct a story or isolate specific key features of a target. However, with continued practice the amount of time taken is likely to decrease and greater levels of practice will also lead to superior benefits for learning and memory.

Visual imagery

It is usually claimed that, to visualise links between targets, or between a target and a peg or location, it will be easier to recall a bizarre image with greater accuracy (see, e.g., Buzan 1986). It may be that bizarre images are more distinctive than plausible images, or that they take more time to form, and that both of these processes help to facilitate memory. However, the evidence is equivocal, with some showing that bizarre imagery is more effective (Andreoff and Yarmey 1976), whilst others report that use of bizarre imagery is no more effective than plausible imagery (see Hauck *et al.* 1976; Wood 1967).

For instance, Wood (1967) found that requiring participants to create a bizarre image of each target word to be remembered did not enhance recall compared to a control group. One suggestion, put forward by Higbee (1979), to account for this lack of an effect is based on the idea that people find it more difficult to create or imagine a bizarre image compared to more everyday images. Nevertheless, constructing an image that is clear, vivid and distinct has been shown to aid recall (see Bower 1972; Campos *et al.* 2004). For instance, Campos *et al.* (2004) found that target words that were rated as highly vivid (i.e. easy to imagine, such as *car*) were recalled more accurately than low-vividness words (i.e. more difficult to imagine, such as *religion*), using both a keyword mnemonic and simple rote rehearsal. Furthermore, Senter and Hoffman (1976) found that creating visual images that interacted was a more effective method for aiding recall than simply constructing a bizarre image.

Related to this issue is the ability of the individual to create or construct a visual image. Previous research has shown that individuals vary in their ability to do this (Clark and Pavio 1991). Such findings led Wyra *et al.* (2007) to examine whether an individual's ability to create a visual image would influence recall using a keyword mnemonic strategy. They found that those rated as having high imagery ability outperformed those with a low imagery ability.

Thus, contrary to many of the claims made about the use of mnemonics, it does not seem necessary to create bizarre images of target items, or between a target and a peg or location, in order to be able to recall the information accurately at a later date. However, constructing images that are clear and vivid and which interact will definitely help, as will being good at creating such images.

Mnemonic type

There are a variety of different mnemonic techniques available and the diverse patterns of data reported in the literature may to some extent be the result of using distinct strategies. For instance, Boltwood and Blick (1970) compared the effectiveness of three different types of mnemonic to the performance of non-mnemonic controls. The specific task was to learn a list of words and the mnemonic techniques included utilising the first letter of the words to spell out another word, conceptual clustering, which involved grouping related words together into meaningful categories, and a descriptive story technique which involved creating a story by linking together the target words. The effects of these techniques were compared to the results of a control group who simply performed rote rehearsal of the list. Recall was tested over a number of different time periods and Boltwood and Blick (ibid.) found that those using the mnemonics recalled more than controls; they also found, however, differences in the level of recall between the groups using different mnemonic strategies. The group using the story method showed the greatest benefit, followed by those grouping words together into categories and then those who used the first letter of each target word to spell out a new word (see Figure 7.10).

Boltwood and Blick (ibid.) suggested that the story mnemonic was more effective because it worked by constructing meaningful links between the target words and it was an easy system for the participants to employ. Such findings support the notion that the degree of benefit seen for a particular memory or learning task when using a mnemonic may depend in part on the specific mnemonic technique used. It may also be the case that the type of

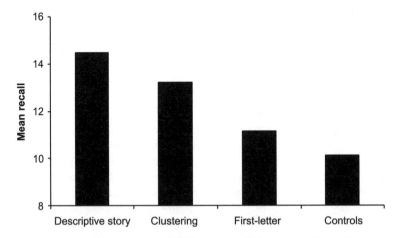

Figure 7.10 Mean recall of target words for those using a descriptive story mnemonic, a clustering mnemonic and a first-letter mnemonic compared to controls using simple repetition.

(Adapted from Boltwood and Blick 1970)

mnemonic interacts with the type of material to be learnt, with specific mnemonics providing a greater benefit for particular types of material.

Control group strategies

The strategy of a non-mnemonic control group may not directly influence the performance of a group trained to use a mnemonic but it can certainly influence the perceived outcome. Attempts to assess the effectiveness of a particular mnemonic often compare the performance of a mnemonically trained group to that of a non-trained control group. The assumption is that those in the control group will simply utilise a basic rote rehearsal strategy. However, evidence shows that, when left to their own devices, many of those allocated to a control group spontaneously utilise a preferred mnemonic technique to help them learn and recall the necessary information (Camp *et al.* 1983; Carlson *et al.* 1976). Camp *et al.* (1983) point out that some of the conflicting findings in the literature may be due to those in the control group utilising a mnemonic technique of their own accord. They also suggest that, because of the bias in the literature of publishing only significant results, there may be numerous unpublished studies failing to show that mnemonic training has any effect on memory simply because the untrained strategy users outperformed those given mnemonic training. Camp *et al.* (ibid.) explored this idea by conducting a recall test on a large group of participants without prescribing any particular strategy. They found that the majority of participants spontaneously utilised a mnemonic to help them recall the list of words. This is consistent with the findings from other researchers showing that participants often spontaneously use a personally developed mnemonic to help them learn (see Boltwood and Blick 1970; Carlson *et al.* 1976). Such findings have important implications in terms of the perceived beneficial effects of mnemonics when performance of a group using a specified mnemonic is compared to that of a control group that is assumed to use only rote rehearsal.

In response to this issue, Higbee (1979) has suggested that participants allocated to control conditions complete a post-test questionnaire asking what, if any, strategy was used. However, Underwood (1972) has noted that, when asked about their strategies, participants' self-reports are not always accurate. On the one hand, they may see the use of a mnemonic strategy as an indicator of intelligence and see reporting such a strategy as a good thing. On the other hand, they may agree to having used a mnemonic strategy simply to please the experimenter. Such points serve to illustrate some of the difficulties faced by researchers and highlight the fact that there is no simple solution to this issue.

Mnemonic transfer

A criticism often aimed at the use of mnemonics is that they aid the memorising of artificial lists of materials, which has little use in everyday life

(Kilpatrick 1985). Furthermore, Kilpatrick suggests that learning based on such processes fails to aid comprehension and is not transferred to new situations. However, a number of researchers have shown that mnemonics can be used to facilitate higher-order thinking and that the cognitive strategies learnt with mnemonic training can be applied and transferred to new situations and new target material (Carney and Levin 2000b; Dretzke and Levin 1996; Pressley and Dennis-Rounds 1980; Rummel *et al.* 2003).

For example, Pressley and Dennis-Rounds (1980) found that adolescents were capable of successfully and spontaneously transferring a keyword mnemonic learnt during one task to another with similar benefits. Rummel *et al.* (2003) also found that participants who used a keyword mnemonic to learn passages of text outperformed free-learning controls when subsequently asked to write a short essay based on the texts, with the essays from the mnemonic group containing significantly more factually relevant information. Similar transferable benefits were reported by Dretzke and Levin (1996) when they utilised an adapted keyword mnemonic approach to help participants learn a passage of information containing various target locations from different geographical sites (e.g. a flower garden in a specific city). Whilst they found that those using the mnemonic recalled more information than controls, they also reported that participants who completed the mnemonic training exhibited superior performance on a separate applied categorisation task, which required them to select and recall previously learnt information according to a variety of newly specified categories (see Figure 7.11).

Dretzke and Levin (1996) argue that such findings indicate that mnemonic training is capable of enhancing performance 'on more than simple measures of rote memory' (p. 88). Specifically, they suggest that learning to utilise a mnemonic may aid in higher-order thinking and the organisation of

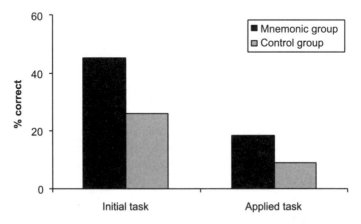

Figure 7.11 Percentage recall of mnemonic group and control group on an initial memory task and a separate applied categorisation task.

(Adapted from Dretzke and Levin 1996)

information. Higher-order thinking refers to the analysis, manipulation and evaluation of information in order to arrive at new interpretations, as opposed to lower-order thinking, which involves the simple recitation of factual information (see Bloom 1956). This proposal is consistent with the suggestions made by Rummel *et al.* (2003) that, rather than simply helping to reproduce facts, mnemonic training can help people to apply such learned information in a flexible and coherent manner. Such findings highlight the potential of a mnemonic to enhance flexible retrieval and intelligent application of learned information, particularly as a large proportion of everyday learning involves identifying, recalling and manipulating factual information.

Nevertheless, researchers do acknowledge that the possible transfer effects of learning a mnemonic technique may be influenced by the difficulty of the task, the similarity between the initial task and the transferred task, and possible instructional variations (Carney and Levin 2000b; Dretzke and Levin 1996).

Long-lasting effects

The above evidence would suggest that information encoded with the aid of a mnemonic strategy is recalled more accurately than using simple rote rehearsal. However, simply recalling more information in the short term, whilst beneficial, is limited. Hence, this section addresses the question of whether mnemonic strategies can facilitate long-term recall.

Despite the fact that a number of researchers have addressed this question, the evidence to date is equivocal. For instance, use of a letter mnemonic (Boltwood and Blick 1970), keyword mnemonic (Levin *et al.* 1986), rhyming mnemonic (Machida and Carlson 1984), story mnemonic (Hill *et al.* 1991), face–name mnemonic (Carney and Levin 2000a) and pictorial mnemonic (Rummel *et al.* 2003) have all been shown to facilitate long-term recall beyond that achieved by simple rote rehearsal. For example, Carney and Levin (2000a) found that an adapted face–name mnemonic led to enhanced levels of recall compared to a non-mnemonic control group when tested immediately and that this benefit was still evident after a delay of two days (see Figure 7.12).

In contrast, others have reported that the method of loci (Carlson *et al.* 1976), the keyword mnemonic (Wang *et al.* 1992) and the pegword mnemonic (Krinsky and Krinsky 1996) failed to elicit any long-term benefits. For example, Carlson *et al.* (1976) compared the memory performance of a group using the method of loci to that of a non-mnemonic control group and, although immediate recall was superior for those using the mnemonic strategy, after a delay of 24 hours the performance of those in the mnemonic group was no better than that of controls (see Figure 7.13).

The different pattern of results often reflects differences in methodology (see the 'Factors influencing mnemonics' section above). One suggestion put forward is that such variation in the data reflects subtle but important

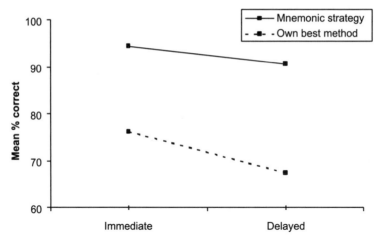

Figure 7.12 Mean recall for those using a mnemonic strategy compared to a non-mnemonic control group when tested immediately and after a delay of two days.

(Adapted from Carney and Levin 2000a)

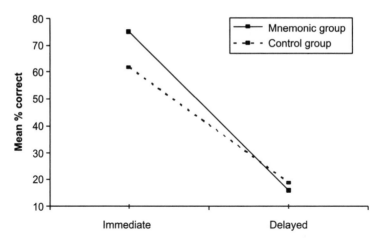

Figure 7.13 Mean recall for the mnemonic group compared to controls immediately after learning and after a one-day delay.

(Adapted from Carlson *et al.* 1976)

differences given in the instructions to participants (Carlson *et al.* 1976). Other possible causes of inconsistent results regarding long-term effectiveness are the use of different mnemonic techniques, variability in the type of information to be remembered, variable lengths of delay between encoding and retrieval, different levels of skill of the individual as well as varying degrees of practice, and the rate and level of exposure to the target (see

Atkinson and Raugh 1975; Boltwood and Blick 1970; Carney and Levin 2000a; Wang and Thomas 1995). Furthermore, Levin *et al.* (1986) have shown that performance can also be influenced by the type of memory task used (i.e. recognition versus recall), with greater mnemonic benefits reported for a mnemonic strategy when tested by an identification or recognition task as compared to a recall task. Wang *et al.* (1993) have also noted that poor long-term mnemonic performance may stem from a susceptibility of the mnemonic-based encodings to interfere with pre-existing associations.

Overview

A mnemonic may refer to a particular technique used to help create associations, which in turn aids in the learning and recall of new information. It is thought that such techniques were initially developed by the early Greeks and Romans as part of a long oral tradition of public speaking and storytelling. Nevertheless, they remain popular and widespread, with many people using them spontaneously when attempting to learn new information. They are also effortful or active devices, in the sense that they rely on the individual to construct a particular strategy or framework which links or associates information in a potentially meaningful way.

There is a wide variety of mnemonic strategies, each aimed at facilitating a particular aspect of learning, and this range is expanding as new systems and strategies are developed to deal with the ever-increasing need to learn more. This chapter has provided an overview of some of the more popular techniques, including the peg system, the method of loci, the major system, the story method, the face–name method and the keyword method.

Mnemonics have been used in a diverse range of settings to enhance a variety of abilities, from memory to language learning. There is a great deal of evidence showing that use of a mnemonic can significantly improve recall. In addition, mnemonics have been shown to enhance recall for factual information embedded in texts, which highlights a potentially beneficial application for use in education. In terms of remembering new names, the use of a mnemonic strategy has been shown to be beneficial but, due to the complexity of the procedure, it often requires additional time and/or practice, which may make it initially less attractive than a simpler procedure such as the expanding retrieval technique. Attempts to learn new foreign language words using a mnemonic have also shown some benefits, but the effectiveness of such techniques may rely on the specific procedure adopted by the individual, as well as how they learnt the particular mnemonic in the first place.

This highlights the fact that, whilst the use of a mnemonic strategy can facilitate performance, such an approach may be influenced by a number of factors, some of which were explored in this chapter. For instance, a certain amount of time is needed initially for using a mnemonic strategy, which means that adopting such an approach may be problematic for information presented very quickly. However, this can improve with additional practice.

The level of practice with a particular mnemonic has also been shown to influence its effectiveness, with greater practice producing more benefits. In terms of the type of images used as part of a mnemonic, contrary to popular belief a bizarre image is not necessary, but using clear and vivid images that interact has been shown to be more beneficial. A comparison between different mnemonic techniques also revealed that some are more effective than others and that this may be influenced by the type of material to be learnt. It was also highlighted that the strategy of control groups, often assumed to be rote rehearsal, was questionable given the finding that a large number report spontaneously using some form of mnemonic. This has led to additional methodological developments, including the use of post-test questionnaires to ascertain which strategies are used by controls.

A criticism often levelled at the use of a mnemonic strategy is that it is artificial, has only limited use for memorising lists of items and doesn't really relate to real-life learning or aid in the comprehension of new material. This was examined by exploring the possibility of mnemonic transfer. This refers to the idea that the information and/or skills learnt using a mnemonic in one situation can be transferred and applied to new and different situations. In fact, the evidence shows that use of a mnemonic can be effective in far more than simple rote learning of lists, yielding improvements in higher-order thinking as well as applications to new situations, including writing an essay based on recalled information and manipulating learned information in new ways. However, such transfer effects may be limited by the extent to which both tasks share certain cognitive processes. Nevertheless, it seems that mnemonics can be used for more than simply list learning.

Finally, evidence showing that use of a mnemonic strategy can enhance memory over long periods of time is encouraging, if inconsistent. Such inconsistencies are largely the result of differing methodologies and, whilst the findings are promising, more research is needed to identify precisely the long-term benefits of mnemonic training.

8   Speed reading

Reading is to the mind what exercise is to the body.

(Sir Richard Steele)

In the last century there was a media explosion resulting in a proliferation of printed material, alongside an expanding amount of information on the World Wide Web. Given this increase in the amount of reading material available, it should come as no surprise that some people feel overwhelmed by the volume of information and have little idea or hope of how to get through it all. Of course, not all material needs to be read in the same way. Sir Francis Bacon once said that some books are to be nibbled and tasted, some are to be swallowed whole, and a few need to be thoroughly chewed and digested. However, despite such a rapid expansion in the amount of material currently available, people invariably read in much the same way as they did 50 or 100 years ago, even though many wish to improve the speed of this process. For instance, when Stevens and Orem (1967) asked their students what they would like to change about the way they read information, 95 per cent expressed a desire to enhance their reading speed. In response to such ambitions, there has been an explosion in the number and availability of speed-reading courses, books, seminars, DVDs and workshops aimed at teaching people how to process large quantities of information rapidly.

Given the wealth of sources available to enhance reading speed, as well as the claims made by advocates of such techniques, this chapter examines how effective speed reading is at enhancing information-processing skills. It begins by outlining the concept of reading and highlights some of the different types of reading. Following this, there is a brief history of the development of speed reading. The chapter then explores factors shown to influence reading speed. The use of speed-reading techniques to enhance reading performance is then examined, along with evidence suggesting that such training can produce long-term benefits. The chapter ends by looking at the effects of speed reading on comprehension.

From reading to speed reading

According to Carver (1985), reading refers to the acquisition of meaning from text in a sentence-by-sentence manner. It is a skill learnt as part of a wider educational training and involves a number of key processes. For instance, the individual begins by learning the associations between the spelling or orthography of a word and its sound, or phonology. It is important to note that, when reading, the reader's eye movements do not flow seamlessly along the text but move in a series of jerky *saccades*, fixating on various words during which visual information is acquired (see Figure 8.1).

Each *fixation* typically lasts for 200 milliseconds, dependent upon the frequency and complexity of the word (Rayner and Duffy 1986). A fixation represents a moment in time when the eye stops to acquire visual information. As can be seen from Figure 8.1, some words may be skipped whilst others elicit multiple fixations. Oftentimes a reader will also move his eyes back over text already covered; this is referred to as a *regression* or regressive saccade, denoted by the grey circles. In addition, the reader invariably voices the words to himself silently as he reads, which is referred to as *subvocalisation* or inner speech. This process is thought to help the reader remember the words of a sentence so that the entire meaning can be understood (Carver 1992).

Not all material, however, is read in the same manner. An individual may read at different speeds depending on the type of material and the specific task at hand. For example, *scanning* may take less time than *skim* reading, which in turn may be faster than *active* reading. Scanning refers to a search-driven exercise such as trying to locate a phone number from the telephone directory. In contrast, skim reading may be useful for processing large quantities of text at a superficial level to identify the main ideas or gist. Meanwhile, active reading, or reading for comprehension, involves the reader

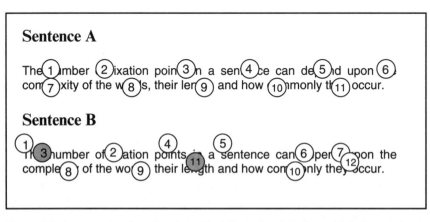

Figure 8.1 An example of eye fixations (circled numbers) for hypothetical smooth eye movements (sentence A) and typical eye movements (sentence B) made during reading.

getting to know the material well enough to be able to recall and/or explain it at a later date.

The similarities between skimming and speed reading have not gone unnoticed (see Carver 1992). However, speed reading is thought to be different from skimming because it aims to maintain levels of comprehension similar to that of active reading. Hence, training in speed-reading techniques has the dual aim of attempting to enhance reading speed whilst maintaining a consistent level of comprehension.

Given that the average college student reads at a rate of approximately 300 words per minute (wpm) (Carver 1992), it is not clear how much faster a reader needs to process text for it to be classified as speed reading. Spache (1962) argued that it is not possible to read at rates of greater than 900 wpm. For example, Spache noted that the shortest effective fixation is 166 milli-seconds, with 33 milliseconds needed to saccade from one fixation point to another, and that during a single fixation the eye can identify between 2.5 and three words. Thus, if an individual is capable of seeing only three words every fifth of a second, this equates to 15 words per second, or 900 wpm. Spache (ibid.) has suggested that this represents an upper limit because a higher fixation rate would be difficult to sustain.

However, Stevens and Orem (1967) were convinced that a proportion of the normal adult population can learn to read in excess of 1500 wpm. Moreover, they observed that rapid readers exhibit a specific pattern of characteristics when reading. First, such readers have high natural reading rates of over 300 wpm and enjoy reading as a recreational pastime. However, none of the fast readers was able to read unfamiliar material at such speeds. Second, faster readers rely more on visual information and were less reliant on subvo-calising words. Stevens and Orem used the term *visual reader* to identify those who bypass the subvocalisation process, relying on visual processes, and they suggest that a consequence of this will be the ability to recognise more words per fixation, leading to superior reading speeds.

In all, a range of reading rates has been suggested for those identified as 'speed readers', from 900 wpm (Spache 1962) up to 10,000 wpm (Homa 1983). All these rates are in excess of the typical reading rate of 300 wpm.

A brief history of speed reading

It's been suggested that speed reading evolved from early research using tach-istoscopes to examine the effects of briefly presented images on an indi-vidual's perceptual ability (Buzan 1997).

According to Buzan (1997), First World War pilots found it difficult to identify planes from a distance. In an attempt to overcome the possible limitations this had on the pilots' ability to distinguish friend from foe, they underwent a series of training sessions. These sessions involved presenting the pilots with silhouettes of various planes on a screen using a tachistoscope at ever-increasing speeds. It was found that, with sufficient training, the pilots became more efficient at identifying the silhouettes, even when they were shown for a fraction of a second.

This led others to wonder whether such a technique could be used to improve reading speeds (see Karlin 1958). This early *tachistoscopic reading* produced some intriguing results showing that individuals were able to identify words at very brief exposures, leading to improved reading rates (Robinson 1934). This technique has been developed over time and the tachistoscope has since given way to the use of computers to present text rapidly in an effort to facilitate reading speed (see Juola 1988).

Alongside these mechanical developments, others promoted the idea that reading speed could be enhanced by using a variety of simple techniques. A prominent approach put forward by Evelyn Wood and Marjorie Barrows in the 1950s later developed into the method called Reading Dynamics (Agardy 1981). Since then, there has been a proliferation of speed-reading books, DVDs and computing software aimed at enhancing reading speed, with many making claims that reading rates ten times that of normal reading speed are possible (see Brozo and Johns 1986).

Speed-reading techniques

It is beyond the scope of this chapter to provide a comprehensive review of all speed-reading techniques. In addition, many organisations remain silent about the precise techniques used as part of their training. However, it is possible to distil a number of common elements contained in many approaches.

One common element is for the reader to tackle material in a number of stages. First, it is suggested that the reader previews material in order to make it easier to access related information (Buzan 1997; Konstant 2000; Scheele 1993). This requires the reader to skim through the text to obtain a general idea of its contents. It may include examination of the table of contents as well as chapter titles. An additional aim is to inspire the reader to think about what it is he hopes to gain from reading such a text. The preview stage is followed by the speed-reading stage. Invariably, each approach identifies this by a particular term, such as active reading (Konstant 2000) or photo reading (Scheele 1993). Following this, there may be a review stage during which the individual needs to reactivate the material presented in the text. This also provides the reader with another opportunity to rehearse the material. If, however, the reader feels that he has not yet achieved the desired level of understanding, Scheele (1993) suggests that he simply scan the text again.

A second common element is the use of a pointer or visual guide. This may be any tool, such as a pen or the reader's finger, which can be placed under the line of text to be read and moved from left to right in a quick, smooth motion. Buzan (1997) outlines a number of different *guidance patterns* that are alleged to aid reading speed. The *traditional pattern* is where the guide is swept along beneath each line at a set rate. The *double sweep* involves the guide moving beneath every other line, encouraging the reader to encode two lines of text at a time, and the *backward sweep*, which is assumed to encourage the reader to encode information during the backward sweep of the guide from the end of one sentence to the beginning of another. Moreover, increasing the sweeping speed of the guide is also assumed to facilitate the pace of reading.

A key benefit of the visual guide is that it is thought to reduce the number of fixations made, thereby encouraging the reader to encode multiple words in each fixation, a shift Maxwell (1973) suggests is essential for readers to enhance their speed. Indeed, Calef *et al.* (1999) found that participants who had completed a speed-reading course showed a significant reduction in the number of eye fixations per 100 words compared to a no-training control group (see Figure 8.2).

An additional benefit of using a visual guide is to reduce the number of regressions made by the reader. Although regressions may occur naturally, most techniques advocating speed reading suggest that it is desirable to reduce them (Brozo and Johns 1986). Consistent with this idea, research has shown that following an intensive speed-reading course those taking part exhibited a significant reduction in the number of regressions made compared to controls (see Figure 8.3) (Calef *et al.* 1999).

However, Hyona and Nurminen (2006) dispute the idea that regressive eye movements are a waste of time and need to be reduced. They argue that looking back at text already covered represents a strategic behaviour and that the more a person looks back over what has been read, the greater his level of recall of the main points of the text. There is thus some debate in the literature concerning the role of regressive eye movements in reading and whether their elimination represents a more efficient mode of reading. For simple text that is easily understood, there may be little need to re-read material. However, for more complex text such regressions may aid comprehension.

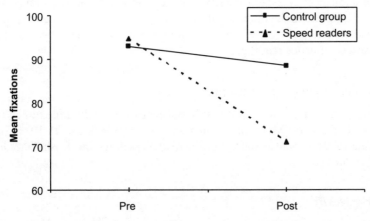

Figure 8.2 Mean number of eye fixations per 100 words before and after training for control group and speed readers.

(Adapted from Calef *et al.* 1999)

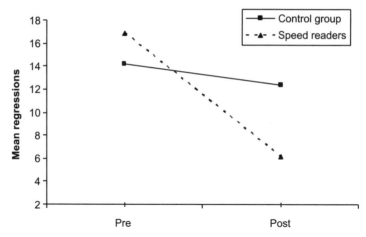

Figure 8.3 Mean number of regressions made pre and post training for control group and speed readers.

(Adapted from Calef *et al.* 1999)

Use of a visual guide is also thought to encourage *visual reading*, with less reliance on subvocalising words (see Konstant 2000). There is a consensus in the speed-reading literature that, by moving away from a reading style which invokes subvocalisation of the words, a reader will enhance his reading speed (Buzan 1997; Konstant 2000; Scheele 1993).

Some proponents also make reference to various *subconscious* processes to facilitate reading speed (e.g., Kurita 2001, 2003; Scheele 1993). For instance, Kurita (2001) suggests that his approach uses the 'mind and body correlation in an original way, to activate the route from the peripheral visual field to the subconsciousness, to establish a new transfer method of information processing, and to improve the intellectual activity' (p. 47). However, such claims are vague and there is little attempt to clarify precisely what they mean and why they would influence reading.

Factors influencing speed reading

Reading can be influenced by a number of factors, including the difficulty of the text (Coke 1974; Miller and Coleman 1972; McConkie *et al.* 1973; Smith and Tate 1953), as well as the age of the reader (Bellows and Rush 1952; Jones and Carron 1965).

Text complexity

The idea that reading speed alters as a function of text difficulty has been debated. Some suggest that, irrespective of the difficulty of the text, the individual's reading rate remains reasonably constant (Coke 1974; Miller and

Coleman 1972), whilst others argue that reading rates alter as a function of difficulty level (Carver 1983; McConkie *et al.* 1973). For example, Smith and Tate (1953) tested individuals' speed-reading rates across a variety of texts and found that they showed a drop in both speed and comprehension as text complexity increased (see Figure 8.4).

It is not just the difficulty of the text that influences reading speed but also the distinction between fiction and non-fiction. For example, Graf (1973) reported on the reading rate of a group of speed readers as they attempted to speed read four different types of literature and found that their reading rate was faster for heavy fiction than light fiction, but for non-fiction the opposite pattern emerged (see Figure 8.5). Thus, increasing text difficulty slowed reading speeds, but only for non-fictional works. This may be due to the more abstract nature of heavy non-fictional text. However, it remains unclear why more difficult fiction should be read at higher speeds.

Age

The age at which an individual begins to develop speed-reading techniques may also influence their effectiveness. Some argue that if such techniques are adopted early on in life, it is more likely they will become the norm and enhance reading speed (Bergquist 1984). There is some support for this idea from research showing that younger participants exhibit greater benefits from speed-reading training than their more mature counterparts. For instance, Bellows and Rush (1952) found a negative correlation between increases in

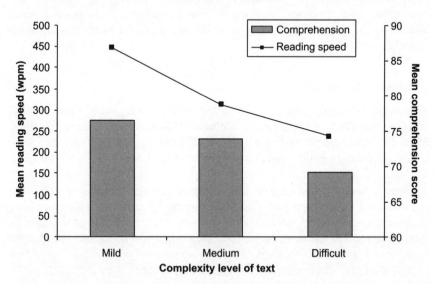

Figure 8.4 Mean reading speed (wpm) and mean percentage comprehension levels for mild, medium and difficult levels of text.

(Adapted from Smith and Tate 1953)

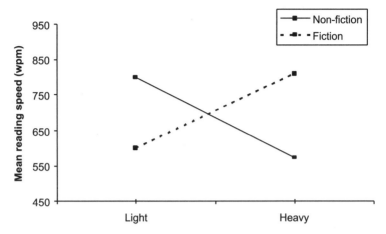

Figure 8.5 Mean reading speed (wpm) for a group of speed readers reading light and heavy non-fiction and fiction.

(Adapted from Graf 1973)

reading speed and age, suggesting that the younger participants benefited more from the training than their older peers. Jones and Carron (1965) also found that age was negatively associated with success in speed reading, with higher levels of success shown by younger participants. They point out that such a finding is not surprising given that such training often requires an individual to modify or extinguish old patterns of reading and establish new ones. Such findings have led to the suggestion that speed reading should be taught in school once the child has mastered basic reading skills (Bergquist 1984).

Enhancing performance

The evidence supporting speed reading is equivocal, with some studies showing that reading speeds can be enhanced (Bellows and Rush 1952; Bond 1941; Breznitz and Share 1992; Calef *et al.* 1999; Just and Carpenter 1987), whilst others fail to elicit any clear improvements (Carver 1970; Homa 1983; McNamara 2000).

Two methods of training have been adopted to enhance reading speed. On the one hand, researchers have adopted a mechanistic approach incorporating tachistoscopic and computerised presentation of text information to facilitate reading speed. On the other hand, speed-reading training has been conducted in seminars and/or workshops, often by speed-reading professionals. This section examines the evidence from each of these areas in turn.

Research by Smith and Tate (1953) examined the effectiveness of using a tachistoscope to aid reading speed. The aim of such training was to encourage the readers to process each word quickly, so that, when they were given standard written text, their reading speeds would improve. Smith and Tate found that six weeks of training using this approach increased reading speeds from 350 to 580 wpm, but without significant losses in comprehension (see Figure 8.6).

Whilst the results were encouraging, Smith and Tate failed to conduct any analysis on the data so it is not clear whether this represented a significant improvement or not. Moreover, even though they suggested that speed reading did not impair comprehension, as can be seen in Figure 8.6 the overall level of comprehension did drop as speed increased.

More recently, Breznitz and Share (1992) utilised a procedure which involved presenting text via computer to schoolchildren and having them read it aloud either at their own pace or at a manipulated fast pace. In both cases, the text was erased letter by letter to minimise regressive eye movements. Using such a presentation device, Breznitz and Share found that the fast-paced process led to a 30 per cent improvement in reading rates compared to self-paced reading, and this increase in speed was accompanied by a 20 per cent increase in comprehension and a 30 per cent improvement in recall. They put such improvements down to changes in short-term memory and noted the possible educational benefits of such a procedure. However, they failed to report the reading speed of each child, making it difficult to know whether this benefit constitutes evidence for speed reading or of facilitating the reading speed of below-average readers to that of a more normative level.

These findings indicate that using technology may enhance reading speed but more needs to be done, particularly in terms of how such an approach may influence comprehension.

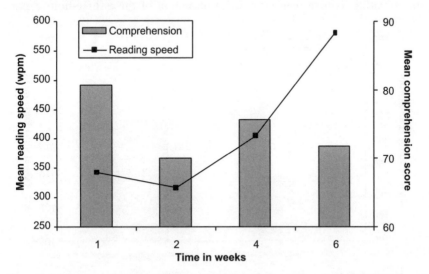

Figure 8.6 Mean reading speed (wpm) and level of comprehension after 1, 2, 4 and 6 weeks of training with a tachistoscope.

(Adapted from Smith and Tate 1953)

Others have adopted a less mechanistic approach, requiring individuals to attend speed-reading training sessions designed to enhance particular visual skills and develop techniques thought to aid the reading process. For instance, Bond (1941) and Bellows and Rush (1952) found that a ten-week speed-reading course significantly enhanced the reading speeds of those taking part. Bond (1941) reported an increase in reading speed from 215 to 335 wpm, while Bellows and Rush (1952) found both speed and comprehension increased (see Figure 8.7).

These findings led the researchers to propose that such training can significantly enhance reading speed, as well as provide benefits for comprehension. However, both studies are flawed because they fail to include adequate controls. Thus, the improvements in reading speed may simply be a function of the additional practice and attention given during the training. Furthermore, a fundamental flaw in the study reported by Bellows and Rush (1952) is that the test of comprehension was computed on a separate piece of text from that used to identify reading speed. This means that, whilst reading speeds improved, the level of comprehension for the material that was 'speed read' may have deteriorated.

A more comprehensive study, conducted by Calef *et al.* (1999), has shown that training in speed-reading techniques leads to more efficient eye movements, which results in enhanced reading speed. Calef *et al.* examined the reading performance of two groups, only one of which completed a speed-reading course. Both groups underwent a number of tests using an infrared monitoring device to measure eye movements and calculate reading speed, as well as the number of words perceived in each fixation. Those completing the speed-reading course then attended a minimum of three three-hour classes

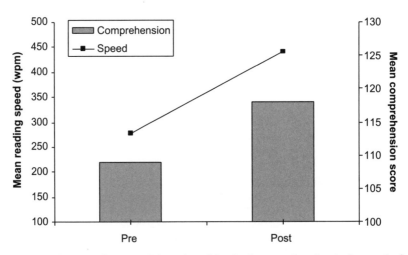

Figure 8.7 Mean reading speed (wpm) and level of comprehension before and after speed-reading training.

(Adapted from Bellows and Rush 1952)

which involved intensive instruction on methods to improve reading speed by a qualified instructor. Before and after the training both groups were instructed to read a passage of text containing approximately 120 words as fast as possible, keeping in mind the need to comprehend the information. Calef *et al.* (ibid.) found that those who had completed the speed-reading course showed a significant improvement in reading speed, from 300 to 400 wpm, with no change in comprehension (see Figure 8.8).

In addition, Calef *et al.* (ibid.) reported that those who took part in the speed-reading training exhibited a 40 per cent increase in their recognition span, which refers to the number of words acquired during a single fixation, compared to only a 4 per cent increase for the control group. They also found

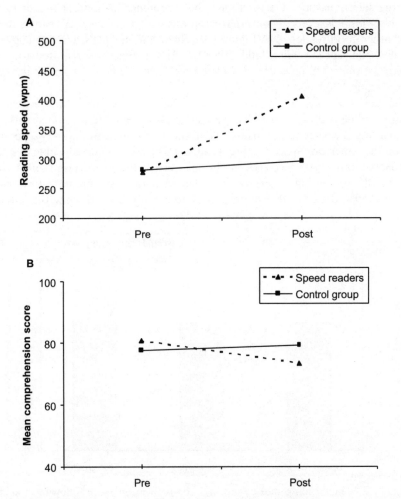

Figure 8.8 Changes in reading speed (Panel A) and comprehension levels (Panel B) from pre to post training for speed-reading and control groups.

(Adapted from Calef *et al.* 1999)

that the speed readers made fewer fixations and regressions. By increasing their recognition span and being able to capture more words per fixation, the speed readers could make fewer fixations. This led Calef *et al.* to suggest that training in speed reading not only enhances the speed with which individuals can read material but also improves specific eye movement characteristics associated with reading.

However, not all researchers have found that speed reading benefits the individual's reading ability. For instance, Carver (1985) compared the reading rates of superior readers, including speed readers and professionals. He measured their typical reading rate, ability to skim-read material, speed, comprehension of text and memory for text presented at various speeds. Using such measures, Carver found that the ability to read at higher rates with reasonable levels of comprehension was no better for speed readers than for other good readers (see Figure 8.9). Such findings led Carver to suggest that, when 'speed-readers and other superior readers are required to give evidence that they have comprehended well, they seem to typically read at rates around 300–600 Wpm' (p. 416).

Homa (1983) also questioned the idea that speed readers attain a greater degree of perceptual sensitivity than normal readers. He examined this by measuring the perceptual sensitivity and speed-reading abilities of two people from the American Speedreading Academy who were reportedly able to read at exceedingly high speeds. Homa initially tested their perceptual sensitivity by briefly presenting letters on a screen in a random manner at various distances from a central fixation point and asking them to name the letters.

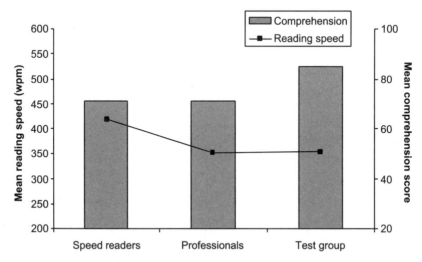

Figure 8.9 Mean reading rate (wpm) and comprehension score following a skim-reading task for speed readers, professionals and a test group of high-ability readers.

(Adapted from Carver 1985)

Their speed reading and comprehension were also tested by having them read a text on human memory and answer a set of standard multiple-choice questions. Unfortunately, the speed readers showed no difference in perceptual sensitivity from that of the controls, with both groups showing a decrease in their accuracy of perceptual sensitivity as a function of target distance (see Figure 8.10).

Nevertheless, Homa (ibid.) noted that the speed readers took, on average, between one and a half minutes to five minutes to read the text on memory, which equates to an approximate word speed of over 10,000 wpm. However, when their comprehension was tested, their performance was so poor that it was classified as a failure. Overall, the speed readers showed no difference in level of perceptual sensitivity and extremely poor comprehension of a text that was allegedly speed read. Homa concluded by stating that the 'only noteworthy skill exhibited by the two speed-readers was a remarkable dexterity in page-turning' (p. 126).

Such a conclusion may be considered rather tongue-in-cheek but others have reached similar verdicts, even when participating in speed-reading training themselves. For example, McNamara (2000) took part in a two-day workshop on PhotoReading (Scheele 1993). At the end of the workshop she compared her reading speed and level of comprehension to that of the expert who led the workshop when reading normally and when attempting to PhotoRead material. Unfortunately, no benefit was found for using the techniques associated with PhotoReading as compared to normal reading practices in terms of speed or comprehension for either herself (the trainee) or the expert (see Figure 8.11).

Nevertheless, McNamara (2000) noted that many people still claim that attending such workshops and/or seminars enhances their reading ability and

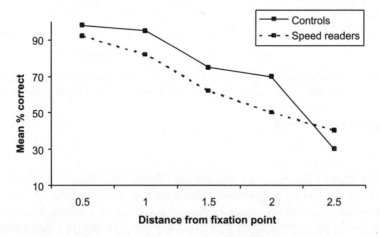

Figure 8.10 Mean percentage of correctly identified targets as a function of target distance from a central fixation point for speed readers and controls.

(Adapted from Homa 1983)

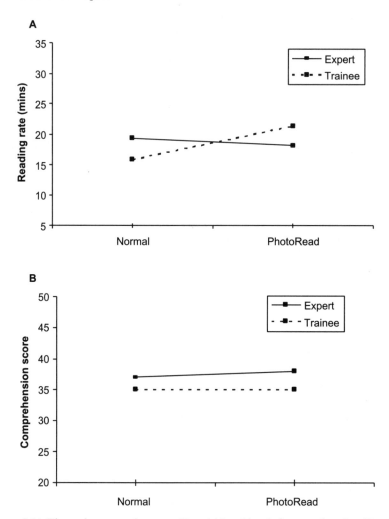

Figure 8.11 Time taken to read test text (Panel A) and level of comprehension (Panel B) for trainee and expert when reading normally and when attempting to PhotoRead material.

(Adapted from McNamara 2000)

that this may be due to a false sense of confidence. Such false confidence may stem from the feeling of familiarity based on the preview of the text and the positive self-affirmations made as part of the training process. McNamara concluded by stating that there is 'clearly no benefit to using the PhotoReading technique' (p. 11).

Such findings have led Carver (1992) to argue that most people read at a constant, typical and optimal rate of around 400 wpm, and that speed readers may be able to process more by skimming over the material. He suggests that what speed-reading courses actually teach are techniques to aid skim reading and therefore, reading rates of over 600 wpm should more accurately be called skimming.

The various outcomes of the above speed-reading studies may be accounted for in part by a range of methodological differences. For example, there is little consensus on how to measure reading rate. Some tests assess reading speed based on two minutes of testing (e.g. Iowa Silent Reading Test), while others utilise longer periods (Minnesota Speed of Reading Test). Furthermore, if the reader sets the reading rate himself he may be more comfortable than when an experimenter sets it. For instance, Rubin and Turano (1992) have shown that higher reading speeds can be achieved when the reader is allowed to set the reading rate. Also, some experimenters do not inform participants how long they will be shown the material for and the reader may not be able to adjust his reading level accordingly (Carver 1985).

Differences in performance can also occur due to variations in the type and difficulty level of text material used, which have been shown to influence reading speed directly (see Graf 1973). There may also be differences in the length, duration and type of speed-reading training, which can range from a few hours (Calef *et al.* 1999) to ten weeks (Bellows and Rush 1952) and may form part of a larger training programme (Bell 2001) or represent an intensive isolated experience (McNamara, 2000).

A variety of different tests have also been used to assess how well the reader remembers the text. This includes fill in the gap and multiple-choice questions (Graf 1973), as well as true/false questions (Calef *et al.* 1999). Carver (1987) criticised such tests as being too simplistic, with potentially high scores resulting from guesswork rather than comprehension. Indeed, McNamara (2000) has shown that the complexity of the question can directly influence the level of perceived comprehension after the speed reading of a text, with more complex, conceptual-based questions resulting in lower comprehension scores than for superficial text-based questions.

Overall, there seems to be a dramatic difference between the levels of speed reading actually achieved and some of the claims made. Evidence shows that an individual can enhance his reading speed from 300 to 400 wpm (Calef *et al.* 1999). However, the claims that reading speeds can be increased to rates exceeding many thousands of wpm are not supported (Homa 1983; McNamara 2000). It would seem that it is certainly possible to enhance reading speed, but that such improvements tend to be relatively modest.

Enduring benefits

Given the potentially high cost of speed-reading training courses, not forgetting the individual's time investment, it would be useful to know whether such training results in long-term benefits. Sadly, there is very little research directly addressing this issue, although some insight can be gained from an early study carried out by Jones and Carron (1965).

Jones and Carron (ibid.) were interested in comparing the effectiveness of two approaches to speed reading. One relied heavily on the use of various technical devices assumed to enhance reading speed by presenting material for very brief periods of time. Showing the text for only a brief period of time challenges the reader to assimilate it very quickly, making fewer fixations and regressions. In addition, it encourages the reader to reduce his reliance on the use of subvocalisations. The alternative approach was referred to as 'book centred training' and involved explanations of efficient eye movements during reading, supervised reading practice and reading materials outlining various speed-reading techniques.

Participants allocated to the two groups underwent a number of reading assessments, which included measuring reading speed and comprehension before the training began, after it had finished and after a delay of between 16 and 18 months. When examining the reading performance of the two groups, Jones and Carron (1965) found that they both exhibited a similar increase in reading speed from pre- to post-training. Furthermore, the gains in reading speed were maintained at a follow-up study conducted 16 to 18 months later (see Figure 8.12).

Such a pattern would indicate that a ten-week course in speed-reading techniques can have reasonably long-term benefits. However, there are a number of caveats relating to the study that need to be highlighted. First, whilst

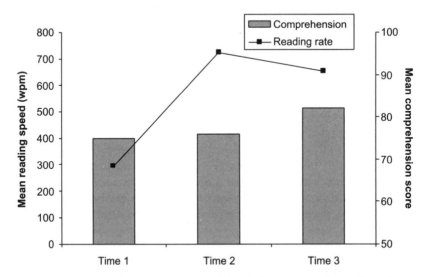

Figure 8.12 Mean reading speed (wpm) and level of comprehension collapsed across the two speed reading groups, before training began (time 1) after it had finished (time 2) and after a 16–18 month delay (time 3).

(Adapted from Jones and Carron 1965)

encouraging, the work by Jones and Carron (ibid.) represents only a single study. More research is needed to ascertain fully the duration of any potential benefits from speed reading. It would also be important to identify whether the level of continued practice influences the individual's reading rate. That is, are such long-term gains maintained only when the individual continually practises the techniques on a regular basis? Second, it should be noted that Jones and Carron (1965) failed to include a no-training control group. That both groups showed an improvement in reading speed without any loss of comprehension may just as easily be accounted for in terms of a combination of practice effects and improved motivation resulting from intensive experi-menter–participant interactions. Furthermore, the speed-reading training contained a range of components, for both groups, making it difficult to identify clearly which element produced the desired effect. It may be the case that a combination of training components produces a more effective outcome. However, again, more research is needed to help clarify this point.

Speed/comprehension trade-off

There are two key issues in speed reading: the first relates to how quickly an individual is able to read the text and the second is how much of the text is understood. Good comprehension requires the individual to extract and retain the ideas from the text, something which it has been argued is essential to the reading process (Bell 2001). There is no clear consensus regarding what specific measure should be used or what the ideal level of comprehen-sion should be for an individual to exhibit full understanding of material covered. Champeau de Lopez (1993) has indicated that a comprehension level of 67 per cent should be deemed as acceptable, whilst Carver (1992) argues that a comprehension rate of 50 per cent or less should be deemed a failure by normal reading teachers. The key issue here is whether attempts made to increase reading speed also lead to a decrease in the level of com-prehension. Carver (1985) has reported that the rate of text comprehension increases linearly as the amount of time spent reading it also increases. Such findings suggest that, whilst training to speed read may improve an indi-vidual's ability to read at a faster rate, it may be at the cost of understanding what the text says. Given this, it may be inappropriate to speed read when attempting to learn new or complex material. Such concerns have led some to suggest that training individuals to enhance the speed of their reading results in a significant decrease in their level of comprehension (Carver 1987, 1992; Graf 1973).

A good example of this can be seen in the study conducted by Graf (1973), who took up the challenge laid down by various proponents of the speed-reading industry to test whether speed and comprehension levels changed as a function of speed reading. Graf found that average reading speed increased from a little over 200 wpm to approximately 695 wpm for those taking part in the training compared to a no-training control group (see Figure 8.13).

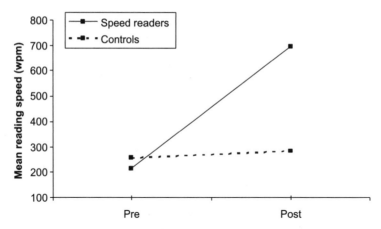

Figure 8.13 Mean reading speed (wpm) before and after taking part in a speed-
reading training course for the speed readers and the control group.

(Adapted from Graf 1983)

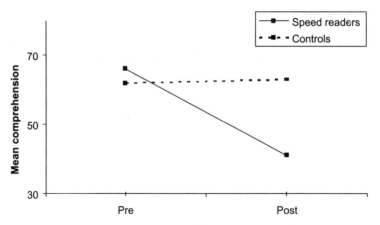

Figure 8.14 Mean comprehension level before and after taking part in a speed-
reading training course for the speed readers and the control group.

(Adapted from Graf 1983)

However, those taking part in the speed-reading course also showed a
39 per cent decrease in their level of comprehension (see Figure 8.14), whilst
controls remained steady across time.

Graf (ibid.) argued, therefore, that it is not possible for a reader to enhance
his reading speed without missing out on information contained in the text.
Others have reported a similar pattern of results, showing that increases in
reading speed can be made only by sacrificing the accuracy of understanding
the text (Carver 1985; Just and Carpenter 1987). This trade-off between speed
and accuracy has led to the suggestion that a reading rate of approximately

300 wpm represents an optimal speed while maintaining good levels of comprehension across texts of different levels of difficulty (Carver 1982). Furthermore, Carver (1987) points out that teaching speed reading to children could be potentially harmful to their natural growth in reading ability. This may be because speed reading instils within the reader a false sense of confidence concerning the material covered and their understanding of it. They may believe that they have understood it when in fact they have not. However, Carver (ibid.) does state that, if such training is portrayed as a skimming process, which is clearly identified as being distinct from reading, it may be useful in certain circumstances. Graf (1973) takes a slightly more pragmatic view, accepting that there may be a speed–comprehension trade-off, and points out that essentially the reader needs to make a decision as to whether it is better to read 'three books at 40 percent comprehension than one book at 70 percent' (p. 113).

It should also be noted that possible gains in reading speed may simply be easier to accomplish than advances in reading comprehension. Given more time and training, it may be that the initial benefits seen for speed could be mirrored by improved levels of comprehension.

Overview

Reading involves a number of distinct processes. The reader's eyes move in jerky saccades from point to point, fixating on a word or group of words for a brief period of time in order to acquire and process them. The eyes then move on to the next set of words, or regress, fixating on a word already encoded. During this process the reader may also subvocalise the words to himself as an aid to understanding. However, not all material is read in the same way. Depending on the type of material and the goals of the reader, material can be scanned, skimmed or actively read. Each respective approach is thought to enable a more comprehensive level of understanding concerning the material covered. Speed reading is distinct from such approaches in that it is assumed to combine the speed associated with skimming along with the comprehension levels seen when material is actively read.

The concept of speed reading is thought to have emerged from the early use of tachistoscopic presentation of material for very brief periods of time. This led to the notion of tachistoscopic reading, which in time gave way to a more computerised approach, often referred to as rapid serial visual presentation. The encouraging findings from using such devices to enhance reading speeds led others to develop a range of different techniques and skills to aid reading speed. Over time, this has led to the development of a wide variety of speed-reading approaches that may be accessed from books and DVDs, or require the individual to take part in a workshop or seminar.

Speed-reading techniques often encourage the reader to cover the material in stages. This includes a preview stage where the reader covers the material, briefly followed by the relevant speed-reading stage. This may be followed by a review stage, which allows the reader to look back and assess what has been covered. During the speed-reading stage, the reader may be encouraged to utilise a pointer or visual guide. This is assumed to help facilitate the pace of reading by encouraging faster visual sweeps from one side of the page to the other. It is also suggested that it helps improve reading speed by reducing the number of visual fixations and regressions. However, there is still some debate concerning the potential benefit of regressive eye movements during reading.

Factors which have been shown to influence the effectiveness of speed reading include the difficulty or complexity of the text, as well as the age of the reader. In terms of text difficulty, the evidence shows that, as text difficulty increases, speed and comprehension levels decrease. However, this has been shown to interact with the distinction between fiction and non-fiction. With regard to age, speed-reading training seems to elicit greater benefits for younger participants, which may indicate a need for greater levels of cognitive flexibility and has led to suggestions that speed reading be taught to young children in school.

Many claims have been made regarding the possibility that an individual can enhance his reading speed from 300 to over 1000 wpm. Unfortunately, many of these claims remain insensitive to the empirical research on speed reading. If reading is to be interpreted in the sense of comprehending most of what is read, then training to enhance reading speeds has only a modest effect. The findings show that training to speed read can help improve an individual's reading speed from 300 to approximately 600 wpm. However, claims that individuals are capable of learning to speed read at rates in excess of 1000 wpm are not supported. There is also some limited work showing that such training may have enduring benefits. Finally, the research suggests that a linear relationship exists between speed of reading and comprehension of the text covered, with comprehension deteriorating rapidly beyond rates of 600 wpm. Whether such a speed–comprehension trade-off is worthwhile remains for the reader to decide.

9 Biofeedback

There is no failure, only feedback.

(Robert Allen)

Physiological states influence physical and cognitive performance, yet many of the body's physiological processes are not under volitional control. Nevertheless, Peper and Schmid (1984) suggest that learning to control aspects of physiology is a necessary component of performing at peak levels. As it turns out, it is possible for an individual to learn how to monitor specific aspects of their own physiology in an explicit manner and, in so doing, possibly learn to alter them, which in turn may help them to enhance some aspect of performance. The technique used to aid such training is called *biofeedback*. Advocates of biofeedback training have suggested that it provides a method of helping people to achieve more confidence in their own behavioural ability, as well as helping to improve focus, reduce stress and enhance composure and power in sports (Costa *et al.* 1984; Croce 1986; Norris 1986).

Thus, the aim of this chapter is to explore biofeedback and examine whether it can be used to enhance human performance. The chapter begins by clarifying what biofeedback is, outlining some of the key processes involved, and notes some of its potential uses. It then focuses on some of the main physiological functions that can be altered during biofeedback training. Following this, the chapter explores the rationale for providing biofeedback to alter specific physiological functions. The chapter also explores some of the more prominent factors that may influence the effectiveness of biofeedback training. Evidence is then examined, which suggests that biofeedback can be used to enhance performance. The chapter ends by asking whether the effects of biofeedback are long lived.

Biofeedback

Biofeedback represents a way of providing an individual with explicit information concerning some aspect of her physiology, such as muscle tension, heart rate or respiration, in a format that is meaningful, rapid, precise and consistent (see Petruzzello *et al.* 1991; Zaichkowsky and Fuchs 1988). The basic premise in biofeedback training is that, if an individual is given information relating to one or more of these biological processes, then over time she may be able to learn to regulate them consciously. Some have suggested that biofeedback acts like a psychophysiological mirror, reflecting back to the individual information concerning their own physiology (Peper and Schmid 1984).

The ultimate goal of biofeedback is really one of self-regulation, where the individual is able to regulate consciously one or more of her own physiological processes without the need for instrumentation or feedback. The implication of this is that, by gaining such control, the individual may be able to enhance behaviours that rely upon such physiological processes. Such learnt control is assumed to help move the individual towards a more optimal level of functioning.

In terms of how biofeedback training is thought to work, Zaichkowsky and Fuchs (1988) suggest that it represents a circular process of recorded information being filtered and fed back to the individual (see Figure 9.1). The process contains three key elements. First, physiological information is recorded from sensors placed on various parts of the body. Second, this information is transduced, filtered, amplified and fed back to the individual in the form of an auditory and/or visual signal. Finally, by paying attention to the information fed back to her, the individual should be able to learn to

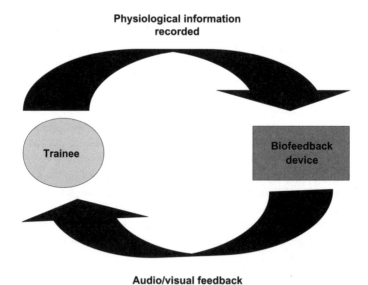

**Physiological information
recorded**

Trainee

**Biofeedback
device**

**Audio/visual feedback
information**

Figure 9.1 A schematic diagram showing the cyclical nature of a biofeedback training paradigm. A variety of physiological information can be recorded from the individual learner which may then be filtered, amplified and fed back to the individual in the form of audio and/or visual information.

alter the physiological activity that forms the basis of the signal. For example, an individual may be attempting to reduce muscular tension. This involves placing sensors on the target muscle region to record information relating to muscular activity, which is filtered, amplified and fed back to the individual in the form of a simple readout relating to the electrical activity measured. The individual then needs to note any changes in muscular tension and identify what cognitive/behavioural processes are influencing it. By becoming consciously aware of such changes in muscular tension, the individual should be able to reconstruct them by recreating the same cognitive/behavioural processes that led to the initial fluctuations.

However, biofeedback training is not complete when the individual has simply learnt to control the feedback from the device, but only when she is able to dispense with the instrument altogether and alter a chosen physiological process at will. The question then arises as to how the individual is able to do this. The answer must be that another type of information, other than the information fed back via the equipment, is available and utilised to help change the target physiological function. This other information may be the subjective experience associated with the feedback. For instance, when an individual receives explicit feedback concerning a specific physiological parameter, such as muscle tension, informing her that her muscular tension is decreasing, at the same time she experiences what it is like to relax the target muscle group. Such feelings are likely to include mental images, memories and thoughts (see Andreassi 2000). If these two processes constantly and consistently occur together, it should be possible for the individual to learn to correlate or associate the two. The assumption therefore is that learning to alter a physiological function via biofeedback requires the individual to learn, by trial and error, which thoughts and feelings are associated with changes in the target physiological processes. The usefulness of the biofeedback equipment is in its initial role in identifying the physiological correlates of particular thoughts and/or feelings.

According to Landers (1985), biofeedback can facilitate performance in three different ways. The first is arousal reduction, which is based on the notion that performance may be less effective when levels of arousal exceed a specific point. This is often referred to as the inverted-U model, first postulated by Yerkes and Dodson (1908), where low levels of arousal may lead to boredom and lack of interest and high levels result in anxious, risk-taking behaviour (see Figure 9.2). Thus, optimal performance may require a level that falls between the two extremes.

Secondly, biofeedback may enhance performance by helping an individual to optimise autonomic control of a particular physiological process. The aim here is that, via a process of learned self-regulation, the individual can become consciously aware of processes such as muscle tension in order to manipulate them to her best advantage. Finally, biofeedback may influence performance by helping to facilitate the rehabilitation of injured athletes.

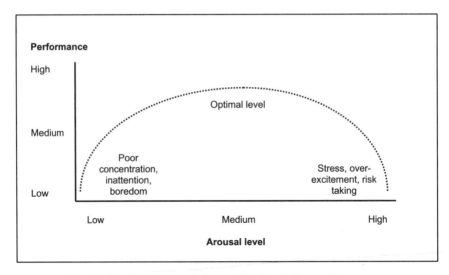

Figure 9.2 Level of performance as influenced by level of arousal.

Although biofeedback has been around for a while, with scientific interest blossoming in the 1960s, its increasing popularity and growth may be the result of a number of factors, including a widening potential for practical clinical applications (see Schwartz and Andrasik 2003). There have also been some dramatic technological developments, particularly with regard to computing speed and power, which have enabled an increasing range of physiological processes to be recorded and displayed in a variety of user-friendly formats. There is also the belief among certain sections of the biofeedback community that such a technique provides a mechanism for accessing higher states of consciousness, greater awareness and improved cognition (Parks 1997).

Physiological functions

There is evidence to suggest that it is possible to learn to modify a range of physiological processes using biofeedback, including muscular tension, heart rate and respiration, and electrodermal activity.

Muscle tension

When a muscle moves, either by contracting or relaxing, it produces a certain amount of electrical activity. This discovery has been attributed to Du Bois-Reymond who, in 1849, made the first recording of electrical activity resulting from muscle movement, termed *electromyography* or EMG (Caccioppo *et al.* 1990). He did this by placing a cloth on each forearm, which acted as a sensor and was connected to a galvanometer, and then immersed his arms into containers of a saline solution. Du Bois-Reymond found that, whenever he flexed the muscles of his hand, he noted a deflection on the galvanometer indicating a change in the level of electrical activity.

Over time, this technique has been developed and refined, leading to modern EMG recording devices which are able to provide a range of information concerning the electrical activity of the target muscle group. In general, this is found in the waveform of the EMG, the main aspects of which are its frequency and its amplitude. Frequency refers to the number of times a waveform oscillates in a second and is often measured in hertz (Hz) or cycles per second (CPS), whereas amplitude refers to half the distance between the high and low points of an oscillation (see Figure 9.3).

The characteristics of EMG recordings include a frequency range of 20–1000 Hz, with most of the EMG activity falling between 100 and 1000 Hz, with an amplitude of between 100 to 1000 μV (Robinson and Snyder-Mackler 1995).

There is a great deal of research that has focused on the EMG–force relationship, examining whether the EMG represents a clear indicator of muscular activity. There is some general agreement on the use of EMG as a measure of muscular activity, showing that increases in EMG amplitude occur in line with increased muscular effort (see Andreassi 2000). However, Lieber (2002) argues that EMG activity is not uniquely related to muscle force because movement can be influenced by muscular tension as well as velocity of movement. Thus, Lieber suggests that, whilst EMG can provide

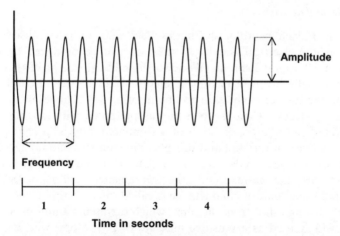

Figure 9.3 Showing the frequency and amplitude of a waveform. Frequency represents the number of times a waveform completes a full cycle in one second and can be measured in cycles per second (CPS) or hertz (Hz). In this instance the waveform completes three full cycles per second, making its frequency 3 CPS or 3 Hz. Amplitude represents the power of the waveform and is often measured in microvolts. Amplitude is measured as half the distance between the high and low points of the waveform.

information regarding muscle activation patterns, caution should be used when interpreting such information to denote a specific level of muscular force applied.

Heart rate and respiration

Heart rate (HR) and respiration represent two measures of cardio-respiratory phenomena that can also provide an individual with a measure of exertional intensity during exercise.

Changes in HR can affect oxygen consumption, with a decrease in HR producing a corresponding decrease in oxygen consumption, and vice versa. Researchers have shown that it is easier to increase HR than to decrease it and that such an increase may be associated with increased blood pressure, but a decrease in heart rate seems to have little or no effect on blood pressure (Stephens *et al.* 1975). Furthermore, Stephens *et al.* noted that individuals with high resting HR may be more able to alter their HR via biofeedback.

Respiration is the process of exchanging oxygen and carbon dioxide between the individual and her external environment. It is invariably measured in terms of the amount of oxygen consumed within a specific time period. Respiratory factors tend to parallel changes in heart rate during exercise, and it has been suggested that individuals may be able to modify their respiration more easily than they can their heart rate, making it a suitable candidate for biofeedback (see Caird *et al.* 1999).

Electrodermal activity

It was the French neurologist Charles Fere who, in 1888, observed that changes in the electrical activity of the skin can be produced by various physical and emotional stimuli (Woodworth and Schlosberg 1954). The procedure originally involved passing a small current between two electrodes placed on the surface of the skin and monitoring any changes in electrodermal activity (EDA) when the person was presented with various stimuli. It was found that the presentation of a stimulus produced a change in the electrical activity of the skin and this phenomenon was initially labelled the *psychogalvanic reflex* (PGR), which was later changed to the *galvanic skin response* (GSR) and, more recently, the *skin conductance response* (SCR).

The traditional unit of conductance is called the mho (ohm spelled backwards) to distinguish it from the ohm, which represents a unit of resistance. EDA is widely used as a sensitive measure of physiology, with changes in SCR occurring alongside variations in the level of arousal of the individual, such that an increase in arousal would lead to an increase in SCR (Dawson *et al.* 2000).

Rationale

A major rationale for using biofeedback to voluntarily control a particular aspect of physiology is when that specific physiological process is directly related to a distinct behaviour.

With regard to EMG biofeedback, it is assumed that enabling an individual to control the level of muscular tension will allow her to reduce any general bodily tension, or tension within a specific muscle group. This is thought to create greater economy of muscular energy, which in turn leads to enhanced performance. However, Druckman and Swets (1988) note that one of the problems traditionally associated with EMG biofeedback is that there is no clear understanding of what a desirable or optimal level of muscle tension should be, though some inroads are beginning to be made into this area, particularly in sports (see Clarys and Cabri 1993). Furthermore, many researchers use the frontalis muscle on the forehead as a general measure of overall muscular tension. This has been shown to be predominantly responsive to changes in head and neck muscle tension, but need not correlate with changes in muscular tension in other areas of the body (see, e.g., Zaichkowsky and Fuchs 1988).

With regard to HR biofeedback, the aim is to improve an individual's anaerobic threshold and thereby enhance her physical performance. For instance, when an individual exercises her muscles she can burn glucose in one of two ways: anaerobically (without oxygen) and aerobically (with oxygen). Depending upon the type of exercise and the effort required, the body can use different proportions of energy from both of these systems.

Hence the rationale for attempting to alter HR via biofeedback is two-fold. First, there is the notion that an ability to alter HR or respiration response consciously during physical exercise will enable the individual to reduce her HR and oxygen consumption while maintaining a stable exercise level (Perski *et al.* 1985). In addition, it has been suggested that, by learning how to control HR and/or respiration level, it may be possible to reduce levels of stress and that this will also help enhance performance (Fredrikson and Engel 1985).

EDA biofeedback is based on the rationale that an increase in autonomic arousal is generally associated with an increase in skin conductivity. Biofeedback training to lower autonomic arousal may therefore result in a reduction in level of stress and anxiety, leading to an increase in feelings of well-being and enhanced performance. For example, there has been some interesting research showing an inverted-U relationship between athletic performance and GSR levels (Landers 1985). Landers found that target shooters reported greater levels of accuracy when their GSR was between 15 and 30 per cent above resting levels, yet lower levels of accuracy when their GSR was either less than 15 per cent or greater than 30 per cent of that seen at rest. Such an association suggests an optimal level of arousal for performance and EDA biofeedback represents a useful tool that could be used to help individuals identify and recreate such levels.

Factors influencing biofeedback training

It would be useful to know what, if any, factors may influence the effectiveness of biofeedback training. Whilst research focusing directly on such issues is limited, it is possible to obtain some insights from previous studies. These include the duration of biofeedback training, the modality of the feedback and the intensity of the task.

Duration of training

Given that attempted control of a particular physiological process is not something normally undertaken, it would seem obvious that a certain amount of time may be needed for the individual to learn how to gain conscious control of a specific physiological function. This is an important point because, given the initial reliance that such training makes upon the biofeedback equipment, and due to the nature of the equipment, this may mean that any attempt to alter physiology will initially be restricted to a laboratory. Thus, the sooner an individual is able to learn how to change her physiology at will, without the need for a device providing explicit information, the more flexible and efficient such training may become.

Surprisingly, there is no clear guidance regarding the number of training sessions, nor the length of each training session, needed to show evidence of 'learning' in terms of a change in physiology. Nevertheless, an examination of the literature provides some insight regarding the number of sessions required to obtain changes in physiology. For instance, changes in muscle tension resulting from EMG biofeedback have been reported following five 30-minute sessions over five consecutive days (Sabourin and Rioux 1979). A similar pattern has been reported for attempts to attenuate heart rate, with changes emerging after five ten-minute trials (Caird *et al.* 1999) and five 45-minute sessions of exercise (Perski and Engel 1980); whilst attempts to alter GSR have been shown to produce successful results following eight 20-minute training sessions (Hashimoto *et al.* 1987). Such findings are consistent with the idea that changes in physiology resulting from biofeedback training are unlikely to be produced instantly but may require a number of sessions to elicit an effect.

Modality of feedback

James (1987) reported on the effects of comparing visual EMG biofeedback with auditory EMG biofeedback on voluntary contraction of a muscle in the right hand. While he found that both types of feedback led to similar improvements in isometric strength of the targeted muscle, he also found that those receiving the visual feedback were quicker to show this increase than those listening to the audio feedback. Of course, this is one study and, as such, caution is needed to not over-interpret the data; nevertheless, it does suggest that, while both modalities may produce an effect, visual feedback may be capable of eliciting such effects in less time.

Task intensity

The ability of the individual to alter a particular physiological function may be influenced by the demands of the task. For instance, it may be more difficult and take longer for an individual to learn to alter an aspect of physiology when exercising at high intensity levels than at lower levels. There is some support for this in the literature, with Moses *et al.* (1986) showing that participants' ability to control their HR deteriorated as demands of the exercise increased (see Figure 9.4)

Furthermore, Goldstein *et al.* (1977) reported that participants were able to reduce their heart rate when walking on a treadmill at a rate of 2.5 mph at an incline of only 6 per cent. Yet Caird *et al.* (1999) found that HR biofeedback produced no differences when participants were required to run on a treadmill at 70 per cent peak velocity for ten minutes. Such findings are consistent with the idea that increasing the intensity of the task may reduce the impact of biofeedback training.

Of course, it is also possible that biofeedback training may be influenced by aspects not mentioned here, including the specific physiological parameter that is altered as well as the motivation level of the individual. Nevertheless, such points serve to highlight the need for more stringent research to examine the various parameters of biofeedback methodology to ascertain what factors influence such training and in doing so identify an optimal training paradigm.

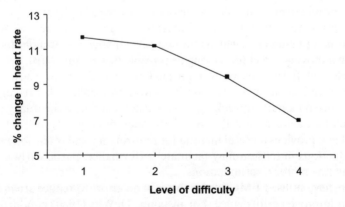

Figure 9.4 Percentage change in heart rate across increasing levels of muscular concentration from low (1) to high (4).

(Adapted from Moses *et al.* 1986)

Enhancing performance

Biofeedback may be used to improve performance through muscular retraining, optimising arousal levels and/or self-regulation of autonomic functioning. The most common physiological processes focused on are EMG, HR and EDA, each of which will be examined in turn.

EMG

EMG feedback is the most widely researched modality of biofeedback and some encouraging results have emerged, with researchers showing that EMG biofeedback can enhance performance on memory tasks (Sabourin and Rioux 1979), improve fine motor performance (French 1980; Sabourin and Rioux 1979), reduce stress (DeWitt 1980) and enhance muscular strength (Croce 1986). However, others have failed to elicit any positive results when examining the effects of EMG biofeedback on muscular flexibility (Cummings *et al.* 1984; Wilson and Bird 1981), the fine motor skills of musicians (Morasky *et al.* 1983), participants' motor response speed (Schultz *et al.* 1987) and shooting performance for basketball players (Kavussanu *et al.* 1998).

Sabourin and Rioux (1979) proposed that an individual's cognitive and motor performance was directly related to her level of muscular tension and that reducing this would lead to enhanced levels of performance. Such a hypothesis led them to examine the effects of EMG biofeedback on the performance of a variety of cognitive and motor skills of two groups, one undergoing biofeedback training and the other acting as controls. They found that both groups exhibited a small improvement in memory performance across the trials, but those receiving the biofeedback training exhibited significantly greater overall levels of recall (see Figure 9.5).

In addition, the biofeedback group also showed faster response times when completing an attentional task that involved pressing a key as quickly as possible in response to a target tone (see Figure 9.6A) and were more accurate during the rotary pursuit task, which required participants to keep a photoelectric wand on a moving target for as long as possible (see Figure 9.6B).

French (1980) later partially replicated these findings by showing that training to reduce muscular tension via EMG biofeedback led to improved performance on a pursuit tracking task, which is similar to the rotary pursuit task used by Sabourin and Rioux (1979). Such findings suggest that EMG biofeedback provides a useful method for reducing muscular tension and that such reductions in tension may facilitate performance, particularly on tasks requiring fine motor discriminations.

Others have utilised EMG biofeedback in an effort to reduce stress and in doing so improve performance. For instance, DeWitt (1980) conducted two studies aimed at helping a group of athletes reduce their levels of competitive stress using EMG biofeedback. The first study involved training a group of

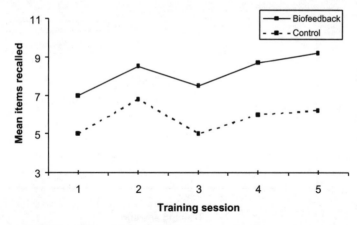

Figure 9.5 Mean number of items recalled across the five testing sessions for the biofeedback and control groups.

(Adapted from Sabourin and Rioux 1977)

six football players to reduce levels of muscular tension in the frontalis, masseter or trapezius muscle groups alongside training in visual imagery. Following the training, he found that four of the six participants showed a reduction in EMG levels and improved game performance. In the second study, DeWitt (ibid.) recruited a group of university basketball players and randomly allocated them to either a treatment group or a control group. Those in the treatment group received EMG biofeedback along with HR biofeedback and were also trained in visual imagery and cognitive strategies. DeWitt found that those in the treatment group were able to reduce both their EMG and HR levels, and were also rated by team managers as exhibiting superior performance compared to those in the control group.

The above studies have produced encouraging results but also display some worrying methodological problems that give cause for concern. For example, Sabourin and Rioux (1979) fail to explain which muscle group was the target for the biofeedback training. In addition, they make no comment on any possible changes in EMG as a function of the biofeedback training, nor why reducing EMG levels would be expected to influence cognitive processing. The results from DeWitt's (1980) studies are also intriguing. However, caution is needed when interpreting the data because, like many of the studies within the field of biofeedback, there are a number of methodological problems. In DeWitt's (1980) first study, treatment type was confounded by combining EMG biofeedback with visual imagery. In addition, there was no control group, making it impossible to isolate the effects of biofeedback training. Although the second study did contain a non-feedback control group, the treatment type was again confounded by combining EMG and HR biofeedback with visual imagery and cognitive strategies. Thus, although

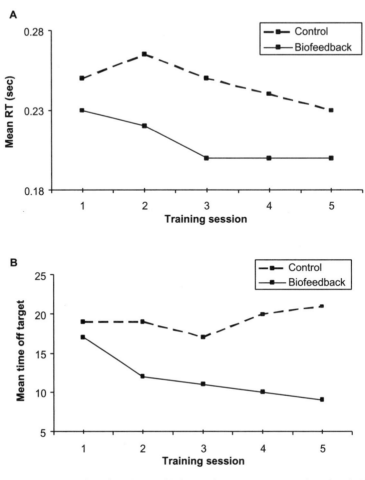

Figure 9.6 Mean reaction time (seconds) for performance on attentional task (A) and
mean time spent off target during pursuit rotor task (B) for biofeedback
and control groups across the five testing sessions.

(Adapted from Sabourin and Rioux 1977)

interesting, it is difficult to attribute the improvements seen in performance to
biofeedback alone.

A more rigorous approach was adopted by Croce (1986), who examined
the effect of EMG biofeedback on muscular strength. According to Croce,
improved muscular performance can occur as a result of changes within the
muscle tissue brought about by physical exercise, or by the development of
neuromuscular patterns that enable muscle groups to work together more
effectively. These ideas led him to propose that EMG biofeedback represents
a potentially useful method for aiding the development of beneficial neuromuscular patterns, by providing explicit information to the athlete concerning

specific muscular activity or joint position. Such information should enable the individual to direct the execution of a particular motor behaviour with a greater level of precision.

Croce (ibid.) tested this idea by examining the effects of EMG biofeedback on possible strength gains of the quadriceps muscle group. To do this, he recruited a number of college students studying physical education and allocated them to one of three groups. The first received EMG biofeedback, the second were given sham ultrasound treatment to control for possible differences incurred as a result of participating in a study, and the final group acted as non-feedback controls. The EMG biofeedback training provided information on the electrical activity and muscle tension levels of the quadriceps muscle group and was performed three times a week for a period of five weeks. Following the five-week period, all three groups exhibited some increase in strength of the quadriceps muscles, but those receiving the biofeedback showed significantly greater gains in terms of muscle strength as measured by peak torque levels (see Figure 9.7A) and higher levels of muscular EMG (see Figure 9.7B).

Thus, muscular strength exhibits greater increases when the training regime is augmented with biofeedback. Such findings led Croce (1986) to conclude that EMG biofeedback can aid in the control of muscle movement by monitoring and feeding back information on the level of activity of a particular muscle group, which in turn facilitates muscle development to produce significant gains.

While the above results, in particular the efforts of Croce (1986), highlight the possibility that EMG biofeedback can enhance muscular performance, not all attempts have met with such success. For instance, Schultz *et al.* (1987) questioned the notion that EMG biofeedback can reduce muscular tension and improve speed of response times. This is because, when they investigated the effects of EMG biofeedback on response times of a group who were given feedback on signals from their triceps compared to a non-biofeedback group, they found no difference in speed of response times between the two groups.

Others have found that, while EMG biofeedback training may result in lowered levels of EMG activity, this does not always translate into enhanced performance for a fine motor skill. For example, Morasky *et al.* (1983) assessed the effects of EMG biofeedback on the trill and scale speed scores of a group of clarinet players. Whilst they found that such training was associated with a reduction in EMG levels, they also found that it had no effect on musical performance. This would suggest that EMG biofeedback has little or no benefit for tasks involving the use of fine motor skills.

Similarly, reports on the effectiveness of EMG biofeedback to improve muscular flexibility have failed to exhibit any positive effects (Cummings *et al.* 1984; Wilson and Bird 1981). Cummings *et al.* (1984) considered the possibility that EMG biofeedback, along with progressive muscle relaxation, would help improve hip joint flexibility for a group of sprinters. However, following the training they found that EMG biofeedback and relaxation were

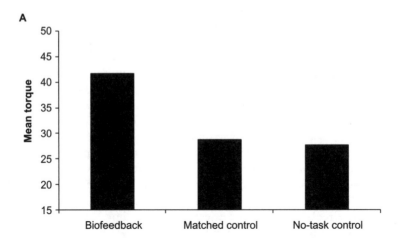

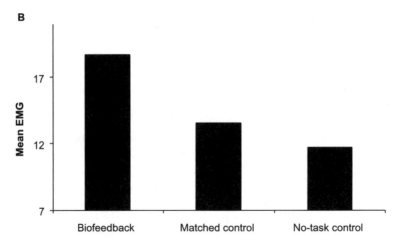

Figure 9.7 Percentage gains in muscular strength, as measured by peak torque
(A) and average changes in muscle tension, as measured by EMG levels
(B) for those receiving biofeedback, a matched contact control group and a
non-contingent control group.

(Adapted from Croce 1986)

no more effective at improving hip flexibility than completing a range of
simple stretching exercises used by a non-contingent control group. Furthermore, both groups showed similar improvements in sprinting performance.
Thus, it would seem that EMG biofeedback, when used alongside progressive
muscle relaxation techniques, has little effect on improving muscle flexibility
and sprinting speed.

More recently, a study was conducted to compare the effectiveness of EMG
biofeedback on basketball free-throw shooting performance (Kavussanu *et al.*

1998). All groups initially completed 60 free throws at a basketball target and then underwent the relevant training. For those assigned to the biofeedback group, this involved completing six 30-minute sessions of EMG biofeedback, with recordings taken from the frontalis muscle. Those assigned to the control group did not complete any training but spent an equal amount of time in the lab to control for participant–experimenter interactions. Following the training, both groups again completed 60 free throws. Kavussanu *et al.* (ibid.) found that those given EMG biofeedback were able to alter their EMG levels according to the training instructions, showing evidence of learning. However, both the EMG biofeedback group and the control group showed similar improvements in basketball shooting performance (see Figure 9.8).

Overall, the results from studies focusing on the effects of EMG bio-feedback to enhance performance seem unclear and inconsistent. On the one hand, some have shown that EMG biofeedback can help to enhance fine motor skills (French 1980; Sabourin and Rioux 1977), whilst others have failed to support such findings (Morasky *et al.* 1983). Such differences may arise because of the different methodologies adopted by the researchers, including training different muscle groups, as well as the nature of the tasks used to assess performance. For example, some lacked control groups (DeWitt 1980) and some included measures of physiological change as an index of learning (Croce 1986; Kavussanu *et al.* 1998), whilst others did not (Sabourin and Rioux 1979). Furthermore, the measures used to assess performance may be crude. For example, Kavussanu *et al.* (1998) assessed performance in terms of scoring a goal when shooting basketball hoops. Such a measure of performance, classified as either a goal or a miss, may lack sufficient sensitivity to discern the possible subtle effects of biofeedback training. Given such distinct methodologies and different outcomes, it should

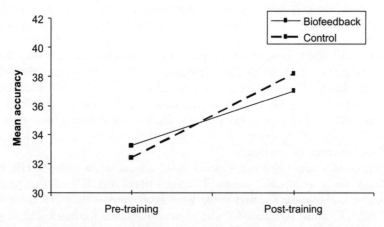

Figure 9.8 Mean accuracy of basketball shooting performance for EMG biofeedback group and control group pre and post intervention.

(Adapted from Kavussanu *et al.* 1998)

come as no surprise that the conclusions people reach concerning the effectiveness of EMG biofeedback are just as varied. While some have suggested that EMG biofeedback can result in improved performance (Zaichkowsky and Fuchs 1988), others conclude that such a technique holds little promise for enhancing performance (Petruzzello *et al.* 1991).

HR

The aim of HR biofeedback training is to increase the cardiovascular efficiency of the individual. Given such information, individuals have shown some success in altering HR, either by increasing it or slowing the rate down (Caird *et al.* 1999; Goldstein *et al.* 1977; Perski and Engel 1980; Perski *et al.* 1985). However, HR biofeedback does not always produce the desired changes in either cardiovascular activity or respiration (Moses *et al.* 1986).

One of the earliest studies to examine HR biofeedback was carried out by Goldstein *et al.* (1977) using healthy individuals walking on a treadmill. They examined whether providing the walkers with feedback on their HR would enable them to decrease it during exercise. They compared the HR of the biofeedback group to that of a control group instructed to try to lower their heart rate without receiving any feedback and found that those receiving biofeedback showed a significant reduction in HR over time (see Figure 9.9A), as well as lower HR during exercise (see Figure 9.9B).

In addition, they found that those initially trained to lower their HR using biofeedback continued to exhibit lower HR levels when asked to control it without the use of biofeedback. Such a pattern indicates that the participants had gained some voluntary control over HR levels and were able to manipulate them by conscious will alone. However, Goldstein *et al.* (1977) point out that the continued low levels of HR activity may have been related to what they called 'the criterion learning features of the study' (p. 121). That is, during the biofeedback training a criterion light would come on to signal attainment of the desired level of HR activity and, once it was attained, no further effort was necessary on the part of the participant and it may therefore have served as a factor that limited their effort. However, when they exercised without biofeedback and attempted to control their HR voluntarily there was no limiting factor and they may have made more effort. Nevertheless, the data would suggest that, once the feedback and instructions result in learned changes in physiology, such changes may be maintained without the need for feedback to continue.

Perski and Engel (1980) reported similar results when utilising HR biofeedback for a group of cyclists. They compared the HR of two groups exercising on bicycles. The first group were asked to slow their HR using HR biofeedback, whilst the second group exercised without feedback. Perski and Engel found that, whilst both groups showed an increase in HR, it was significantly smaller for those receiving the feedback than for controls (see Figure 9.10). Consistent with the findings from Goldstein *et al.* (1977),

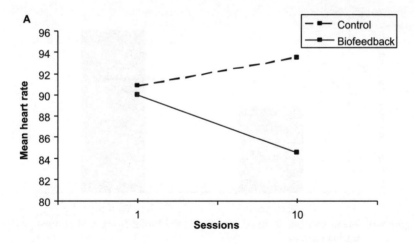

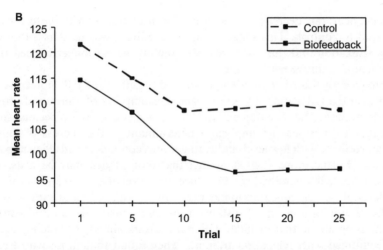

Figure 9.9 Mean heart rate at the first and tenth training session (9.9A) and mean
heart rate during exercise for the biofeedback and control groups (9.9B).

(Adapted from Goldstein *et al.* 1977)

they also found that, once the participants had learnt to modulate their heart
rate, they could maintain this skill without the need for explicit biofeedback.

In a follow-up study, Perski and colleagues were able to replicate their
earlier findings at a more demanding exercise intensity level (Perski *et al.*
1985). Here, they found that participants exercising at 65 per cent of their HR
maximum were able to use biofeedback to help them lower their HR by over
20 per cent compared to a non-feedback control group. In addition, they
found that those receiving feedback showed reduced ventilation and used less
oxygen. Perski *et al.* (ibid.) also found that, even when exercising without

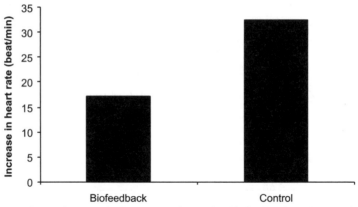

Figure 9.10 Mean increase in heart rate (bpm) for biofeedback and control groups during exercise.

(Adapted from Perski and Engel 1980)

feedback, heart rate decreases were greater for those trained with biofeedback compared to controls. This suggests that biofeedback was used as a tool to enable relaxation and that, once learned, the athlete no longer needed the equipment to improve performance.

More recently, Caird *et al.* (1999) examined the effects of HR biofeedback training on the HR variability and oxygen consumption of a group of long-distance runners. They focused on levels of oxygen consumption because this is thought to represent an important determinant in the success of long-distance runners, with low levels indicating more economical and efficient performance. Furthermore, they suggested that biofeedback may be a useful technique for helping individuals to reduce their level of arousal and optimise their level of oxygen consumption as they run. Caird *et al.* (ibid.) tested this idea by recruiting a group of distance runners to participate in a six-week training programme that included HR biofeedback aimed at reducing heart rate, combined with relaxation training. They found that those who took part in the training exhibited lower levels of oxygen consumption, which led them to conclude that the 'use of a combined biofeedback and relaxation intervention improved running' (p. 721).

The findings from the above-mentioned studies would indicate that, if an individual is healthy, she should be able to learn to use biofeedback to alter HR levels during exercise. Thus, HR can be brought under volitional control through use of an appropriate technique. However, none of the studies report any changes in the physical behaviour of the participants. That is, while there are reported changes in HR levels, there is no reported change in physical performance. A central assumption of HR biofeedback is that, if an individual can manage to learn to reduce her HR, she will perform more efficiently. This is based on the notion that an individual should, in such circumstances, be able to accomplish the same amount or duration of physical exercise but with less effort. This is consistent with the suggestion by Perski and Engel (1980), that biofeedback training improves the efficiency of a physical training pro-gramme because the changes in HR obtained via such training are 'compar-able to the changes obtained during 2 or 3 months of training of physical conditioning' (p. 103). However, it remains to be seen whether such changes in performance consistently accompany the changes occurring in physiology. Furthermore, Caird *et al.* (1999) confound their findings by including HR biofeedback as part of a larger, more comprehensive training package. Thus, caution is needed when interpreting such results.

Although the above studies exhibit some methodological pitfalls, it is important to note that they were successful in showing that modulation of HR is possible with biofeedback. However, not all researchers have been so successful. For instance, Moses *et al.* (1986) recruited two groups of students, both of which were told to try to control their HR at rest, during a static isometric muscular exercise, and when recovering from physical exertion, though only one of the groups was given biofeedback relating to their HR. Moses *et al.* found that both groups showed an increase in HR (see Figure 9.11A) and a decrease in HR when instructed to do so (see Figure 9.11B), but there was no difference between the two groups.

The fact that both groups showed similar patterns in HR suggests that such changes are more likely to be the result of an instructional effect than relying on information fed back to individuals. Because HR biofeedback failed to produce any changes in HR levels, either during rest or during exercise, Moses *et al.* (ibid.) concluded that providing feedback on HR did not influence a participant's ability to alter their HR levels.

Overall, the data from HR biofeedback studies fail to provide a clear and coherent message. It would seem that a number of issues relating to the use of HR biofeedback have yet to be resolved. These include establishing whether attenuating HR during exercise will enable those involved to exercise for longer periods of time, as well as clarifying whether the exercise intensity level interacts with the individual's ability to alter her heart rate. The effectiveness of HR biofeedback also highlights a distinction between dynamic and static exercise regimes. For instance, HR biofeedback seems to be more effective at helping the individual alter HR levels during dynamic exercises, such as walk-ing (Goldstein *et al.* 1977), cycling (Perski and Engel 1980) and running (Caird *et al.* 1999) than during a static regime of isometric arm exercises (Moses *et al.* 1986). It is likely that dynamic and static exercise regimes both influence, and are influenced by, HR in different ways, making HR biofeedback training more suitable for certain types of exercise regime.

EDA

In trying to assess the possible benefits of EDA biofeedback, one is hampered by a noticeable lack of empirical research. While some have suggested that EDA biofeedback may be a powerful tool that can help athletes to enhance

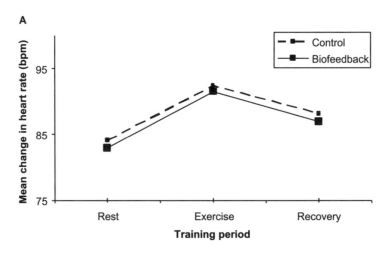

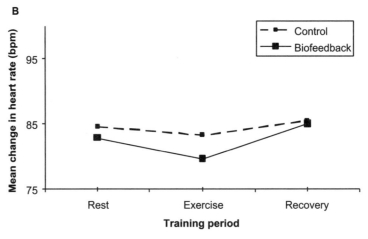

Figure 9.11 Mean change in heart rate (beat/min) for biofeedback and control groups when instructed to increase (9.11A) and decrease (9.11B) their heart rate.

(Adapted from Moses *et al.* 1986)

their performance (Peper and Schmid 1984), there is little or no evidence supporting such claims.

What limited research there is has focused on using EDA biofeedback to reduce the anxiety experienced by athletes, particularly during the pre-competition stage (Costa *et al.* 1984). Focusing on anxiety in sports may be a productive area because high levels of pre-competition anxiety have been suggested to directly influence the level of athletic performance. For example, increases in anxiety may reduce the focus of the individual, which in turn could have a detrimental effect on concentration and performance. This is consistent with the view reported by athletes that their pre-competition mental attitude accounts for 80 per cent of their success (Peper and Schmid 1984). Thus, learning how to modulate levels of arousal and anxiety could aid performance.

Peper and Schmid (1984) have suggested that athletes could use portable EDR biofeedback devices to help them maintain a relaxed state as they rehearse for their event. This may help to identify possible stress-evoking components or cues during their routine or event that lead to increased levels of anxiety and decreased performance. By monitoring their physiological state during rehearsal, athletes would be able to identify possible anxiety-provoking events and attempt to address them by perceiving themselves performing the task perfectly without any anxiety.

Costa *et al.* (1984) examined the performance-enhancing effects of EDA biofeedback by comparing the anxiety levels of athletes who received bio-feedback training with those that did not. They found that those undertaking EDA biofeedback training exhibited a 'decrease in anxiety level' (p. 104), whilst no such changes were found for those allocated to the control group. This led them to conclude that such training could help athletes reduce and control levels of pre-competition anxiety. However, this study was plagued by a number of methodological pitfalls making interpretation of the data difficult. To begin with, the changes found in anxiety levels were measured psychologically and not physiologically, as would be expected with such a study. Furthermore, no statistical analysis was conducted on the data and Costa *et al.* (ibid.) seem satisfied with merely reporting descriptive information. Moreover, there was no reported change in the behaviour of the athletes resulting from this intervention. In order to be considered an effective technique for enhancing performance, in this case by reducing pre-competition stress levels, the intervention needs to have a demonstrable effect on the behaviour of the athlete. Thus, more research is needed to ascertain whether EDA biofeedback is truly effective at enhancing performance.

Overall, there is only limited evidence to support the notion that bio-feedback can be used to enhance human performance. Landers (1988) has suggested that biofeedback as a mechanism to enhance performance has yet to be clearly demonstrated because its benefits are often compromised by combining it with other techniques and performance evaluations are often subjective. Nevertheless, researchers need to be careful not to throw the baby out with the bath water. As things stand, more research is needed in order to provide a clear answer to the question of whether biofeedback can enhance human performance.

Long-term effects

As with any training technique, it is important to know how long the effects resulting from such training will last and whether the individual can transfer the knowledge gained during the training to other episodes of behaviour. Surprisingly, no research has directly addressed this question within the field of biofeedback for optimal performance, as yet. Nevertheless, it is possible to obtain some insights by looking at the literature.

It may be the case that HR biofeedback produces longer-lasting effects than either EMG or EDA biofeedback. Such speculation is based on the limited data available showing that, of the different biofeedback protocols, only HR biofeedback produced effects that continued after the feedback had been removed (Goldstein *et al.* 1977; Peski and Engel 1980). Of particular interest is the finding from Goldstein *et al.* (1977) showing that such effects were maintained for a period of five weeks following the initial training. These findings led researchers to suggest tentatively that, once individuals have learnt to control a physiological function via biofeedback, it should be possible for them to maintain it without feedback for a number of weeks.

Once again, caution is needed to ensure that the limited data are not over-interpreted. In addition, it should be kept in mind that the studies of both Goldstein *et al.* (1977) and Perski and Engel (1980) were focusing on effects of biofeedback on a particular physiological process, not on the duration of such effects. Furthermore, simply because the long-term effects of EMG or EDA biofeedback have not been reported, this should not be taken to indicate that they do not exist. More research is needed to address this question directly by comparing the effects of biofeedback on both physiology and behaviour over clearly segmented periods of time.

Overview

Biofeedback refers to a technique that can be used to provide an individual with information about a variety of physiological processes, such as muscle tension, heart rate and skin conductance. The aim of providing an individual with such information is for them to learn to control the associated physiological function.

Although such training may be able to help an individual learn to control a wide range of physiological parameters, this chapter focused on the most common protocols, which included EMG, HR and EDA biofeedback. The general aim with EMG biofeedback is to reduce muscular tension, thereby allowing the individual to perform a task with greater economy of muscular energy. However, there is a lack of consensus regarding what constitutes a desirable or optimal level of muscular tension for any particular task. This problem is exacerbated by researchers failing to use a standardised approach when making comparisons between different research studies. Furthermore, it is not always made clear why researchers target a particular muscle group during feedback training. In contrast, HR biofeedback training is based on the as yet untested assumption that training to achieve a lower heart rate will ensure that the individual can exercise for a longer period of time and/or more effectively, and EDA biofeedback is based on the relationship between variations in arousal levels, changes in skin resistance and conductivity. Such a technique may be of particular use in helping reduce arousal levels of athletes prior to competing. However, there is a need for more research to establish clearly what represents an optimal level of physiological performance for all types of feedback.

A number of factors were examined which have either shown, or exhibit the potential to influence, the effectiveness of biofeedback training. These included the duration of the biofeedback training, the modality of the feedback and task intensity. For example, the duration of the biofeedback training needs to be sufficiently long to enable individuals to exhibit adequate changes in their physiology. In terms of feedback modality, even though the data are limited, there is some evidence to suggest that visual feedback may be more efficient than auditory feedback. For tasks of varying intensity a consensus is emerging which shows that, as the level of task intensity increases, the ability to alter physiology via biofeedback decreases. Biofeedback may represent an effective technique for gaining control over physiological processes as long as sufficient training time is provided and the level of task intensity is low.

The results showing that biofeedback can enhance human performance are, at best, equivocal. However, to a great extent this may be due to differences in methodology between the various studies. In particular, whilst the most researched, EMG biofeedback has produced the least consistent results. However, as mentioned above, it is important not to fall into the trap of thinking that such inconsistencies denote no real potential benefit. A more consistent and rigorous approach is needed to identify clearly the possible benefits of such training. For HR biofeedback, an emerging pattern suggests that it may be more effective for dynamic exercise than for static exercise. Evidence supporting the use of EDA biofeedback, meanwhile, is limited.

At present, there is also very little evidence providing information on the duration of effects resulting from biofeedback training. It seems that, despite the considerable technical advances that have taken place over the past few decades, the understanding and application of biofeedback programmes to enhance human performance remain quite limited. More specifically, the implication for its use within a variety of athletic skills remains largely unexplored. It falls to future researchers to address some of these shortcomings. In particular, if some of the methodological limitations can be adequately dealt with, the sports science fields may benefit a great deal from the applied use of biofeedback as part of their training.

10 Neurofeedback

> Whatever happens in the mind of man is represented in the actions and interactions of brain cells.
>
> (C. E. Boklage)

Given that biofeedback may help train muscular strength, wouldn't it be useful if such a technique could be used to train cognitive strength, or mental agility, based on brain activity? Whilst this may sound a little like science fiction, it is precisely what advocates of electroencephalographic (EEG) biofeedback, or neurofeedback, propose is possible. This chapter continues to explore the potential of biofeedback by extending the focus to include neurofeedback. The use of neurofeedback has risen dramatically in recent years, alongside claims that it can be used to enhance behaviour and/or cognition. Such training is thought to enable better mind management, facilitate enhanced self-awareness and improve mental performance, attention and memory, as well as enhance creative, athletic and academic performance (see Gruzelier *et al.* 2006; Vernon 2005, 2008; Vernon and Gruzelier 2008).

The chapter begins by explaining how information relating to the EEG is recorded and fed back to the individual during neurofeedback training (NFT). This is followed by a brief history of the development of neurofeedback and an examination of some of the specific parameters of NFT. The chapter then explores the rationale for using NFT to enhance performance in a variety of areas. This is followed by an examination of the evidence from the fields of sport, cognition and artistic performance to ascertain whether NFT to alter brain activity leads to improved performance. Finally, the chapter addresses the question of whether or not the effects of NFT are long lived.

Neurofeedback

Throughout the day the brain of an individual is constantly active, producing a range of electrical activity that can be measured using an electroencephalograph to identify the various frequency components (see Table 3.1). Such electrical signals are measured in terms of their frequency and amplitude (see Figure 9.3), and are thought to stem from the synchronised firing of many thousands of neurons in the cortex.

Once the EEG has been recorded and the different frequency components separated out, information relating to these components in terms of their frequency range and/or amplitude can be fed back to the individual using an online feedback loop, which is often referred to as NFT (see Figure 10.1).

Neurofeedback, also referred to as EEG biofeedback and, more recently, brain–computer interface training, represents a sophisticated form of bio-feedback based upon specific frequency components of the EEG. By making information recorded from the EEG available, the individual is encouraged to learn how to modify it in a particular way, which may include learning to alter the amplitude of a particular frequency wave, the speed at which it oscillates, or its consistency with brain waves emerging from different regions of the brain. The goal of NFT is to teach the individual what specific states of cortical arousal feel like and how to activate them so that, with sufficient training, he will be capable of inducing such changes voluntarily, without the need for either equipment or feedback.

For example, the goal of NFT may be to encourage the individual to increase the amplitude of his alpha brain wave activity. Such a process involves recording the individual's EEG, extracting the alpha frequency wave and feeding this back to the individual using an online feedback loop in the form of audio and/or visual information (see Figure 10.1). For instance, the alpha frequency component may be depicted on a computer by a coloured moving bar, with the height of the bar representing the amplitude of the frequency,

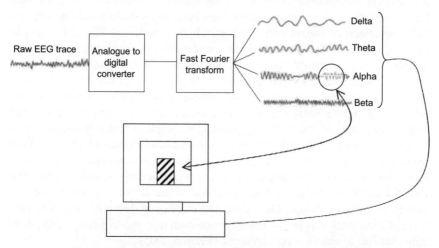

Figure 10.1 The neurofeedback loop. The raw EEG signal is recorded from the scalp, amplified and then separated into its distinct frequency components using a Fast Fourier transform. Information relating to a target wave-form, in this instance the amplitude of alpha activity, is then fed back to the individual in the form of a moving bar on a computer screen, with the height of the bar representing the amplitude of the target frequency.

such that the higher the bar, the greater the amplitude. The individual's task is then to increase the height of the bar and, in doing so, increase the amplitude of the alpha rhythm. Such training provides the individual with the opportunity to learn to alter a variety of brain wave activity, including amplitude, coherence and the peak frequency within a specified target range.

A brief history of neurofeedback

The development of neurofeedback owes a great deal to the work of Joe Kamiya and Barry Sterman. Kamiya's (1968) research focused on distinct states of consciousness and how they correlated with changes in the EEG. In particular, he was interested in the activity of alpha, as this was associated with a calm resting state. As part of his early research, he examined whether an individual could learn to influence this component of his EEG when information relating to it was fed back to him. Kamiya found that some people were not only able to identify when their brain was producing alpha, but were also able to increase the production of this activity. These results were the first to show that an individual could gain a degree of voluntary control over the production of his own brain activity.

Meanwhile, Sterman produced some serendipitous findings that proved to have important implications for patients suffering from epilepsy. While recording the EEG of cats, he found that they exhibited an increase in activity ranging from 12 to 16 Hz when reinforced to suppress motor activity. This 12–16 Hz activity was referred to as the sensorimotor rhythm (SMR), because it occurred predominantly over the sensorimotor cortex. The story may have ended there if Sterman hadn't then been requested to test the seizure-inducing effects of rocket fuel. He began by testing the ability of the fuel to induce a seizure in cats and found that, whilst most of them suffered a seizure, its onset was considerably later for a particular subset. Trying to understand why this might have occurred, he realised that the resilient cats were the ones involved in the previous EEG conditioning tests. This led him to surmise that enhancing the SMR rhythm produced an increased resilience to seizure onset. This idea spawned a study to examine whether training patients with epilepsy to enhance their SMR rhythm would have similar beneficial effects (Sterman and Friar 1972). Later, this approach was developed into a treatment for children with attention deficit hyperactivity disorder (ADHD; Lubar and Shouse 1976), and has since led to the use of neurofeedback in a variety of clinical settings. Over time, the increasing desire of people to perform at their peak has led to the incorporation and use of neurofeedback as a mechanism to enhance performance (Vernon 2005).

Parameters of NFT

There are a number of technical and logistical considerations that need to be taken into account when completing NFT. These include the precise recording montage used, the specific target frequency, the nature of the feedback and the duration of the training. Each of these factors is explored in turn.

Neurofeedback montage

The location of sensors placed on the scalp follows the 10–20 system (Jasper 1958). It is called this because sensors are placed at distances of either 10 or 20 per cent apart from one another. In addition, each site is identified by a letter, corresponding to the underlying cortical tissue, and another letter or number to denote the particular location. For example, the letters F, T, C, P and O are used to refer to the *Frontal, Temporal, Central, Parietal* and *Occipital* regions of the brain, with accompanying even numbers (2, 4, 6, 8) referring to the right hemisphere and odd numbers (1, 3, 5, 7) the left hemisphere, with the letter z denoting the midline. Thus, Cz refers to the central-midline region and C3 to the central-left position of the scalp (see Figure 10.2).

The precise number of sensors placed on the scalp during NFT is referred to as the *montage*. This may be referential (monopolar) or sequential (bipolar). A referential montage involves placing one active recording sensor on the scalp over an area of interest (e.g. Cz) and another reference sensor on an inactive area, such as the earlobe. This is thought to provide a measure of cortical activity at a particular location (e.g. Cz). The assumption is that learning to alter EEG activity using a referential montage can only be achieved by altering the relevant EEG frequency at or near the site of the

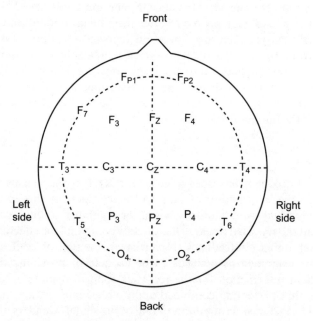

Figure 10.2 Common EEG sensor locations using the 10–20 system.

active sensor. However, this assumption is not well established and training using a referential montage has been shown to elicit changes in the EEG beyond the target frequency and across the scalp (see Egner *et al.* 2004). In contrast, a sequential montage involves placing two active recording sensors on the scalp to provide a picture of the relationship between the level of cortical activity across two different sites (e.g. Cz and Fz). Identifying which montage is the more effective depends to a great extent on what it is that the participant is training to do. If the aim is for the participant to identify and train a specific component of his EEG at a particular site, the referential montage may be best. However, if the aim is to focus on the level of synchrony between two distinct areas, a sequential montage may be more effective. Fehmi and Collura (2007) have suggested that, because the different types of montage can influence the information recorded and therefore the information fed back to the participant, the decision to use one montage over another can have serious implications in terms of neurofeedback training.

EEG frequency components

Over time, researchers have shown that NFT can be used to alter a wide range of components extracted from the raw EEG trace. For example, such training has been shown to alter theta (3–7 HZ) (Beatty *et al.* 1974), alpha (8–12 Hz) (Bauer 1976), the sensorimotor rhythm (12–15 Hz) (Vernon *et al.* 2003), beta (16–22 Hz) (Rasey *et al.* 1996) and gamma (40 Hz) (Bird *et al.* 1978). Neurofeedback can also be used to train one frequency in relation to another, often referred to as ratio training. For instance, Egner and Gruzelier (2003) have shown that it is possible for people to alter their theta-to-alpha ratios using neurofeedback. As yet there have been no reported attempts to use neurofeedback to train aspects of cortical coherence in a healthy population, although coherence training has produced some positive effects on the residual symptoms of patients with mild closed head injury (Walker *et al.* 2002). Such findings indicate that neurofeedback can be used to alter many, if not all, aspects of the human EEG.

Modality of feedback

Once a frequency component has been selected for NFT, it then needs to be decided whether the information relating to this component should be fed back to the individual using auditory, visual or combined audio-visual feedback. At present, no reported research has directly compared the effectiveness of these different modes of feedback. Nevertheless, the type of feedback provided should be examined as it needs to be capable of providing the trainee with sufficient information for the feedback loop to operate effectively. It is possible that presenting combined audio-visual information may be more effective. For instance, as attention to one of the signals wanders, the remaining signal may be capable of redirecting attention back to the task. To some extent this notion is supported by research showing that people respond more efficiently to a target presented in more than one modality than to a single modality alone (Giray and Ulrich 1993). Furthermore, using combined audio-visual biofeedback has proved to be more effective at lowering blood pressure than using audio feedback alone (Lal *et al.* 1998). Thus, providing both audio and visual feedback may be a more effective way of producing changes with neurofeedback.

Duration of training

Attempts to examine the beneficial effects of NFT have focused predominantly on outcome measures, with little thought given to either the duration or number of training sessions needed to elicit such effects. For instance, some have shown changes in the EEG resulting from neurofeedback sessions that last from 15 minutes (Vernon *et al.* 2003) up to one hour (Bauer 1976). Similar variation can be seen concerning the number of training sessions required to produce significant changes, with some showing limited changes in the EEG after a single session (Hanslmayr *et al.* 2005), whilst others have produced effects only after eight training sessions (Vernon *et al.* 2003). Of course, such variability may to some extent be the result of training to alter different frequency components of the EEG, differences in the duration of the individual sessions, the use of a referential as opposed to a sequential montage and the type of feedback given. However, Konareva (2005) has suggested that successful regulation of the EEG via neurofeedback may require a minimum of three to four sessions in order for the trainees to become accustomed to the equipment, setting and training regime.

Rationale for NFT

A number of reports have shown clear associations between specific frequency components of the EEG and particular physical and/or cognitive behaviours, which provides a route by which alteration of the relevant EEG component may result in changes in behaviour and thus provides a rationale for the use of neurofeedback training. Such associations have been found in sport and cognition, as well as in the arena of artistic performance.

Sport

The use of EEG measurements to gain some insight into the mental state of athletes prior to, during and after they complete a set task has grown over the years. Such research has reported a range of hemispheric asymmetries in the EEG of athletes prior to the execution of a skill. For instance, Hatfield *et al.* (1984) reported an increase in alpha activity in the left hemisphere during shot preparation for skilled marksmen, a pattern that has been replicated when skilled archers prepare to shoot and golfers get ready to putt (Landers *et al.* 1991). This increase in alpha has been suggested to represent a reduction in cortical activation of the left temporal region, decreasing the level of covert verbalisations of the left hemisphere, which in turn reduces potentially distracting cognitions and allows the visual-spatial processes of the right hemisphere to become more dominant (Salazar *et al.* 1990). If this is the case, then NFT to enhance alpha activity over the left hemisphere may benefit those participating in such sports.

Cognition

Probably more is known about the psychophysiological correlates of cognition than many other aspects of behaviour. For example, the alpha frequency range has been associated with a variety of cognitive processes, including memory performance (Klimesch *et al.* 1990), problem solving (Jausovec 1996), creativity (Fink *et al.* 2006) and intelligence (Doppelmayr *et al.* 2005). These studies have shown that those identified as more intelligent, or highly creative, tend to exhibit higher amplitude alpha than those classified with low intelligence. Given the consensus that alpha power is inversely related to cognitive effort, these differences have been interpreted as indicating that gifted, or high IQ, individuals exhibit more alpha because they activate fewer cortical areas when required to complete a task (Jausovec 1996). It may, then, be that intelligence is not represented so much by how hard the brain works, but by how efficiently it works, and efficiency in this instance refers to the level of cortical activity needed to complete a task successfully. Fewer, less relevant areas active may indicate a more efficient and task-focused use of available resources.

These findings represent only a small subset of the associations found between specific frequency components of the EEG and particular aspects of cognition and behaviour. Nevertheless, they offer a plausible rationale for using neurofeedback to enhance a particular aspect of cognition. For example, if high-amplitude alpha activity is associated with more effective memory performance, then using neurofeedback to enhance the amplitude of alpha may lead to improvements in memory performance.

Artistic performance

Research focusing on the modification of cortical activity related to music has invariably concentrated on changes in brain activity occurring as an individual is listening to, as opposed to playing, music. To some extent, this is no doubt influenced by the logistics of attempting to measure cortical activity, itself a sensitive process, whilst a musician physically plays an instrument. Nevertheless, researchers have shown that trained musicians exhibit a pattern of cortical activity when listening to music that is distinct from that seen in non-musicians. This includes increased levels of alpha activity (Wagner 1975), as well as enhanced levels of beta and gamma coherence

(Bhattacharya and Petsche 2001; Petsche *et al.* 1993). These differences in cortical activity between trained musicians and non-musicians may be a result of the training that musicians undergo. Wagner (1975) suggested that such differences could represent the musicians' ability to access and retrieve musical pattern information from memory. If so, NFT to enhance such frequency components, or levels of coherence, may aid musical perception and understanding.

Not a one-to-one relationship

It is important to note that, whilst the associations outlined above between spectral components of the EEG and specific behaviours have been found, this does not represent a one-to-one relationship. To some extent this may seem obvious given that the human EEG is traditionally subdivided into a range of five to eight distinct frequencies and people are capable of carrying out more than five to eight different types of behaviour. Hence such subdivisions represent an extremely crude measure of intellectual processing. No doubt, over time, as more research is conducted, the neural correlates of specific abilities will be isolated and identified, and further sub-divisions of the traditional EEG frequency ranges may occur. To some extent this has already begun to happen within the alpha frequency range, with researchers suggesting that the traditional alpha EEG frequency range of 8–12 Hz should be subdivided into low-alpha (7–9.5 Hz) and upper-alpha (9.5–12 Hz), with the low-alpha frequency range predominantly associated with attentional processing and the upper-alpha frequency range primarily associated with semantic memory processes (Klimesch 1999).

Enhancing performance

This section focuses on evidence from the areas of sport, cognition and artistic performance.

Sport

Data showing reduced levels of cortical activity in the left hemisphere of athletes prior to completion of a skill led Landers *et al.* (1991) to examine whether NFT to alter hemispheric activity would benefit target shooting for archers. They examined three groups of pre-elite archers, two of which received NFT to reduce the level of activity in either the left or right hemisphere by inducing a negative shift in electrocortical activity, whilst the third acted as non-feedback controls. Pre- and post-training, all groups were assessed by completing a total of 27 shots at a target positioned 45 metres distant, with the level of performance measured as the distance between the arrow and the centre of the target. Landers *et al.* (ibid.) found that those trained to reduce cortical activity in the left temporal region of their brain showed a significant improvement in performance, whilst those trained to reduce right cortical activity showed significantly poorer performance, and controls showed no significant change (see Figure 10.3).

However, examination of participants' EEGs from pre- to post-training failed to reveal any clear changes as a result of the neurofeedback training. For instance, all groups, including the non-feedback controls, showed an increase in power between 5 and 11 Hz and between 13 and 30 Hz in the left hemisphere, and between 5 and 11 Hz in the right hemisphere. Nevertheless, the group given right-temporal feedback did exhibit a greater increase in power in the 13–30 Hz range in the right hemisphere compared with both the left-temporal feedback group and the control group. These findings led Landers *et al.* (1991) to suggest that there was some support for the notion that NFT could help enhance the athletic performance of pre-elite archers.

These findings are encouraging, but are by no means conclusive, especially given the lack of any clear change in the EEG. The fact that previous research has shown significant increases in left-hemisphere alpha activity (8–12 Hz) during the shot preparation of skilled marksmen (Hatfield *et al.* 1984) suggests that a more effective NFT procedure may be one that focuses on enhancing the level of alpha activity within the left hemisphere, as opposed to inducing a negative shift. Furthermore, focusing on a specific frequency component may make it easier to identify possible changes in the EEG associated with such training.

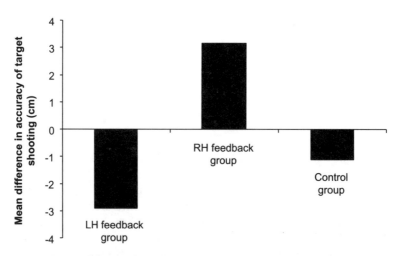

Figure 10.3 Mean difference in target shooting performance (pre–post) for left hemi-sphere trained group, right hemisphere group and control group. A lower score indicates a shot closer to the centre of the target and a higher score a shot further away from centre.

(Adapted from Landers *et al.* 1990)

Cognitive performance

Neurofeedback has been utilised to enhance a variety of cognitive processes, including attention, memory, creativity and imagery skills.

Attention

A number of researchers have suggested that NFT can benefit attentional performance (Beatty *et al.* 1974; Egner and Gruzelier 2001, 2004; Rasey *et al.* 1996). For instance, Beatty *et al.* (1974) noted that theta (3–7 Hz) activity was a reliable correlate of vigilant attention and, as such, NFT to alter theta levels may be expected to influence performance on a task requiring such sustained levels of attention. They tested this idea by having two groups of participants complete a radar monitoring task, which involved each person monitoring a screen for long periods of time and depressing a switch when a target was detected. Whilst completing the vigilance task, one group underwent NFT to suppress theta, whilst the remaining group trained to enhance theta.

Beatty *et al.* (ibid.) found that the neurofeedback produced changes in participants' EEG in line with the direction of the training. Those trained to enhance theta showed higher theta ratios and those trained to suppress theta exhibited lower theta levels compared to baseline measures (see Figure 10.4A). In addition, they found that the group trained to suppress theta activity performed significantly better at the radar detection task, identifying more targets than those trained to enhance their theta activity (see Figure 10.4B).

These findings show that it's possible for people to alter the level of their theta activity using neurofeedback and that training to suppress such levels can enhance attentional performance on a vigilance detection task. However, because the NFT and the monitoring task were carried out simultaneously, it would indicate that for such training to have an effect on performance the individual would need to complete both the NFT and the cognitive task simultaneously. If this is the case, it would severely limit the applicability of this training beyond the laboratory.

However, others have reported benefits for attentional processing on tasks that are completed after the NFT has finished (Egner and Gruzelier 2001, 2004; Rasey *et al.* 1996). Nevertheless, these studies are not without their limitations. For instance, the study conducted by Rasey *et al.* (1996) had a sample size of four participants, only two of whom showed any evidence of learning to alter their EEG via neurofeedback, with only very limited improvements in attention. Egner and Gruzelier (2001) reported that NFT to enhance low beta EEG frequency components led to some improvements in attention as measured by a continuous performance task. However, there were no reported changes in the participants' EEG levels, limiting the inference that NFT was responsible for any changes in attention, and they failed to include a control group, which means that any improvements in attention may be accounted for in terms of a practice effect.

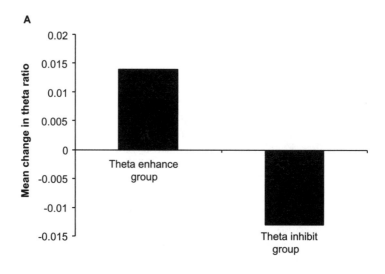

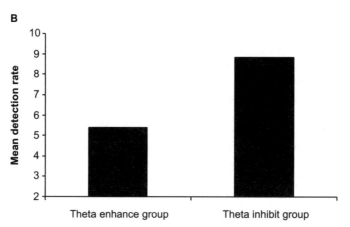

Figure 10.4 Mean change in theta ratio as a function of neurofeedback training
(10.4A) and mean detection rate during radar monitoring task (10.4B)
for both theta enhance and theta suppress group.

(Adapted from Beatty *et al.* 1974)

A more rigorous follow-up study conducted by Egner and Gruzelier (2004)
examined the differential effect of enhancing low beta (12–15 Hz) and beta1
(15–18 Hz) on attention. To do this they recruited three groups of participants and allocated each to a different training regime. The first group used
neurofeedback to enhance their low beta amplitude. The second group were
required to enhance their beta1 amplitude and the third group engaged in a
non-NFT regime utilising the Alexander technique. All groups completed a
range of attentional measures pre- and post-training. Following the training,
analysis of attentional performance revealed that the low beta group showed

a significant reduction in omission errors (see Figure 10.5). Omission errors reflect a failure by the participant to identify and respond to a target and are thought to represent a measure of attentional focus and distractibility. Furthermore, those trained to enhance beta1 activity exhibited an improvement in response times from pre- to post-training when completing a computerised attention task (see Figure 10.6).

These findings led Egner and Gruzelier to conclude that NFT to enhance the amplitude of low beta and beta1 EEG components leads to significant and specific effects on attention, with training to enhance low beta improving

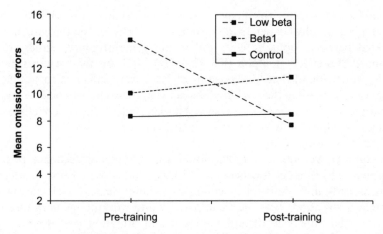

Figure 10.5 Mean omission error rate pre- and post-training for low beta neurofeedback group, beta 1 neurofeedback group and control group.

(Adapted from Egner and Gruzelier 2004)

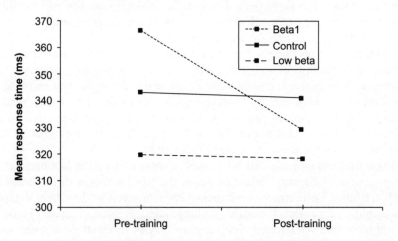

Figure 10.6 Mean response time (ms) pre- and post-training for beta1 neurofeedback group, control group and low-beta neurofeedback group.

(Adapted from Egner and Gruzelier 2004)

perceptual sensitivity and attentiveness and training to enhance beta1 leading to enhanced speed of response. However, Vernon (2005) noted that there were no reported changes in EEG levels for either neurofeedback group. This makes it difficult to clearly attribute the changes in behaviour to the neurofeedback training. Thus, while these findings are supportive of the performance-enhancing effects of neurofeedback, more needs to be done to determine the scope of such effects.

Memory

Researchers attempting to enhance memory performance via NFT have produced mixed results (Bauer 1976; Vernon *et al.* 2003). Given the associations reported between alpha activity and memory performance, Bauer (1976) examined the effect of alpha (8.5–12.5 Hz) NFT on two memory tasks. Whilst Bauer found that four sessions of NFT were sufficient to produce a 25 per cent increase in the level of alpha activity, these changes had no impact on participants' memory performance. This led Bauer (ibid.) to conclude that changes in alpha activity have no functional significance for short-term memory processing.

In contrast, Vernon *et al.* (2003) found that using neurofeedback to train participants to enhance low beta (12–15 Hz) brain activity led to significant improvements in a short-term semantic working memory task. Given the reported associations between theta activity and working memory (see von Stein and Sarnthein 2000) and low beta and attention (see Rossiter and LaVaque 1995), Vernon *et al.* (2003) were interested in comparing the differential effects of theta and low beta NFT on measures of memory and attention. To do this, they recruited three groups of participants, one trained to enhance theta activity, the second trained to enhance low beta and the third group acting as non-feedback controls. All three groups completed a number of pre- and post-measures of attention and memory.

Contrary to expectations, they found that those trained to enhance theta showed no clear shift in their EEG and no change in cognitive performance. However, those trained to enhance low beta showed a significant increase in the level of low beta activity from the beginning to the end of each neurofeedback session (see Figure 10.7). Moreover, only those who trained to enhance their low beta activity showed a significant improvement in the semantic working memory task (see Figure 10.8).

These findings indicate that NFT used to enhance levels of low beta activity is capable of eliciting clear changes in the EEG in line with the goals of such training. Furthermore, enhancing cortical levels of low beta activity significantly improved semantic working memory performance. Thus, it would seem that NFT to enhance memory may be more effective when such training focuses on the higher frequency range of 12–15 Hz rather than 8–12 Hz. However, it should be noted that a follow-up study attempting to delineate further the effects of low beta NFT on memory performance failed

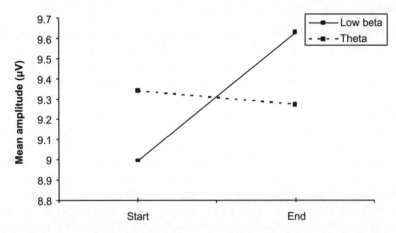

Figure 10.7 Mean amplitude (μV) of low beta and theta activity at the beginning and the end of the neurofeedback training sessions.

(Adapted from Vernon *et al.* 2003)

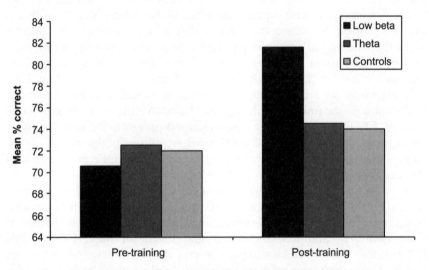

Figure 10.8 Mean percentage recall on semantic working memory task pre- and post-training for low beta neurofeedback group, theta neurofeedback group and control group.

(Adapted from Vernon *et al.* 2003)

to replicate these initial findings (Vernon *et al.* 2004). This may in part be due to differences in the precise methodology and neurofeedback protocols between the studies. Nevertheless, it remains unclear at present what the precise benefits on memory are following neurofeedback training.

Creativity

Martindale and Hines (1975) reported that highly creative individuals exhibit higher levels of alpha EEG activity than those classified as less creative. Others have also shown that training participants to use divergent thinking techniques, which aim to help the individual identify a range of possible solutions and are often linked to creativity, was associated with increased alpha power (Fink *et al.* 2006). Vernon and Gruzelier (2008) note that such findings have led to two strands of research regarding neurofeedback training: one to ascertain whether highly creative individuals are better able to regulate their EEG using neurofeedback, and the other which focuses on utilising neurofeedback to enhance creativity. For instance, Martindale and Armstrong (1974) reported that individuals classified as highly creative are able to learn to regulate their alpha activity using neurofeedback in less time than those identified as less creative. Such cortical flexibility may be what helps creative people shift their thinking strategies, facilitating the generation of novel ideas.

In contrast, Boynton (2001) suggested that the innovative ideas forming the basis of creativity may stem from an altered state of consciousness similar to the hypnogogic reverie experienced when falling asleep. She noted that it may be possible to induce this altered state of consciousness by utilising alpha/theta neurofeedback training. Alpha/theta NFT represents a modification of a traditional NFT paradigm, whereby the individual attempts to increase the level of theta activity over that of alpha. Boynton (ibid.) utilised this approach to see whether such training would enhance creativity. Unfortunately, she found that the training failed to elicit any change in participants' EEG activity and the small increases in creativity seen for those undergoing neurofeedback were mirrored by those in the non-feedback control group. This suggests that alpha/theta NFT has little or no effect on creative ability.

Boynton (2001) attempted to account for the failure to find an effect by suggesting that the lack of any clear changes in behaviour may have resulted from a confound in the training programme, which included several different components. In addition, she noted that length of the NFT schedule (20 minutes) and the small sample size may also have acted as mitigating factors. Given the known relationship between alpha activity and creativity, if such points were addressed and the NFT focused on enhancing only the alpha component of the EEG, it might prove to be more successful.

Mental rotation

Based on research showing a distinct relationship between EEG alpha activity and cognitive performance, Hanslmayr *et al.* (2005) were keen to distinguish whether such a relationship was correlational or causative in nature. To test this, they had a group of participants undergo a 20-minute session of

NFT to enhance alpha activity in the parietal regions of the brain. To assess any possible changes in cognition, all participants completed a mental rotation task before and after the neurofeedback training. This involved presenting two versions of a cube on screen and asking participants to identify whether they were the same, with one simply rotated, or whether they were different. Of the 18 participants who took part, only eight exhibited enhanced levels of alpha following neurofeedback training. They classified these as 'responders' and when they examined performance on the mental rotation task found that the responders showed a significant improvement in the accuracy of their performance compared to non-responders (see Figure 10.9).

The fact that only a subset of the participants showed any evidence of learning to regulate their EEG may be due in part to the short single session of neurofeedback training. Others have found effects following only multiple sessions of neurofeedback (e.g. Vernon *et al.* 2003). Nevertheless, the fact that those who did manage to increase their alpha activity also showed enhanced cognitive performance would imply that alpha may be more than a correlational factor.

Overall, the evidence suggesting that neurofeedback can be used to enhance cognition is encouraging but inconclusive. The strongest findings by far are those identifying neurofeedback as a potential mechanism for enhancing attention, either by suppressing theta or by enhancing low beta. The results of neurofeedback to enhance memory and mental rotation ability are also positive. Yet, in all cases, more work needs to be done to clearly delineate the effects such training can have on cognition.

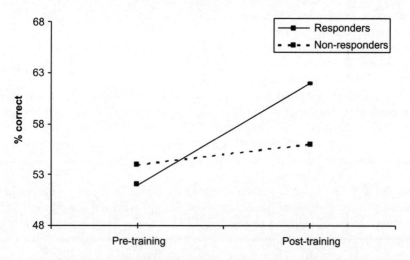

Figure 10.9 Mean percentage correct responses for mental rotation task, before and after neurofeedback training for responders and non-responders.

(Adapted from Hanslmayr *et al.* 2005)

Artistic performance

Recent years have seen an expansion of the use of NFT into the arena of performing arts. This has included music (Bazanova and Lubomir 2006; Egner and Gruzelier 2003), dance performance (Raymond *et al.* 2005) and singing (Leach *et al.* 2006).

Music

Egner and Gruzelier (2003) conducted a multi-EEG component NFT regime to see what effects such training would have on the musical performance of conservatoire music students. They recruited a group of music students and had them complete a schedule of ten NFT sessions that involved attempting to enhance low beta, followed by beta1 and then high theta-to-alpha ratios. A subset of this group also completed a regime of physical exercises and mental skills training, whilst a third group acted as no-training controls. Prior to and at the end of the interventions all participants were assessed on a piece of music of their choice, which was judged by experts from the Royal College of Music. Egner and Gruzelier (ibid.) found that only those completing the neurofeedback training, without the physical and mental skills training, showed improvements in their musical performance. A correlation conducted to examine which of the three NFT protocols was most efficacious revealed that success in learning to enhance theta-to-alpha ratios was associated with improved musical performance. This led to a second study, which randomly allocated a different set of music students to six distinct training groups. They included three different neurofeedback protocols (theta/alpha, low beta and beta1) and three other non-NFT techniques (aerobics, mental skills training, Alexander technique). Once again, Egner and Gruzelier (ibid.) found that only those completing the NFT to enhance theta-to-alpha ratios exhibited improved musical performance as rated by expert judges blind to the training conditions. They concluded that NFT to enhance theta over alpha can lead to improved musical performance for healthy participants.

These findings inspired Bazanova and Lubomir (2006) to try to enhance the musical performance of musicians by encouraging them to learn to regulate their individual alpha frequency (IAF). The use of IAF ranges stems from research showing that the peak alpha frequency can vary from person to person and may be influenced by a number of factors, including age and cognitive ability (Klimesch 1999). Bazanova and Lubomir (2006) suggested that NFT based upon a person's individual alpha frequency range rather than a pre-set traditional frequency range may provide a more efficient and effective means of learning to regulate EEG activity. They reported on two case studies of musicians, in both of which the musicians underwent NFT to enhance IAF activity. They found that such training led to significant increases in alpha activity and that this was associated with a decrease in levels of anxiety and enhanced musical performance as rated by expert judges.

These findings are certainly encouraging and would suggest that NFT may well be able to enhance musical performance. However, Vernon (2005) has noted some limitations concerning the study by Egner and Gruzelier (2003). For instance, in their first experiment they confounded the effects of NFT by having participants attempt to regulate three different components of their EEG. Furthermore, the correlation reported between changes in alpha/theta and improved musical performance is confounded by including those who also completed the physical exercise regime and mental skills training. The implication here is that, at best, any improvement in musical performance is the result of a combination of alpha/theta neurofeedback training, physical exercise and mental skills training. In their second experiment they also failed to report any changes to EEG activity following neurofeedback training, which limits the interpretation that such training influenced brain function and, as a consequence, enhanced behaviour. The findings from Bazanova and Lubomir (2006), whilst encouraging, also need to be treated with caution due to the fact that they are based on only two case studies. It would be interesting, and useful, to know whether such a training scheme utilising the IAF range can be replicated with larger groups.

Dance performance

Extending the work showing potential benefits for NFT on musical ability, Raymond *et al.* (2005) compared the effectiveness of alpha/theta NFT to that of heart rate variability (HRV) biofeedback as a mechanism to aid dance performance. It was thought that both approaches could reduce performance anxiety and, in addition, that NFT might also benefit artistry in performance, as reported by Egner and Gruzelier (2003). To test these ideas, three groups of male–female pairs of competitive ballroom dancers were recruited. The first group completed the neurofeedback training, the second underwent HRV biofeedback training and the third acted as non-contingent controls. Before and after the relevant training programme the dance performance of each pair was evaluated by experts. These ratings showed that the dance performance of both the neurofeedback and HRV biofeedback group improved beyond that of the control group (see Figure 10.10).

These findings led Raymond *et al.* (2005) to suggest that both alpha/theta training and HRV biofeedback training can improve dance performance. They also pointed out that the level of improvement elicited by the training was of professional significance. However, there were no reported changes in EEG for those completing NFT and no change in HRV for those completing the biofeedback training. Given this, the improved dance performance shown by both feedback groups may be nothing more than a confound of partici-pant–experimenter interaction. The failure to ensure that the control group maintained an equal level of experimenter contact gives rise to the possibility that both feedback interventions resulted in improved performance merely as

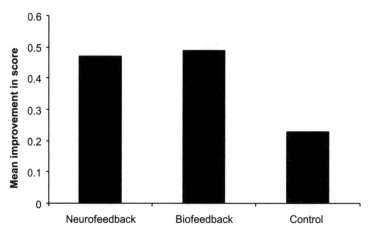

Figure 10.10 Mean improvement in dance scores for neurofeedback, biofeedback and control groups.

(Adapted from Raymond *et al.* 2005)

a function of taking part in a training scheme, irrespective of what that scheme provided.

Singing

As part of an ongoing study to extend the work carried out by Egner and Gruzelier (2003) on elite musicians, Leach *et al.* (2006) examined the effect of NFT on the performance of a group of novice singers. The singers were randomly allocated to either theta-to-alpha or low beta neurofeedback training. Leach *et al.* reported that only those singers training to enhance theta-to-alpha ratios showed a change in EEG levels in line with the training. Moreover, those completing such training were also rated as showing improved confidence and expressivity in their singing performance. Although such data represent the preliminary findings of a larger project, they are encouraging in that they suggest that singing performance can be improved with neurofeedback training.

In terms of neurofeedback benefiting artistic ability, there is some evidence to suggest that such training may enhance musical performance and singing, but very little evidence to suggest that such training can also improve dance performance.

Long-term benefits

NFT may require a large number of sessions in order to produce changes in behaviour, so an important issue is whether the effects produced are long lived or not. Unfortunately, none of the studies outlined above have conducted any long-term follow-up examinations of those undergoing such training. However, some insights into this issue can be obtained by looking at the use of NFT for clinical populations. For instance, Tansey and colleagues (Tansey 1993; Tansey and Bruner 1983) have shown that NFT to alleviate the clinical symptoms of hyperactivity can lead to long-term benefits. They reported on the case study of a ten-year-old boy who suffered from reading difficulties and hyperactivity. This individual underwent a series of NFT sessions to help normalise an irregular EEG profile and improve his learning. Following 20 sessions of neurofeedback, they found that the boy showed clear changes in his EEG and exhibited improved reading behaviour, which subsequently helped to boost his academic performance. An initial follow-up study conducted after a delay of two years showed that the boy maintained these improvements and an additional follow-up study conducted ten years after the termination of his treatment showed that he had maintained his academic and personal success, as well as a normalised EEG profile. Although based on a single case study, this would seem to suggest that the possible benefits resulting from NFT may be long lived.

However, not all clinical studies following up on the outcome of their patients have shown such long-lasting effects. For instance, Wadhwani *et al.* (1998) utilised NFT within a school setting and were able to show that the individual in question improved his academic performance. However, a follow-up examination one year later revealed that these initial gains were not maintained. Thus, evidence supporting the notion that neurofeedback can have long-term benefits, whilst primarily based on data from clinical studies, remains equivocal. Of course, it may be that NFT using healthy participants is capable of producing more consistent long-term effects – only time will tell.

Overview

Using modern equipment, it is now possible to record the electrical activity of the brain, amplify and filter this signal and identify the constituent frequency components. Information relating to one or more of these components, such as its amplitude, can then be fed back to the individual in the form of audio and/or visual information. This feedback loop represents a technique that is commonly referred to as neurofeedback training. The aim of such training is to enable the individual to identify on-line changes in his own brain activity associated with distinct patterns of thought, states of arousal or feelings. Once such a level of awareness has been achieved, the individual should then be capable of recreating these states of arousal, or thoughts, by learning to regulate their own EEG activity.

The development of neurofeedback as a plausible mechanism for altering brain function and thereby influencing behaviour stems from the early work of Kamiya and Sterman. These researchers were among the first to show that it was possible for an individual to learn to regulate his own brain activity and that such control could have a beneficial effect on the behaviour of clinical groups exhibiting abnormal EEG activity. The beneficial effects of such training, once noted by those outside the clinical domain, led to its use as a mechanism to enhance the performance of healthy individuals in a variety of settings.

Scrutiny of the NFT regime has revealed a number of factors that may influence its effectiveness. Whilst not comprehensive, this list includes the precise montage used during the training, the various frequency components of the EEG that are extracted and fed back to the individual, the modality of the feedback information and the duration and length of the training. In addition, the chapter outlined the rationale for NFT to enhance performance, showing that it's based upon associations between specific components of the EEG and particular aspects of cognition and/or behaviour. However, it was noted that current classification of the various EEG components may represent only a crude measure of the underlying neural processing. Furthermore, training to alter a single frequency component has been shown to produce changes in the EEG beyond that of the targeted frequency.

The evidence showing that NFT can enhance performance is suggestive, but inconclusive. To some extent, the ambiguity of these findings results from a combination of limited research and a problematic methodology shown by much of the research conducted to date. Nevertheless, some promising results have been reported, particularly with regard to improvements in attention and memory. However, it is unclear at present whether the potential benefits of such training are short lived or can be maintained for longer periods. Thus, whilst the findings suggesting that neurofeedback can be used to enhance performance are both intriguing and encouraging, more work needs to be done to fully explore the possibilities of such training and clearly identify what the potential benefits may be.

11 Mental imagery practice

> Mental life is indeed practical through and through.
> It begins in practice and it ends in practice.
>
> (Samuel Alexander)

A sportsperson may be encouraged to *see* herself scoring a vital match point, or *feel* herself lifting a heavy weight, while a musician may be told to *hear* herself perform Mozart's piano sonata in C major with perfection and ease. Such forms of encouragement are commonplace, with the individual in question being told to 'imagine' herself performing the task easily and accurately in order to enhance her actual performance. The idea that simply thinking about completing a task can help to enhance performance is well documented. According to Suinn (1997), the goal of such training is to enable the individual to achieve peak levels of performance by strengthening the correct physical and mental skills and providing the maximum opportunity to practise the performance. The potential benefits of such a technique may be large, given that it can be carried out virtually anywhere and needs little or no additional resources or equipment.

Hence, this chapter examines the technique of using mental imagery practice (MIP) to enhance performance. It begins by outlining what MIP is, what it involves and why it might be used. The chapter then provides a brief outline of the two main theories that have been put forward to explain how MIP influences behaviour. This is followed by an examination of a number of factors that have been shown to influence the effectiveness of MIP. The chapter then reviews evidence from the fields of sport, cognition and music which suggests that engaging in MIP can enhance performance. The possibility that such performance-enhancing effects are long lived is also explored. Finally, the chapter outlines two key methodological issues that have permeated the research on MIP: the use of adequate controls and identifying the processes involved in MIP.

Mental imagery practice

MIP signifies the introspective or covert rehearsal that takes place within the individual when she is attempting to learn a new skill or behaviour, or to practise a skill mentally without any overt physical movement taking place. However, there is no clear agreement on the processes involved and this has led to a variety of terms being used, including symbolic rehearsal, visualisation, imagery exercise, covert practice and introspective rehearsal, to name but a few (see, e.g., Driskell *et al.* 1994; Grouios 1992a; Suinn 1997). This lack of agreement has hindered interpretation of research, given that different researchers suggest that distinct processes are involved. Nevertheless, there is some general agreement that MIP involves perceptual and sensory experiences that are distinct from those experienced in day-dreaming, and that they occur in the absence of any external stimulus input (Murphy 1994; Richardson 1967a, 1967b). According to Murphy (1994), any experience that satisfies both conditions can be regarded as MIP. Thus, musicians rehearsing a piece of music in their mind or athletes thinking about competing are examples of MIP.

The specific nature of MIP may be visual, verbal, kinaesthetic, or a combination of these, with visual thought to be the most dominant form (Sackett 1935). Its use is widespread, particularly within sport. For instance, surveys of athletes found that between 85 and 99 per cent report using MIP as part of their training (Orlick and Partington 1988; Ungerleider and Golding 1991). Many coaches also use MIP to enhance performance and positively rate its effectiveness (Murphy 1994). Indeed, the use of MIP in sport has become so well accepted that it is regarded as a basic field of study within sport psychology.

Richardson (1967a) proposed three reasons for using MIP. First, it may be used to acquire new skills; second, it may help maintain these newly acquired skills; and, third, it can help to improve them. There are a number of possible reasons why MIP may be used instead of, or alongside, physical practice. It may be that there are few opportunities to practise physically or that physical practice is inconvenient, expensive, fatiguing or possibly injurious. According to Cohn (1990), MIP can provide two advantages. First, mental rehearsal can be used to help reinforce unconscious processes that are used to execute specific motor skills to enhance performance. This is because conscious control of quick and complicated movements may be too slow and could potentially disrupt performance. Second, optimal performance of a behaviour requires a specific level of arousal and attention for efficient execution. MIP allows for the mental rehearsal of such processes, which are thought to translate into the formulation of a specific goal-oriented response.

Theories of mental imagery practice

A number of theories have been put forward to account for the findings from MIP, including psycho-neuromotor theory, symbolic learning theory, attentional/arousal theory, motivational theory and bioinformational theory (see Grouios 1992a). However, it is beyond the scope of this chapter to review all these theories and it therefore focuses on the two most prominent accounts: psycho-neuromotor and symbolic learning theory.

Psycho-neuromotor theory

According to this theory, conducting MIP to influence a skill or behaviour can trigger identical motor actions for that skill and thus assist in its development. Two lines of research have been developed in order to test this idea. The first focuses on measuring muscular activity during MIP and the second focuses on brain activity.

As an individual imagines herself carrying out a specific behaviour, going through the sequence of actions one by one, she will be producing minute innervations of the relevant muscles. As the imagined performance improves, or becomes more accurate, the level of neuromuscular coordination should also be facilitated. Although no overt movement takes place, the effects of low-level innervation are presumed to transfer to physical action. For example, the innervation resulting from MIP may provide a degree of kinaesthetic feedback, allowing the learner to alter and strengthen specific motor patterns that, in turn, help to facilitate physical performance.

Support for this idea comes from researchers showing that imagined movement produces an increase in electrical potentials recorded in the muscle groups used to make that movement. For example, Harris and Robinson (1986) demonstrated that simply thinking about moving a muscle produced a muscular pattern of activity that mirrored the action of the movement. Furthermore, Bakker *et al.* (1986) reported greater levels of electrical activity resulting from muscle movement, or electromyography (EMG; see Chapter 9) in the muscles of one arm compared to another when participants imagined lifting a weight with that arm. These findings are consistent with the proposal that simply thinking about making a movement can produce low-level activity in the relevant muscle groups.

In a similar way, brain regions responsible for motor execution are also activated during MIP. Research has shown that the neural operations involved in executing a particular behaviour may also play a role in mentally rehearsing those actions. For instance, changes in regional cerebral blood flow (rCBF), which provides an index of cortical activity, have been reported in the supplementary motor area during MIP of muscle movement (Roland *et al.* 1981). Roland *et al.* compared the level of rCBF activity throughout the completion of a physical movement and during MIP of the same movement. They found rCBF activity in the same cortical region during the imagery training as during the physical movement, despite no overt movement taking place. Furthermore, the level of rCBF during MIP was as high as 60 per cent of that seen during the actual physical movement. Similar findings were reported by Roth *et al.* (1996) when conducting a functional magnetic resonance imaging study of cortical activity during MIP. They found increased levels of activity in the primary motor cortex during muscular movement and when participants imagined the same movement. Such patterns have also been found in the auditory association cortex when participants imagine hearing sounds (Kraemer *et al.* 2005). Thus, MIP activates many of the neural components in the brain that are responsible for directing movement and perceiving stimuli. This would suggest that there is some degree of overlap in the neural substrates involved during an imagined event and the real thing and that MIP may strengthen such patterns of activity, leading to more efficient levels of behaviour.

However, this account is not without its critics. For example, Hale (1982) found EMG activity in the biceps *and* triceps of participants mentally practising bicep curls, suggesting a more general and less focused degree of muscular activation. Of course, it should be noted that, when an individual imagines completing a bicep curl, she may envisage her forearm moving upwards in an arc as her bicep muscle contracts. However, relaxing her bicep would of necessity involve a contraction of her tricep muscles in order for her to move her forearm back down to its starting position. Some muscular activity in the triceps may thus be expected when she is imagining such a movement.

Symbolic learning theory

According to symbolic learning theory, during MIP an individual will mentally rehearse the symbolic elements of the task, rather than the specific physical actions, which leads to enhanced performance (Sackett 1934). The idea of symbolic learning theory is that MIP provides the individual with an opportunity to rehearse the sequence of movements, identified as symbolic components, contained within the task. These symbolic elements could involve temporal or spatial elements of the skill, as well as possible courses and sequences of action. Thus, when mentally rehearsing a task, the symbolised elements become more familiar and retention of these components may subsequently facilitate performance.

Support for this approach comes from research showing that MIP often results in greater benefits for tasks that contain a high degree of symbolic content, such as spatial tasks, sequential learning tasks and tasks that involve planning (Grouios 1992b; Richardson 1967b). For example, Ryan and Simons (1983) found that participants trained to use MIP performed better than no-training controls on tasks containing fewer motor components but were no better than controls on tasks containing high levels of motor components. This led them to suggest that the effectiveness of MIP is primarily related to the cognitive aspects of the task. Driskell *et al.* (1994) also found that MIP training led to greater gains in performance for cognitive relative to physical tasks. Such findings are consistent with the idea that MIP facilitates skills in which there is a degree of symbolic control of the movements involved.

However, Suinn (1997) reports that the effects of MIP are often greater for experienced individuals than for novices. Given that the acquisition of any new task would be expected to involve a higher level of symbolic learning, the effects of MIP would be expected to influence novice performance to a much greater extent than expert performance. Such a pattern is contrary to what would be expected from symbolic learning theory. Thus, while symbolic learning may be able to account for some of the gains resulting from MIP training, it cannot account for all of them.

Factors influencing MIP

A number of factors have been shown to influence the effectiveness of MIP, including age, the task in question, the individual's level of skill at performing the task and the level of practice, as well as imagery ability, perspective and content. Each of these factors is briefly considered in turn.

Age

Researchers have suggested that older people are better able to generate, scan and manipulate mental images than children (Kosslyn *et al.* 1990). This would imply that age may be an important factor that needs to be considered when examining the effects of MIP.

For instance, when Jarus and Ratzon (2000) examined the effects of MIP on a motor coordination task using three different age groups – children (9 years), younger adults (21–40 years) and older adults (65–70 years) – they found that older adults exhibited a significant reduction in response times when using MIP compared to physical practice alone but there was no difference in performance for the children or the younger adults (see Figure 11.1).

Thus, MIP proved to be beneficial for older adults learning a novel coordination task but not for children. The fact that MIP was of no benefit for younger adults was contrary to expectations. However, the low response times for both of the younger groups suggests that they may be more dextrous than their elders. It may also be that no differential effect was found because the younger participants were performing at ceiling. Thus, the idea that MIP is mediated by age is only partially supported.

Task and level of skill

The nature of the task being carried out would seem an obvious factor that could potentially influence the outcome and there is a degree of consensus in the literature noting that MIP tends to be more effective for tasks that contain a larger symbolic component (Ryan and Simons 1983). That is, MIP may be more effective for tasks that contain a large proportion of mental or cognitive events but less effective for predominantly physical tasks. For instance, Driskell *et al.* (1994) compared the effectiveness of MIP on both cognitive

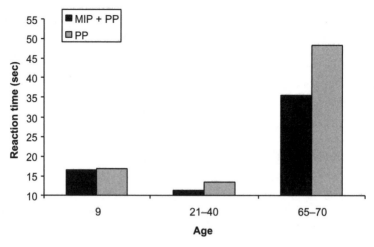

Figure 11.1 Mean reaction time for participants from the three different age groups
completing either physical practice (PP) or a combination of mental
imagery and physical practice (MIP + PP).

(Adapted from Jarus and Ratzon 2000)

and physical tasks, and found that MIP was more effective at enhancing
performance on cognitive tasks.

There also seems to be little doubt that individual differences in terms of
familiarity, knowledge and level of skill in completing the assigned task
play a part in the effectiveness of MIP training. According to Richardson
(1967a, 1967b), knowledge of and familiarity with the task are essential for
MIP to elicit positive effects, with those who are more familiar with the task
exhibiting greater gains. Furthermore, Lawther (1968) suggested that it is
necessary for the learner to be able to conceptualise the whole task, rather
than just the various components, if MIP is to have a beneficial effect.
This implies that MIP may be more effective for experienced performers who
have better cognitive models of the task in place. There is some support for
this from researchers showing differential effects of MIP training as a function
of experience. For instance, Clark (1960) found that MIP of goal shooting
elicited greater benefits for experienced basketball players than for novices. In
addition, others have found that MIP may have a detrimental effect on the
sporting performance of low-ability players compared to those of high ability
(Noel 1980) and that it may be detrimental when used in the early stages of
learning a new task (Zecker 1982).

Nevertheless, it may be the case that the type of task (cognitive versus
physical) interacts with the level of skill (expert versus novice) of the individual
to influence the effectiveness of MIP. For example, Driskell *et al.* (1994)
compared the effects of MIP for experienced versus novice participants and
found that the effects of MIP were no stronger for one group than the other.

However, they did find that, while experienced participants benefited equally when completing both cognitive and physical tasks, novice participants benefited more from MIP training on cognitive than physical tasks.

These findings indicate that experienced participants are more likely to benefit from using MIP to enhance performance on *both* cognitive and physical tasks. Novice participants, in contrast, may benefit more from using MIP to enhance cognitive as opposed to physical tasks.

Practice

Wollman (1986) suggested that both the duration of the MIP training period and the number of training trials conducted could influence outcome. There is no consistency in the literature regarding the duration of MIP training, with training periods varying in length from less than a minute to over an hour (Feltz and Landers 1983). An intuitive assumption might be that more practice would equate to more effective results from MIP. However, Twining (1949) noted early on that a single period of five minutes is probably the longest amount of time an individual can concentrate without rest. Thus, multiple MIP sessions of short duration may be more effective at maintaining efficient levels of concentration.

In terms of the number of training trials, some have suggested a positive link between the number of training trials and the degree of improvement (Sackett 1935; Smyth 1975). For instance, Sackett (1935) found that, as the number of MIP training sessions increased, the number of trials needed to relearn a task and the time taken to complete it decreased (see Figure 11.2). This suggests that a greater level of practice elicits more beneficial effects. However, Weinberg (1982) notes that there may be an optimal length of practice for eliciting beneficial effects from MIP and that continued practice beyond this point may be detrimental. There is some support for this idea from the findings of Driskell *et al.* (1994), who examined not just the number of training sessions but the total duration of MIP training. This revealed no clear relationship between the number of practice trials and the magnitude of the MIP effect. However, they did find that, as the length of the MIP training increased, its effect on performance decreased. Thus, while MIP can benefit performance, the longer the individual practises, the less beneficial it may become. This drop in effectiveness over time may be because MIP represents an intensive training regime and the continued training may lead to a loss of concentration (Richardson 1967a). Alternatively, Driskell *et al.* (1994) point out that continued MIP without knowledge of the results of the practice may decrease levels of motivation and increase negative affect. Overall, such findings indicate that more MIP is not always necessarily better.

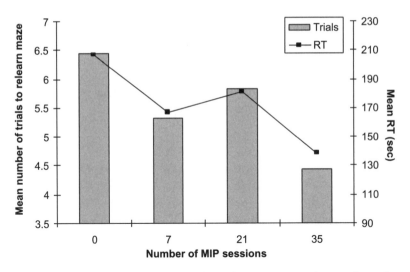

Figure 11.2 Mean number of trials needed to relearn a maze and mean time taken to complete the maze as a function of increasing numbers of MIP training sessions.

(Adapted from Sackett 1935)

Imagery ability

Good imagery ability is thought to rely on an individual's capacity to generate vivid images and to manipulate or control them (Murphy 1994). Given that individuals exhibit different levels of ability with regard to forming mental images, it should come as no surprise that researchers suggest that such differences may influence the effectiveness of MIP (Murphy 1994; Richardson 1967a), with those exhibiting good imagery skills benefiting more from MIP training than those with less efficient imagery skills (Goss *et al.* 1986; Marks 1977; Start and Richardson 1964). For instance, when Start and Richardson (1964) measured the relationship between vividness and control of imagery, and benefits from MIP, they found that individuals who were able to produce more vivid images and demonstrate greater control over their images exhibited greater benefits from MIP training. A similar pattern was reported by Marks (1977), who found that MIP led to greater gains for individuals classified as high-vivid imagers compared to low-vivid imagers. Furthermore, it is not just the vividness of the image that counts but also its clarity, with those able to construct images of high clarity exhibiting greater benefits from MIP (Goss *et al.* 1986). Such findings illustrate that an individual who is capable of creating clear, vivid images is more likely to benefit from the performance-enhancing effects of MIP training.

Imagery perspective

The use of MIP may involve the individual either imagining herself performing a task and experiencing the various multi-sensory responses (using an
internal/first-person perspective) or she may opt for an external/third-person
perspective, which involves imagining the action as if she is watching herself
from a distance. The benefit of using imagery to create a third-person perspective is that it may help to make the process more objective than it would
be if she is using a first-person perspective. By taking such a perspective,
participants may be able to distance themselves from becoming emotionally
involved in the task, which in turn may enable them to make a more critical
evaluation of their own performance.

Nevertheless, Suinn (1997) points out that individuals will ultimately have to
master the use of a first-person perspective in order to simulate fully the actual
event. By adopting such a perspective to construct an image, it may be easier
for the individual to imagine the sequence of events involved in the behaviour,
leading to more effective performance. The evidence supporting this idea is
equivocal. On the one hand, researchers monitoring muscle activity in terms
of EMG levels during MIP, and utilising an internal and an external imagery
perspective, found greater levels of EMG activity associated with the internal
perspective (Harris and Robinson 1986). In addition, Hale (1982) has suggested that external imagery fails to evoke the feeling of muscular action that
internal imagery does, which may be a fundamental factor in terms of
enhancing performance. Thus, use of an internal imagery perspective may
lead to greater levels of muscular innervation of the muscles normally utilised
in the task, which in turn elicits greater benefits in terms of task performance.

However, on the other hand, Meyers *et al.* (1979) found no evidence of an
association between the imagery perspective taken and performance levels.
Nevertheless, it is possible that the lack of consistent effects is the result of
the different skill levels of those taking part in such research, as well as their
familiarity with the task. For instance, Mahoney *et al.* (1987) reported that
elite athletes are more likely to use an internal perspective than are non-elite
athletes. In addition, Murphy (1994) has noted that this distinction between
imagery perspectives may be more influential in sport due to the kinaesthetic
nature of the tasks. Tasks requiring, or utilising, kinaesthetic feedback, such
as motor skill learning, may be more influenced by adopting an internal
perspective. In contrast, the use of external imagery may facilitate performance on tasks utilising different processes. In terms of task familiarity,
Hinshaw (1991) found that familiar tasks or scenes have a tendency to be
evoked using an internal perspective, whereas unfamiliar scenes are generally
imagined according to an external perspective.

Thus, while the data show a trend supporting greater effectiveness of an
internal perspective compared to an external perspective, this may be influenced by the level of skill of the individual as well as the nature and familiarity
of the task.

Imagery content

According to Lee (1990), the content of the imagery used in MIP is crucial for eliciting a beneficial effect. The assumption is that positive images are likely to be effective at enhancing performance, while negative images may be detrimental. For instance, Powell (1973) found that encouraging participants to imagine throwing a dart at a board and missing the target had a detrimental effect on performance compared to a group using positive imagery. A similar pattern of effects was reported by Woolfolk *et al.* (1985), who compared the performance of a positive imagery group to that of a group using negative imagery and found that the positive group exhibited a 30.4 per cent improvement in golf putting scores, while performance of the negative group deteriorated by 21.2 per cent (see Figure 11.3).

Such findings highlight a distinct pattern of effects based on the nature of the imagery used, with positive images enhancing performance and negative images inhibiting it. Murphy (1994) pointed out that negative imagery may interfere with the motor programme of the individual, creating a decline in performance, and may also impact on participants' motivation, self-confidence and concentration.

Apart from the positive or negative nature of the image, participants can also focus on using information from more than one modality. That is, not only are visual and acoustic information used, but also olfactory and kinaesthetic. By drawing on as much sensory information as possible concerning the conditions of the behaviour, a more realistic, and possibly more effective, imagery process may be created. Due to the inherent difficulty associated with trying to identify which imagery modality an individual has used, the limited research to date has invariably used post-training questionnaires. These show

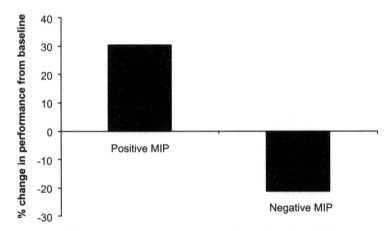

Figure 11.3 Percentage change in performance from baseline for groups using positive and negative MIP, where a positive score indicates an improvement in performance.

(Adapted from Suinn 1997)

that, when using MIP, the majority (80 per cent) report using visual images, with only a small minority (20 per cent) utilising verbal information (Sackett 1934). However, Richardson (1967b) has proposed that combined visual and kinaesthetic imagery may be more effective, though there is no empirical support for this claim. Perhaps with the advent of ever more accurate brain imaging techniques, it may be possible to identify with a greater degree of accuracy the particular modality of imagery used and its contribution to the overall effect.

Enhancing performance

The majority of research on MIP shows a consistent positive effect, with significant improvements in a variety of areas (Driskell *et al.* 1994; Feltz and Landers 1983; Grouios 1992a; Murphy 1994; Richardson 1967a; Suinn 1997; Taktek 2004). These include sport, cognition and, more recently, music, each of which will be explored in turn.

Sport

The use of MIP in sport is widespread and has been shown to enhance a range of skills, including basketball shooting (Savoy and Betiell 1996), dart throwing (Vandell *et al.* 1943), diving (Grouios 1992c), golf (Martin and Hall 1995), figure skating (Garza and Feltz 1998), tennis (Noel 1980) and table tennis (Lejeune *et al.* 1994) to name but a few.

In order to refine and develop any skill, an element of practice is needed and the suggestion is that MIP represents a useful option because athletes can conduct such practice bet...... trials or during physical rest periods. According to Keele (1982), the basis of all skilled performance relies on the ability of the individual to generate an appropriate sequence of motor commands from the feedback of performing a set task, creating a template of ideal performance. Grouios (1992c) suggests that a skill may be developed and enhanced by using MIP to generate a set of behaviours that are compared to the template, which can then help modify and refine the positive aspects of the behaviour. For example, Grouios (ibid.) had a group of divers complete a 30-minute MIP session for a period of 21 days and compared their diving performance to an equal contact no-training group and found that the imagery group performed significantly better (see Figure 11.4).

Such beneficial effects suggest that MIP is a powerful activity which can significantly enhance motor performance. Grouios (1992c) argued that the benefits resulting from MIP stem in part from the individual's ability to match her imagined performance to an internal template, modifying behaviour as needed in order to improve it. MIP practice may also help to reactivate memory processes associated with the task, bringing about a more robust memory of what an accurate performance should be.

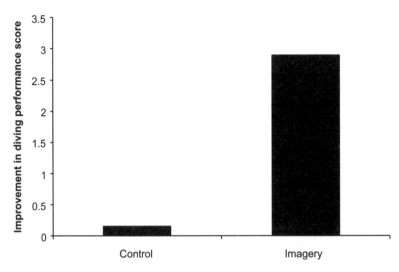

Figure 11.4 Mean improvement in diving performance score for mental imagery and control groups.

(Adapted from Grouios 1992b)

Others, however, have not been so fortunate in their attempts to use MIP to enhance motor performance (Linden *et al.* 1989; Ryan *et al.* 1986). For instance, when Linden *et al.* (1989) examined whether MIP could improve walking balance for a group of elderly people, they found that those taking part in the MIP training exhibited no improvement compared to controls. Ryan *et al.* (1986) also found that MIP was ineffective when used to help individuals learn how to bounce a ball to a target. Such findings add a necessary cautionary note to the effectiveness of MIP.

Nevertheless, there is an emerging consensus that, while MIP may be better than no practice, combining it with physical practice can lead to even greater benefits (Garza and Feltz 1998; Lejeune *et al.* 1994; Savoy and Beitel 1996). For instance, Savoy and Beitel (1996) found that combining MIP with physical practice produced an 18 per cent improvement in basketball players' shooting performance compared to physical practice alone. In addition, Lejeune *et al.* (1994) found that, while a small level of improvement was found for those who completed physical practice alone or combined physical practice with observational learning, which involved watching a film explaining how to complete the task, the most significant and largest improvement was obtained for those who completed combined training which included MIP (see Figure 11.5).

Thus, combining MIP with physical practice may be a more efficient method of enhancing performance, particularly for sporting athletes, than either physical practice or MIP alone.

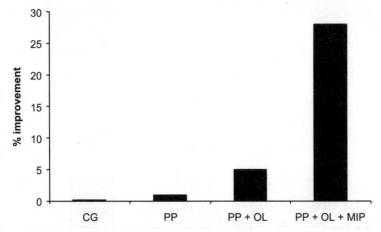

Figure 11.5 Percentage improvement in accuracy of table tennis shots for control group (CG) and those completing physical practice (PP), physical practice combined with observational learning (PP + OL), and physical practice combined with observational learning and mental imagery practice (PP + OL + MIP).

(Adapted from Lejeune *et al.* 1994)

Cognition

MIP has also been shown to benefit aspects of cognitive processing, including memory (Sackett 1934) and speed of processing (Grouios 1992b). Sackett (1934) was one of the first to show that MIP benefits cognition. He compared the ability of different groups to relearn a maze following initial learning to a standard criterion. Once they had learnt how to complete the maze, each group was given different instructions with regard to how they should then rehearse such information. One group were required to redraw the maze from memory as often as possible. A second group were asked to mentally rehearse completing the maze as often as possible, and a third control group were required not to think about the maze. After a delay of seven days, all participants were called back and asked to complete the maze once again. Sackett (ibid.) found that those required to physically produce a drawing of the maze performed the best, needing fewer trials and taking less time to relearn it. In addition, the MIP group also took less time and required fewer trials than the controls (see Figure 11.6). This led Sackett (ibid.) to conclude that both physically drawing and mentally rehearsing a maze pattern were sufficient to aid recall of the spatial information needed to relearn the maze.

However, Shanks and Cameron (2000) reported that MIP failed to elicit any benefit when it was used to aid recall of a target-matching task. The task involved a visual target appearing in one of four distinct locations in a pre-specified sequence, so that, over time, participants could learn the sequence

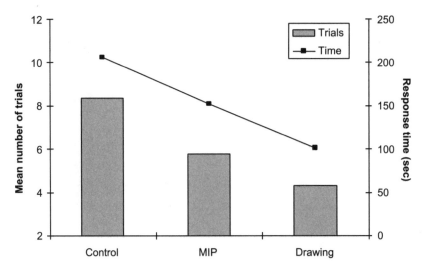

Figure 11.6 Mean number of trials and mean response time (seconds) taken to relearn a maze for the control, MIP and drawing groups.

(Adapted from Sackett 1934)

and improve the speed of their responses. Once familiar with the task, participants were allocated to one of four groups. The first physically practised the task, the second and third groups both completed MIP, one rehearsing the correct target sequence and the other an incorrect target sequence, and the final group acted as no-training controls. Following the training, all participants again performed the task to identify possible improvements. Shanks and Cameron (2000) found that only those completing the physical practice regime showed a significant improvement in their response time. The response times of those completing MIP were no different from controls. This led them to propose that MIP is ineffective in enhancing speed of performance on a target-matching task.

The lack of an effect for MIP found by Shanks and Cameron (2000) is inconsistent with the benefits reported by Sackett (1934). However, this discrepancy may be accounted for in part by differences in their respective methodologies. For example, Sackett found a cognitively beneficial effect from MIP after participants were required to practise daily for a period of seven days. In contrast, Shanks and Cameron failed to find any positive effects from MIP after a single session lasting only seven minutes. Such a short duration of practice for such a cognitively complex task may have been insufficient to enable the effects of MIP to emerge. This is consistent with research showing that MIP can produce effects equivalent to those obtained via physical practice after ten days of training (Rawlings *et al.* 1972). Furthermore, Grouios (1992b) found that 14 days of MIP training were sufficient to elicit improvements on a speeded matching task. When Grouios conducted the study, he matched participants on a number of variables known to affect MIP, such as age, imagery ability and intelligence, and assessed the differential performance of MIP, physical practice and combined MIP and practice compared to no-training controls. Grouios (ibid.) found that all those completing some form of training showed significantly faster response times than did the controls (see Figure 11.7).

That MIP alone was sufficient to improve response times relative to controls shows that it is capable of enhancing cognitive performance. The improvement may be the result of MIP positively influencing the memory comparison and/or response selection stages of processing, which manifest themselves in shorter response times. According to Grouios (ibid.), the benefits of MIP result from the formation of associations between stimuli and responses, creating what he referred to as an 'additional degree of memory organisation' (p. 152), which in turn makes the comparison process more efficient. Such findings indicate that MIP has the potential to enhance cognition, leading to gains in memory performance.

Thus, MIP may be capable of enhancing recall and speed of processing as long as sufficient training is provided. In addition, it is interesting to note that, consistent with the findings from the sporting literature, the combined effects of MIP and physical practice elicit greater benefits than physical practice or MIP alone.

Music

Musicians are aware of the fact that in order to improve their playing skills they need to continually practise. Whilst many agree with this sentiment, it

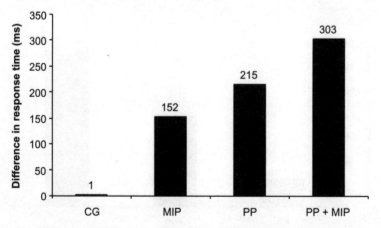

Figure 11.7 Mean improvement measured as a difference in response times from pre- to post-training, for control group (CG), mental imagery practice group (MIP), physical practice group (PP) and combined physical practice and mental imagery group (PP + MIP).

(Adapted from Grouios 1992b)

has been suggested that constant physical practice can become a tedious chore (Coffman 1990). Thus, MIP may represent a useful adjunct to physical practice, providing a degree of variety to the musician's training regime which may help maintain motivation levels. MIP can also be used to practise during musical rest periods, making more efficient use of available time. Furthermore, Theiler and Lippman (1995) noted that many of the skills required by musicians are predominantly cognitive in nature, including the need to assimilate and understand patterns of scales, arpeggios, rhythmic motifs, structure, tonality and musical style. Given the suggestion that imagery may be more effective for tasks that contain a high number of cognitive components, such skills could be particularly amenable to the benefits of MIP.

Coffman (1990) was one of the first to examine the possible benefits of MIP on musical training. He did this by comparing physical rehearsal and MIP to no-training controls in the learning of a set piece. Coffman found that those completing either physical or MIP training played the piece faster than controls without any noticeable decrement in accuracy, although the physical practice group were faster than those using MIP (see Figure 11.8).

This shows that MIP is sufficient to produce significant benefits in terms of improved speed of a musical recital. Hence, utilising MIP as part of a musician's training regime may lead to greater improvements in performance, particularly if it is combined with physical practice. Indeed, researchers have shown that combining physical and MIP training can elicit positive effects on musical performance that are greater than those found with either physical practice alone (Theiler and Lippman 1995), MIP alone (Lim and Lippman 1991), or when MIP alone fails to elicit any benefit (Ross 1985). According to Ross (ibid.), the physical practice helps to provide auditory, visual and

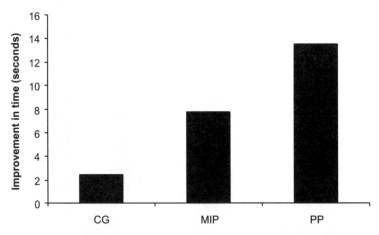

Figure 11.8 Mean improvement in speed of playing (seconds) for the control group (CG), the mental imagery practice group (MIP) and the physical practice group (PP).

(Adapted from Coffman 1990)

kinaesthetic feedback, whereas MIP may help focus the performer's attention on the more cognitive aspects of the task. Thus, combining the two approaches allows the individual to benefit from the feedback as well as the cognitive consideration given to the task. Such findings indicate that, while MIP alone may be less effective than physical practice, when combined with either physical practice or musical listening training it may be more successful.

Long-term benefits

Given the relative ease with which MIP can be conducted, it would be useful to know how robust the effects it produces are. The duration of any positive effect also has implications in terms of the need to conduct additional MIP training sessions to maintain enhanced levels of performance. Suinn (1997) notes, however, that there is a lack of sufficient research conducting follow-up analyses to address this issue fully.

There is some indication that a negative relationship exists between the strength of effect elicited from MIP and the length of time since the last practice session, implying that the possible benefits are short lived. For instance, a meta-analysis conducted by Driskell *et al.* (1994) compared the efficiency of MIP to physical practice across increasing delay periods and found a decrease in the effect of both physical and MIP training as the number of days since the last training session increased (see Figure 11.9). This pattern indicates that MIP is more beneficial in the short term than the long term.

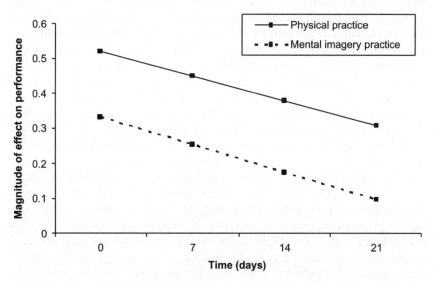

Figure 11.9 Decreasing magnitude of effect resulting from MIP and physical practice as time from last practice session increases (in days).

(Adapted from Driskell *et al.* 1994)

To some extent this is not surprising, as the effects from physical practice also show a decline in magnitude over time. Nevertheless, it would suggest that refresher training sessions need to be implemented reasonably often in order to maintain the initial benefits of the training.

Methodological issues

While there is some consistency in the literature regarding the beneficial effects of MIP training, researchers have outlined two key methodological issues that remain to be addressed before a full understanding of the effects of such training can be made clear (Driskell *et al.* 1994; Taktek 2004). The first relates to the use of adequate controls and the second to the processes involved in MIP training.

Adequate controls

The classic paradigm in MIP research is to compare the pre versus post-intervention performance of three groups: one conducting physical practice, one using MIP, and a no-training control group. The performance of the MIP group is then compared to both the physical practice group and the controls. However, one problem noted by researchers is that a no-practice control group receives less contact time than either intervention group, thus potentially confounding the data (Driskell *et al.* 1994; Grouios 1992a; Taktek 2004). It may be that those participating in the MIP training are simply more motivated because they are taking part in some form of training, whereas the controls are not. In an attempt to address this, some have utilised what are referred to as 'equivalent control groups' (Linden *et al.* 1989). This involves the control group engaging in some form of non-MIP activity for a period of time equivalent to those receiving the MIP training. Having the controls engage in some form of activity has been shown to influence the magnitude of effects resulting from MIP. For example, Driskell *et al.* (1994) reported a trend showing that the effects of MIP were lower when compared to equivalent controls versus a no-contact control group. That is, the benefit seen for MIP training is less robust when the effects are compared to a control group who maintain equivalent levels of contact and perform a specified activity.

Such issues led Wollman (1986) to suggest the need for a greater variety of control groups within MIP research. More specifically, he noted that stringent control groups should be used to help identify the effects of the various images used and the type of cognitive information incorporated, as well as the level of individual motivation. Wollman proposed that better use of single case designs may help to elucidate such issues by complementing the traditional group designs, particularly for highly skilled athletes, whose improvements, while significant, may be small and masked when their scores are combined within a group. Furthermore, rather than adopting a 'one size fits all' approach to the use of MIP, he suggests that specific imagery routines could be introduced to suit the style and needs of the individual. In addition, it may make more sense for controls to complete non-task-relevant MIP, because if imagery can influence performance, then it is essential that the level and nature of imagery used by the control group is also monitored.

Defining MIP

MIP represents an internal subjective experience which relies primarily on the cognitive activity of the individual. Those completing MIP are invariably seated with eyes closed and told to imagine the execution of a particular task or behaviour. This may involve visual, kinaesthetic and/or auditory imagery. The fact that it is impossible to tell with any degree of accuracy which of these processes is involved during such training highlights the problem that MIP represents a generic term used to denote a diverse set of activities, ranging from an individual closing her eyes and simply thinking about the task without any overt activity, to full-blown imaginal experiences with auditory, visual, emotional and proprioceptive components.

The difficulty is that MIP is often defined so loosely that it is not always clear what it entails (Driskell *et al.* 1994). For instance, Murphy (1994) points out that simply to say that 'an athlete is mentally practising can mean several activities are going on' (p. 491). It may involve thinking about the task, talking through the various stages, imagining an expert performing the task and the use of positive imagery and affirmations, as well as emotional arousal.

In addition, the MIP procedure is not always made clear. Unless very clear guidance is given with regard to the specific type of MIP that should be used, participants may utilise a range of mental procedures in an attempt to aid their performance. This makes cross-comparisons between studies difficult and also means that it's not clear precisely what aspect of the mental rehearsal process is having an effect. For instance, a positive effect may emerge from emotional arousal or self-affirmations, or both.

Proposals have been made suggesting that MIP research consistently includes questionnaires to asses the type, content and nature of the imagery experiences of the individuals (Wollman 1986). This is essential because researchers have shown that, even when given clear instructions regarding the type of imagery to be used, participants often report modifying the approach to suit their own tastes and abilities (Woolfolk *et al.* 1985).

Thus, the concept of MIP needs to be clearly defined and ideally agreed upon. The imagery procedure itself also needs to be made clear, with specific guidance provided to the trainees regarding the type and nature of the imagery they should use. While it may be difficult, if not impossible, to limit or control the various aspects of imagery incorporated by an individual, the use of post-training assessment may go some way to address this. Future studies incorporating brain imaging techniques may also help provide insights into the various imagery processes involved. These are important issues as the different studies utilising MIP may be examining distinct phenomena, which makes attempts to interpret them under a single heading problematic.

Overview

MIP represents a generic term used to denote the mental rehearsal of a skill or behaviour in imagination rather than by overt physical practice. Such rehearsal may take the form of visual, verbal, kinaesthetic or a combination of these processes. It is a widespread technique, with many people using it of their own accord to help acquire new skills as well as maintain and enhance existing ones.

Several theories have been proposed to account for the effects of MIP, with the psycho-neuromotor and symbolic learning approaches dominating the field. Although no single theory is able to account for all of the data, each offers some insights that may be useful in understanding the processes involved. The fact that no single theory has emerged led Suinn (1997) to suggest that it may be more effective to try to integrate the various theories into a single framework in an attempt to provide a more comprehensive understanding.

A number of factors have been shown to influence the effectiveness of the MIP training process. In general, these indicate that more effective results are associated with MIP that maintains a clear, vivid and controllable image. Imagery ability is also a mediating factor, with those showing greater ability to produce vivid and controllable images exhibiting greater benefits from MIP. In addition, negative images exert a powerful detrimental effect on performance. Imagery perspective differences are less consistent and may be related to the preferred cognitive style of the individual as well as the specific task in hand.

Evidence from the use of MIP to enhance sporting, cognitive and musical performance all show consistent beneficial effects. However, the improvements seen in performance are invariably not as robust as those found for physical practice alone. Thus, although MIP is certainly better than no practice at all, it may be best used as an adjunct to physical practice rather than as a replacement. Furthermore, there is an emerging consensus that combining MIP with other types of practice often leads to a more effective outcome than that obtained by physical practice alone. However, clear and comparative controls need to be used and more work needs to be done to identify the specific processes involved in MIP.

Part III
Peak performance

12 Techniques, themes and directions

Investigators should be bold in what they try, but cautious in what they claim.

(Miller 1974)

After an exploration of a variety of techniques, this final chapter brings them together, identifying which may be more successful and whether there is a difference between passive and active techniques. The chapter also draws attention to some of the themes that have emerged from research into the use of these techniques. Finally, the chapter outlines some future directions in terms of application of a particular technique and future possibilities.

Techniques

There is often a desire when faced with a complex issue or, as is the case here, a complex technique that elicits ambiguous and often contrary evidence, to want a simple answer to the question, 'does it work?' Unfortunately, the answer is not so simple, which usually means it's couched in terms of a 'yes but' or a 'yes to some extent' response. This is because attempts to simplify the question into a yes/no outcome fail to do justice to the complexity of the issues or the level of supporting evidence. Nevertheless, in an effort to provide a synopsis of the various techniques along with the level of supporting evidence, a summary is provided in Table 12.1.

When we look at the evidence in Table 12.1, it's important to remain aware of a number of key points. First, the level of evidence supporting each technique has been classified as ranging from poor to very good to help the reader identify the efficiency of a particular technique. Nevertheless, it is important to keep in mind that the level of supporting evidence may be poor or limited for two reasons. First, because the research examining the effectiveness of the technique has found little or no evidence that it has the capability to enhance performance, as in the case of subliminal verbal messages. Or that, while positive effects have been found, only a limited amount of research has been conducted, as in the case of auditory entrainment. To help clarify the effectiveness of each technique, providing an overall view of its performance-

Table 12.1 An overview of the various techniques. The table identifies the specific nature of the technique (passive vs. active), whether it has a supporting theory or rationale and lists the main behaviours that have been targeted. It also identifies the level of evidence* supporting the use of each technique as well as the potential long-term benefits and/or negative effects. Finally, each technique has been given an overall rating to classify how effective it is at enhancing performance.

Techniques	Theory/rationale	Targeted behaviours	Evidence	Long-term effects	Negative effects	Rating
Hypnosis	Non-state vs. state theory	Memory	Limited		Poor accuracy	4
		Academic performance	Limited			4
		Motor performance	Poor			2
		Sporting performance	Limited			4
Hypnopaedia	No	Behaviour adaptation	Poor		May impair quality of sleep	2
		Verbal learning	Limited			4
		General knowledge	Poor			2
Subliminal verbal Subliminal visual	No	Memory, self-esteem, academic performance	None		Costs	0
		Verbal behaviour	Poor			2
		Academic performance	Reasonable	Limited		6
Audio entrainment Visual entrainment Audio-visual	Rationale	Memory	Limited			4
		Creativity	Poor			2
		Attention	Limited			4
		Imagery	Poor	Poor	Linked to seizure episode	2
		Recognition memory	Reasonable	Poor		6
		Academic performance	Limited			4
Meditation	Rationale	Attention	Good		Predisposition to exhibit epileptic-like behaviours	8
		Perceptual sensitivity	Reasonable			6
		Memory	Limited			4
		Academic performance	Limited			4
Mnemonics	Rationale	Memory	Very good	Good – but may depend on mnemonic		10
		Faces and names	Reasonable			6
		Facts	Reasonable			6
		Language learning	Good			8

Speed reading	No	Reading	Limited	Limited	May decrease comprehension	4
Biofeedback	Rationale	Memory	Limited	Limited		4
		Motor skills	Limited			4
		Muscular strength/endurance	Limited			4
		Muscular flexibility	Limited			4
Neurofeedback	Rationale	Target shooting	Poor			2
		Attention	Good			8
		Memory	Limited			4
		Creativity	Poor			2
		Artistic performance	Limited			4
Mental imagery practice	Various	Sporting performance	Very good	Limited		10
		Cognition	Reasonable			6
		Musical skill	Reasonable			6

* The level of supporting evidence has been classified as: none (0), poor (2), limited (4), reasonable (6), good (8) and very good (10). Where a section has been left blank, this is because there is no evidence.

enhancement capabilities, each approach has been given a rating. This rating is not meant to represent a precise index but rather provides, in a general sense, an indication of the effectiveness of each of the techniques. Furthermore, cells that remain blank do not indicate a lack of supporting evidence but, rather, denote a lack of empirical support because few, if any, studies, have directly addressed the issue. For example, no comment is made for the long-term effects of hypnosis because, as yet, there is no research directly addressing this issue. This idea is nicely encapsulated in the phrase 'an absence of evidence is not the same as evidence of absence'. These empirical gaps in knowledge concerning the effectiveness of the techniques, while limiting current understanding, can however be addressed in future research. Thus, rather than being seen as limitations, they can be viewed as signposts pointing the way to potentially fruitful future studies.

The techniques that have been examined were classified using a framework of passive versus active approaches. Two questions emerge from grouping them in this way. First, which are the most effective techniques within each classification and, second, is one approach more or less effective than another? The following summaries deal with each of these questions in turn.

Passive techniques

Passive techniques, so called because they require no additional effort by the participant taking part, included hypnosis, sleep learning, subliminal stimulation and entrainment. Of these techniques, the most effective are visual subliminal stimulation and audio/visual entrainment. In particular, use of the subliminal visual message 'Mommy and I are one' was shown to improve academic performance across different cultures (Ariam *et al.* 1992; Cook 1985); visual entrainment elicited clear improvements in memory (Williams 2001); and binaural beat entrainment benefited memory and attention (Kennerly 1996; Lane *et al.* 1998). Unfortunately, the level of evidence supporting the use of hypnosis to enhance performance is limited, often by methodological inadequacies, and the support for sleep learning is even less robust. Meanwhile, research examining the effectiveness of audio subliminal messages has consistently shown that such messages fail to elicit any beneficial effects. Thus, visual subliminal messages and visual entrainment represent the best of the passive techniques.

Active techniques

Active techniques, in contrast, require the individual to actively process information in a specific way, learn new ways to process information or learn to control physiological processes not normally under volitional control. These included meditation, mnemonics, speed reading, biofeedback, neurofeedback and mental imagery practice (MIP). Of these, meditation, mnemonics and MIP all show good supporting evidence of enhancing performance.

In particular, meditation improved attentional processing (Chan and Woollacott 2007; Valentine and Sweet 1999), mnemonics improved memory performance (e.g. Hill *et al.* 1990; Krinsky and Krinsky 1996) and the use of MIP was shown to benefit sporting performance (Grouious 1992c; Lejeune *et al.* 1994). The findings from biofeedback and neurofeedback are limited, although for different reasons. Evidence supporting biofeedback is often limited by methodological problems producing inconsistent results. In contrast, only a limited amount of research has explored the potential benefits of neurofeedback training, which has produced some encouraging results, particularly in terms of enhancing attention (e.g. Beatty *et al.* 1974; Egner and Gruzelier 2001). Unfortunately, evidence supporting the use of speed reading is limited and shows that, whilst such training may have a small effect, depending on the reader's initial reading speed (e.g. Calef *et al.* 1999), there is no support for claims that it is possible to read at speeds in excess of 1000 wpm. Overall, meditation, mnemonics and MIP represent the most effective active techniques.

Passive versus active

By and large, it would seem that there is less supporting evidence for passive than for active techniques. More specifically, the passive techniques of subliminal visual training and visual entrainment are the only areas that exhibit reasonable levels of supporting evidence. In contrast, the active techniques of meditation, mnemonics and MIP all show robust levels of empirical support. Such differences may at first glance seem intuitively obvious. After all, it has long been known that making more of an effort is associated with better performance (Kanfer 1987; Norman and Bobrow 1975). This is also consistent with the idea that, in order to improve or enhance a particular aspect of behaviour, the individual needs to actively engage in or work on improving his behaviour. Despite such differences it is important not to fall into the trap of thinking that this means passive techniques are ineffective. The use of visual subliminal messages and audio/visual entrainment has produced some intriguing findings, which deserve further scrutiny to determine their full potential. The same is also true for neurofeedback, which shows only limited evidence due to a paucity of research. Thus, at this moment in time, performance-enhancing techniques classified as active may be capable of eliciting greater benefits, though with the advent of additional research this may change.

Themes

Two themes emerged from reviewing the evidence of these performance-enhancing techniques. The first, which permeated much of the research, relates to methodological issues. The second highlights the finding that effectiveness of any one technique is not reliant solely upon that technique alone, but can be mediated or influenced by a variety of factors relating either to the individual or to the procedure.

Methodological issues

Throughout the preceding chapters a number of methodological issues have arisen which can influence the level of supporting evidence for a particular technique. This includes the lack of a clear theory, which not only limits understanding of the processes involved but may also hinder development. In addition, poor controls and confounds restrict the interpretation of available data.

Lack of clear theory

The aim of a theory is to provide a conceptual framework which can be used to help describe and understand the phenomenon. However, as can be seen in Table 12.1, not all techniques benefit from theoretical support. For instance, there is no clear theory outlining why information played to a sleeping individual would be remembered or why simply scanning pages at high speeds would enable someone to speed read material and be capable of recalling it at a later date. This is an important point because research is not simply about gathering ever greater quantities of data but about improving conceptual understanding of a particular phenomenon, and the absence of a theory means that conceptualisation of the relevant issues is more difficult. Theories are also a useful way of generating ideas that can be used to test the boundaries of understanding. The lack of a clear theory can act as a limiting factor because a clear theory can drive research, encouraging researchers to ask specific questions regarding the particular processes involved. In this way, each step becomes a refinement of the theory as it is modified in the light of new information.

In some instances, whilst no clear theory has emerged, a rationale can be produced for using a specific technique. For instance, the rationale behind entrainment is similar to that of neurofeedback, in that both aim to modify some aspect of electrocortical activity and, in doing so, influence behaviour. To some extent a rationale may represent the early stages of theoretical development, as it identifies a plausible reason for using a technique, which needs to be developed into a full-blown theory.

Adequate controls

The evaluation of a specific technique should, of necessity, involve comparing the effectiveness of a technique given to an experimental group to that of a control group who do not receive it. In this way, the controls act as a baseline against which the behaviour of the experimental group may be compared to ascertain whether the technique in question is capable of enhancing performance. Unfortunately, a number of studies examining the potential benefits of a particular technique failed to include a control group (e.g. DeWitt 1980; Pates *et al.* 2002). This means that, even if the technique elicits a positive effect, the failure to include no-training controls leaves the research open to the criticism that the improved performance stems from practice as opposed to the intervention.

Simply including a no-training control group, while necessary, may not always be sufficient. This is because many of the performance-enhancing techniques require the individual to participate in a number of training sessions in order to become accustomed to using the technique and extract its full benefit. Such prolonged training often means that individuals spend more time interacting with researchers than those allocated to the no-training control group. The increased level of contact for those in the experimental group creates an additional confound. Given the greater level of experimenter– participant interaction, those in the experimental group may be more motivated to help the experimenter with his research and simply try harder than controls. Thus, a more effective control group is one that receives the same amount of contact as the experimental group and ideally undergoes some form of intervention. This could be training in an associated technique, such as relaxation in the case of studies examining the effects of meditation (e.g. King and Coney 2006), or providing a modified version of the performance-enhancing technique itself, as in the case of mock neurofeedback suggested by Vernon (2005). It may also be worth having controls complete post-session questionnaires to ascertain exactly what they did do, given that researchers have shown that when required to do nothing, or utilise a prescribed strategy, they often adopt strategies of their own (e.g. Camp *et al.* 1983). Thus, it is essential to ensure that adequate controls are utilised and that ideally the strategies used in the research are monitored.

Confounds

A final methodological issue to arise is that of confounding the intervention by combining it with one or more additional techniques. Some of the examples seen in the previous chapters include combining hypnosis with sleep learning (Cooper and Hoskovec 1972), combining presentations of multiple frequencies during an auditory entrainment paradigm (Lane *et al.* 1998) and combining biofeedback with a range of other interventions (Caird *et al.* 1999). The rationale for combining one technique with another is not always clear. It may be that a combination of techniques will be more effective. However, the problem with this approach is that it makes it impossible to identify which component is responsible for producing the effect. It is essential for an intervention to provide the researcher with information concerning the effectiveness of each technique *alone*. Of course, it may be that some techniques are *only* effective, or are *more* effective, when used in combination. For example, given the similarities in rationale between entrainment and neurofeedback, it is not difficult to imagine a scenario which involves combining them to alter cortical activity in an effort to enhance memory. However, while combining techniques may in some cases lead to greater benefits, it is essential to obtain an understanding of the effects of each technique alone prior to combining them.

Mediating factors

Whilst a technique may elicit a positive effect, it is unlikely to elicit the same effect for everyone, or in all situations. The effectiveness of many of the techniques may be mediated by a variety of mitigating factors which relate either to the individual or the procedural process.

Individual factors

Two key individual factors to emerge relate to an individual's *susceptibility*, or responsiveness to suggestions, and *age*. For instance, researchers from the fields of hypnosis and sleep learning found that people who are more respon-sive to suggestions often exhibited greater effects (Dinges *et al.* 1992). This may mean that the overall impact of such techniques is limited to a subset of the population identified as being highly suggestible.

In terms of age, it is often the case that younger participants exhibit greater benefits from using one of the techniques to enhance performance (see, e.g., Bar-Eli and Blumenstein 2004). This may occur for a number of reasons. Younger participants may be more open and flexible in their approach to learning and, as such, find it easier to alter their cognitive style and adopt a new method or incorporate a new technique into their learning regime. In contrast, older participants may be more set in their ways and find such changes difficult to adapt to. However, in the case of MIP, which requires the individual to be capable of creating a vivid image that can be manipulated in an effort to facilitate performance, Jarus and Ratzon (2000) found that MIP was more beneficial for older adults. This difference was accounted for in terms of the older adults having developed better imagery abilities. Thus, in general many of the techniques may elicit greater effects with younger participants, as long as they are sufficiently capable of carrying out the requirements of the technique.

Nevertheless, it should be noted that age and suggestibility are unlikely to represent a comprehensive list of all possible mitigating factors. It may be that factors such as an individual's baseline level of performance or their level of motivation can also influence the outcome.

Procedural differences

Two factors relating to procedural differences which have been shown to mediate the effectiveness of the various techniques are *time* and *task*.

Time can refer to the length or duration of the training session, the overall length of the training or how often such training is conducted. In general, the length and duration of time given to practise a technique has been shown to be a key factor, with longer and more frequent sessions producing more robust effects for sleep learning (Levy *et al.* 1972; Tani and Yoshi 1970), hypnosis (Pates *et al.* 2001; De Vos and Louw 2006), biofeedback training (Caird *et al.* 1999), meditation (Brown and Engler 1980; Chan and Woollacott 2007) and MIP (Wollman 1986). The fact that the remaining techniques do not show clear effects of time doesn't mean they remain unaffected by time, but may be because research has yet to test such a notion.

These effects of time may be the result of learning and/or practice. For some techniques (such as mnemonics and biofeedback), sufficient time needs to be provided for the individual to learn how to use the technique in the first place. For instance, Wood (1967) found that initially using a mnemonic actually slows down performance until the individual becomes familiar with it. In addition, Caird *et al.* (1999) suggested that, due to the complexity of attempting to control physiological processes that are not traditionally under volitional control, sufficient training time needs to be allocated for the individual to learn how to do this. Once the individual has learnt how to use the technique, it is then a matter of practising to become more adept, with continued practice, in many instances, leading to greater benefits.

However, it is important not to over-practise. Such a concept may sound counterintuitive but Driskell *et al.* (1994) found that more MIP did not simply translate into better performance. Rather than a linear effect positively linking practice to outcome, Driskell *et al.* suggest that there may be an optimal level of practice and that if the individual continues to practise beyond this point, performance may deteriorate. According to such a view, extensive practice may have a detrimental effect on an individual's level of motivation, particularly if he doesn't get the opportunity to use the skills he is developing and obtain much-needed feedback regarding his performance. Thus, whilst additional practice is generally considered to be a good thing, there may be an ideal level of practice beyond which performance may deteriorate. However, precisely what this optimal level of practice is remains to be seen.

With regard to the task, both the type and intensity of the task have been shown to influence performance. It may seem an obvious point that differences in the type of task used to measure performance when assessing the effectiveness of a particular technique can result in different outcomes. For example, hypnotically induced hypermnesia is thought to elicit greater benefits for tasks that contain meaningful material (DePiano and Salzberg 1981) and variations in the task have been suggested to influence the effectiveness of mnemonics (Carney and Levin, 2000b). Attempts to speed read complex material can elicit a different result from that of a simple text (Graf 1973) and MIP is thought to be more effective for tasks that contain a higher number of cognitive elements than physical elements (Driskell *et al.* 1994). Furthermore, it is not just the differences between tasks that are significant but also the variations in intensity within the same task. For example, Moses *et al.* (1986) found that the effects of biofeedback were mitigated by the intensity of the task, such that high-intensity tasks reduced the effectiveness of biofeedback training. Thus, differences in the type of task as well as the difficulty level of the specific task may influence the effectiveness of a particular technique.

Directions

Given the current findings, there are a number of possibilities for applying some of the techniques in specific circumstances. It is also possible to provide some speculative indications of possible future developments.

Application

Given the clear benefits demonstrated for using MIP within sport, it would seem obvious that this technique should be used in a wider range of settings, including artistic and cognitive performance. MIP also has the added benefit of requiring few resources beyond the time needed to practise. In addition, the benefits seen in attention for those who meditate and the improvements in memory for those using mnemonics make such techniques viable candidates to include within mainstream education. Such ideas mirror suggestions by others that young children could benefit from exposure to such techniques at an early age (Fisher 2006). It is possible that, by embedding them within mainstream education, they would become part of an individual's natural repertoire of learning techniques. In addition, they may also enhance quality of life, particularly given the health-related benefits associated with meditation (see Kelly 2008).

Future possibilities

Thinking about future possibilities is by its very nature a speculative process. Nevertheless, such possibilities can at least be informed by what has gone before. Given this, it seems likely that the number of people prepared to use a technique to enhance some aspect of their performance will increase. To some extent, this increasing desire is already visible in the use of off-label drugs to boost performance. For instance, a recent newspaper article stated that, of those people surveyed, one in five had used some form of medication to enhance performance (Randerson 2008). Such claims are not original or new, as many people start the day with a mind-sharpening boost of caffeine. This desire to optimise performance may be fuelled by an individual's needs or by the increasing and intense levels of competition that form much of modern society. The point is that the desire to enhance performance is likely to increase, with more people opting for this as a way of improving their life.

To meet this growing desire, the range of current techniques will need to be refined and new ones developed. For example, it is already possible to have subliminal visual messages flashed up on the screen of a computer. It is not difficult to imagine a scenario where the use of such messages becomes the norm and the individual, after logging on to his PC in the morning, simply selects the message that best suits his needs. If such messages positively influence the individual's performance and in turn the productivity of the organisation, their use may be actively encouraged.

In future, the more effective techniques are likely to be the ones embedded in the lifestyle of the individual and the more easily they can be assimilated, the more likely it is that they will be used. For example, many people, young and old, currently wear a watch and carry mini media players with headphones. It is easy to imagine a scenario whereby an individual's watch has a range of sensors capable of measuring physiological processes, such as blood pressure and heart rate. If one or more of these measures exceeds a predetermined threshold, an alerting signal is given and the individual uses this information to regain control or alter the physiological process. With regard to mobile media players, these already have the capacity to present audio and/ or visual messages that could be used to hypnotise the individual, help him learn to meditate or entrain brain activity. It doesn't take a great leap of the imagination to see such devices interacting directly with the individual's brain activity via a simple sensor connected to an extending cable which can be attached to the scalp. Such a sensor would be able to record information regarding brain activity and, using entrainment, neurofeedback or a combination of the two, help the individual to learn how to alter the profile of his brain activity to that of a more optimal or desired state. Such a procedure could also be used to help the individual enter into a specific receptive state during which meditative guidance or hypnotic suggestions are given.

What the ethical and social issues are of such potential developments is difficult to know. There may be concerns about people becoming too reliant on the use of such devices. However, if their use does confer an advantage there may be increasing pressures to utilise them. The development and use of such devices may also create divisions in society between those who have access to and use them, and those who do not.

Such possibilities may sound more like fiction than fact, but a look back at how far we have come may give some indication as to how far we are prepared to go. What does seem clear is that the continued developments within the field of optimal performance will ensure that the people of tomorrow have a greater opportunity to explore and reach their full potential than those alive today.

References

Aarons, L. (1976). Sleep assisted instruction. *Psychological Bulletin*, *83*(1), 1–40.

Abrams, R. L., Klinger, M. R. and Greenwald, A. G. (2002). Subliminal words activate semantic categories (not automated motor responses). *Psychonomic Bulletin and Review*, *9*(1), 100–106.

Adkins-Muir, D. L. and Jones, T. A. (2003). Cortical electrical stimulation combined with rehabilitative training: Enhanced functional recovery and dendritic plasticity following focal cortical ischemia in rats. *Neurological Research*, *25*, 780–788.

Adrian, E. and Matthews, B. (1934). The Berger rhythm: Potential changes from the occipital lobes in man. *Brain*, *57*, 355–384.

Aftanas, L. I. and Golocheikine, S. A. (2003). Changes in cortical activity in altered states of consciousness: The study of meditation by high-resolution EEG. *Human Physiology*, *29*, 143–151.

Aftanas, L. I. and Golocheikine, S. A. (2005). Impact of regular meditation practice on EEG activity at rest and during evoked negative emotions. *International Journal of Neuroscience*, *115*, 893–909.

Agardy, F. J. (1981). *How to Read Faster and Better – The Evelyn Wood Reading Dynamics Program: How To Get Everything You Want from Anything You Read as Fast as You Can Think*. New York: Simon and Schuster.

Alexander, C. N., Langer, E. J., Newman, R. I., Chandler, H. M. and Davis, J. L. (1989) Transcendental meditation, mindfulness, and longevity: an experimental study with the elderly. *Journal of Personality and Social Psychology*, *57*(6), 950–964.

Andreassi, J. L. (2000). *Psychophysiology: Human Behavior and Physiological Response*, 4th edition. Mahway, NJ: LEA.

Andreoff, G. R. and Yarmey, A. D. (1976). Bizarre imagery and associative learning: A confirmation. *Perceptual and Motor Skills*, *43*, 143–148.

Ariam, S. and Siller, J. (1982). Effects of subliminal oneness stimuli in Hebrew on academic performance of Israeli high school students: Further evidence of the adaptation-enhancing effects of symbiotic fantasies in another culture using another language. *Journal of Abnormal Psychology*, *91*(5), 343–349.

Atkinson, R. C. (1975). Mnemotechnic in second-language learning. *American Psychologist*, *30*, 821–828.

Atkinson, R. C. and Raugh, M. R. (1975). An application of the mnemonic keyword method to the acquisition of a Russian vocabulary. *Journal of Experimental Psychology: Learning, Memory and Cognition*, *104*(2), 126–133.

Bakker, F., Boschker, M. and Chung, T. (1986). Changes in muscular activity while imagining weight lifting using stimulus or response proposition. *Journal of Sport and Exercise Psychology*, *18*, 313–324.

Balkhashov, I. (1965). The rapid teaching of a foreign language by lessons heard during sleep. *Soviet Psychology and Psychiatry*, *4*(2), 20–21.

Barabasz, A. F. (1985). Enhancement of military pilot reliability by hypnosis and psychophysiological monitoring: Preliminary inflight and simulator data. *Aviation, Space and Environmental Medicine*, *56*(3), 248–250.

Bar-Eli, M. and Blumenstein, M. (2004). The effect of extra-curricular mental training with biofeedback on short running performance of adolescent physical education pupils. *European Physical Education Review*, *10*(2), 123–134.

Bauer, R. H. (1976). Short-term memory: EEG alpha correlates and the effect of increased alpha. *Behavioural Biology*, *17*, 425–433.

Bazanova, O. and Lubomir, A. (2006). Neurofeedback efficiency increases by using individual EEG alpha activity peculiarities. Paper presented at the Society of Applied Neuroscience, Swansea University, Wales, 16–19 September.

Beatty, J., Greenberg, A., Diebler, W. P. and O'Hanlon, J. F. (1974). Operant control of occipital theta rhythm affects performance in a radar monitoring task. *Science*, *183*(4127), 871–873.

Bell, T. (2001). Extensive reading: Speed and comprehension. *Reading Matrix*, *1*(1), 1–13.

Bellows, C. S. and Rush, C. H. (1952). Reading abilities of business executives. *Journal of Applied Psychology*, *36*(1), 1–4.

Benham, G., Rasey, H. W., Lubar, J. F., Frederick, J. A. and Zoffuto, A. C. (1998). EEG power-spectral and coherence differences between attentional states during a complex auditory task. *Journal of Neurotherapy*, *2*(3), 1–9.

Bergquist, L. (1984). Rapid silent reading: Techniques for improving rate in intermediate grades. *Reading Teacher*, *38*(1), 50–53.

Bhattacharya, J. and Petsche, H. (2001). Musicians and the gamma band: A secret affair? *NeuroReport*, *12*(2), 371–374.

Bierman, D. and Winter, O. (1989). Learning during sleep: An indirect test of the erasure theory of dreaming. *Perceptual and Motor Skills*, *69*, 139–144.

Bird, B. L., Newton, F. A., Sheer, D. E. and Ford, M. (1978). Biofeedback training of 40-Hz EEG in humans. *Biofeedback and Self Regulation*, *3*(1), 1–11.

Bloom, B. S. (1956). *Taxonomy of Educational Objectives: The Classification of Educational Goals. Handbook I: Cognitive Domain*. New York: McKay.

Boersma, F. J. and Gagnon, C. (1992). The use of repetitive audiovisual entrainment in the management of chronic pain. *Medical Hypnoanalysis Journal*, *7*(3), 80–97.

Boltwood, C. and Blick, K. A. (1970). The delineation and application of three mnemonic techniques. *Psychonomic Science*, *20*(6), 339–341.

Bond, E. A. (1941). The Yale–Harvard freshmen speed-reading experiment. *School and Society*, *54*, 107–111.

Bornstein, R. F. (1989). Subliminal techniques as propaganda tools: Review and critique. *Journal of Mind and Behaviour*, *10*(3), 231–262.

Bottiroli, S., Cavallini, E. and Vecchi, T. (2007). Long-term effects of memory training in the elderly: A longitudinal study. *Archives of Gerontology and Geriatrics*, *47*(2), 277–289.

Bower, G. H. (1972). A selective review of organizational factors in memory. In E. Tulving and W. Donaldson (eds), *Organization and Memory*. New York: Academic Press.

Bower, G. H. and Clark, M. C. (1969). Narrative stories as mediators for serial learning. *Psychonomic Science*, *14*, 181–182.

Boynton, T. (2001). Applied research using alpha/theta training for enhancing creativity and well-being. *Journal of Neurotherapy*, *5*(1/2), 5–18.

Breznitz, Z. and Share, D. L. (1992). Effects of accelerated reading rate on memory for text. *Journal of Educational Psychology*, *84*, 193–199.

Briggs, G. G., Hawkins, S. and Crovitz, H. F. (1970). Bizarre images in artificial memory. *Psychonomic Science*, *19*(6), 353–354.

Brosgole, L. and Contino, A. F. (1973). Intrusion of subthreshold learning upon later performance. *Psychological Reports*, *32*(2), 795–798.

Brown, D. P. and Engler, J. (1980). The stages of mindfulness meditation: A validation study. *Journal of Transpersonal Psychology*, *12*, 143–192.

Brozo, W. G. and Johns, J. L. (1986). A content and critical analysis of forty speed-reading books. *Journal of Reading*, *30*, 242–247.

Bruce, D. J., Evans, C. R., Fenwick, P. B. C. and Spencer, V. (1970). Effect of presenting novel verbal material during slow-wave sleep. *Nature*, *225*, 873–874.

Budzynski, T. H. and Budzynski, H. K. (2000). Reversing age-related cognitive decline: Use of neurofeedback and audio-visual stimulation. *Biofeedback*, *28*(3), 1–7.

Budzynski, T. H. and Tang, J. (1998). Biolight effects of the EEG. *SynchroMed Report*.

Budzynski, T. H., Jordy, J., Budzynski, H. K., Tang, H. Y. and Claypoole, K. (1999). Academic performance enhancement with photic stimulation and EDR feedback. *Journal of Neurotherapy*, *3*(3/4), 11–21.

Bugelski, B. R., Kidd, E. and Segman, J. (1968). Image as a mediator in one trial of paired-associate learning. *Journal of Experimental Psychology*, *76*(1), 69–73.

Burgess, C. A. and Kirsch, I. (1999). Expectancy information as a moderator of the effects of hypnosis on memory. *Contemporary Hypnosis*, *16*(1), 22–31.

Buzan, T. (1986). *Use your Memory*. London: BBC Books.

Buzan, T. (1997). *The Speed Reading Book*. London: BBC Books.

Cacioppo, J. T., Tassinary, L. G. and Fridlund, A. J. (1990). The skeletomotor system. In J. T. Caccioppo and L. G. Tassinary (eds), *Principles of Psychophysiology*. New York: Cambridge University Press, pp. 325–384.

Cahn, B. R. and Polich, J. (2006). Meditation states and traits: EEG, ERP, and neuroimaging studies. *Psychological Bulletin*, *132*(2), 180–211.

Caird, S. J., McKenzie, A. D. and Sleivert, G. G. (1999). Biofeedback and relaxation techniques improve running economy in sub-elite long distance runners. *Medicine and Science in Sports and Exercise*, *31*(5), 717–722.

Calef, T., Peiper, M. and Coffey, B. (1999). Comparisons of eye movements before and after a speed-reading course. *Journal of the American Optometric Association*, *70*(3), 171–181.

Camp, C. J., Markley, R. P. and Kramer, J. J. (1983). Naive mnemonics: What the 'do nothing' control group does. *American Journal of Psychology*, *96*(4), 503–511.

Campos, A., Amor, A. and Gonzalez, M. A. (2004). The importance of the keyword-generation method in keyword mnemonics. *Experimental Psychology*, *51*(2), 1–7.

Campos, A., Gonzalez, M. A. and Amor, A. (2003). Limitations of the mnemonic-keyword method. *Journal of General Psychology*, *130*(4), 399–413.

Canavero, S. and Bonicalzi, V. (2002). Therapeutic extradural cortical stimulation for central and neuropathic pain: A review. *Clinical Journal of Pain*, *18*(1), 48–55.

Carlson, R. F., Kincaid, J. P., Lance, S. and Hodgson, T. (1976). Spontaneous use of mnemonics and grade point average. *Journal of Psychology, 92*(1), 117–122.

Carney, R. N. and Levin, J. R. (2000a). Mnemonic instruction, with a focus on transfer. *Journal of Educational Psychology, 92*(4), 783–790.

Carney, R. N. and Levin, J. R. (2000b). Fading mnemonic memories: Here's looking anew, again! *Contemporary Educational Psychology, 25*, 499–508.

Carsello, C. J. and Creaser, J. W. (1978). Does transcendental meditation training affect grades? *Journal of Applied Psychology, 63*(5), 644–645.

Carver, R. P. (1970). Effect of a chunked typography on reading rate and comprehension. *Journal of Applied Psychology, 54*(3), 288–296.

Carver, R. P. (1983). Is reading rate constant or flexible? *Reading Research Quarterly, 18*(2), 190–215.

Carver, R. P. (1985). How good are some of the world's best readers? *Reading Research Quarterly, 20*(4), 389–419.

Carver, R. P. (1987). Teaching rapid reading in intermediate grades: Helpful or harmful? *Reading Research Instruction, 26*(2), 65–76.

Carver, R. P. (1992). Reading rate: Theory, research, and practical implications. *Journal of Reading, 36*(2), 84–95.

Champeau de Lopez, C. (1993). Developing reading speed. *English Teaching Forum, 31*(2), 50–51.

Chan, D. and Woollacott, M. (2007). Effects of level of meditation experience on attentional focus: Is the efficacy of executive or orientation networks improved? *Journal of Alternative and Complementary Medicine, 13*(6), 651–657.

Cheesman, J. and Merikle, P. M. (1986). Distinguishing conscious from unconscious processing. *Canadian Journal of Psychology, 40*(4), 343–367.

Chin-Yen, L., Tsung-Hsien, K., Yen-Ku, K., Yen-Lin, K., Li-An, H. and Chien-Ting, L. (2007). Practice makes better? A study of meditation learners in a classroom environment. *Educational Studies, 33*(1), 65–80.

Clark, J. M. and Pavio, A. (1991). Dual coding theory and education. *Educational Psychology Review, 3*(3), 149–210.

Clark, L. V. (1960). Effect of mental practice on the development of a certain motor skill. *Research Quarterly, 31*, 560–569.

Clarys, J. P. and Cabri, J. (1993). Electromyography and the study of sports movements: A review. *Journal of Sports Sciences, 11*(5), 379–448.

Cobb, J. C., Evans, F. J., Gustafson, L. A., O'Connell, D. N., Orne, M. T. and Shor, R. E. (1965). Specific motor response during sleep to sleep-administered meaningful suggestion: An exploratory investigation. *Perceptual and Motor Skills, 20*, 626–636.

Coffman, D. D. (1990). Effects of mental practice, physical practice, and knowledge of results on piano performance. *Journal of Research in Music Education, 38*(3), 187–196.

Cohn, P. J. (1990). Preperformance routines in sport: Theoretical and practical applications. *Sport Psychologist, 4*, 301–312.

Coke, E. U. (1974). The effects of readability on oral and silent reading rates. *Journal of Educational Psychology, 66*, 406–409.

Cook, H. (1985). Effects of subliminal symbiotic gratification and the magic of believing on achievement. *Psychoanalytic Psychology, 2*(4), 365–371.

Cooper, L. M. and Hoskovec, J. (1972). Hypnotic suggestions for learning during Stage I REM sleep. *American Journal of Clinical Hypnosis, 15*(2), 102–111.

Corbett, A. T. (1977). Retrieval dynamics for rote and visual image mnemonics. *Journal of Verbal Learning and Verbal Behaviour*, *16*, 233–246.

Costa, A., Bonaccorsi, M. and Scrimali, T. (1984). Biofeedback and control of anxiety preceding athletic competition. *International Journal of Sport Psychology*, *15*, 98–109.

Crawford, H. J. and Allen, S. N. (1983). Enhanced visual memory during hypnosis as mediated by hypnotic responsiveness and cognitive strategies. *Journal of Experimental Psychology: General*, *112*(4), 662–685.

Crawford, H. J. and Allen, S. N. (1996). Paired associate learning and recall of high and low imagery words: Moderating effects of hypnosis, hypnotic susceptibility level, and visualization abilities. *American Journal of Psychology*, *109*(3), 353–372.

Croce, R. V. (1986). The effects of EMG biofeedback on strength acquisition. *Biofeedback and Self Regulation*, *11*(4), 299–310.

Crovitz, H. F. (1969). Memory loci in artificial memory. *Psychonomic Science*, *16*, 82–83.

Csikszentmihalyi, M. (1990). *Flow: The Psychology of Optimal Experience*. New York: Harper and Row.

Cummings, M. S., Wilson, V. E. and Bird, E. I. (1984). Flexibility development in sprinters using EMG biofeedback and relaxation training. *Biofeedback and Self Regulation*, *9*(3), 395–405.

Davidson, R. J. (2005). Meditation and neuroplasticity: Training your brain. *Journal of Science and Healing*, *1*(5), 380–388.

Davidson, R. J. and Goleman, D. J. (1977). The role of attention in mediation and hypnosis: A psychobiological perspective on transformations of consciousness. *International Journal of Clinical and Experimental Hypnosis*, *58*, 291–308.

Davidson, R. J., Goleman, D. J. and Schwartz, C. E. (1976). Attentional and affective concomitants of meditation: A cross sectional study. *Journal of Abnormal Psychology*, *85*(2), 235–238.

Davidson, R. J., Kabat-Zinn, J., Schumacher, J., Rosenkranz, M., Muller, D., Santorelli, S. F., Urbanowski, F., Harrington, A., Bonus, K. and Sheridan, J. F. (2003). Alterations in brain and immune function produced by mindfulness meditation. *Psychosomatic Medicine*, *65*, 564–570.

Dawson, M. E., Schell, A. M. and Filion, D.L. (2000). The electrodermal system. In J. T. Cacioppo, L. G. Tassinary and G. G. Berntson (eds), *Handbook of Psychophysiology*, 2nd edition. New York: Cambridge University Press.

DePiano, F. A. and Salzberg, H. C. (1981). Hypnosis as an aid to recall of meaningful information presented under three types of arousal. *International Journal of Clinical and Experimental Hypnosis*, *29*, 383–400.

De Vos, H. M. and Louw, D. A. (2006). The effect of hypnotic training programs on the academic performance of students. *American Journal of Clinical Hypnosis*, *49*(2), 101–112.

DeWitt, D. J. (1980). Cognitive and biofeedback training for stress reduction with university students. *Journal of Sport and Exercise Psychology*, *2*(4), 288–294.

Dhanes, T. P. and Lundy, R. M. (1975). Hypnotic and waking suggestions and recall. *International Journal of Clinical and Experimental Hypnosis*, *23*(1), 68–79.

Dinges, D. F., Whitehouse, W. G., Orne, E. C., Powell, J. W., Orne, M. J. and Erdelyi, M. H. (1992). Evaluating hypnotic memory enhancement (hypermnesia and reminiscence) using multitrial forced recall. *Journal of Experimental Psychology: Learning, Memory and Cognition*, *18*(5), 1139–1147.

Doppelmayr, M., Klimesch, W., Hodlmoser, K., Sauseng, P. and Gruber, W. (2005). Intelligence related upper alpha desynchronisation in a semantic memory task. *Brain Research Bulletin, 66,* 171–177.

Dretzke, B. J. and Levin, J. R. (1996). Assessing students' application and transfer of a mnemonic strategy: The struggle for independence. *Contemporary Educational Psychology, 21,* 83–93.

Driskell, J. E., Copper, C. and Moran, A. (1994). Does mental practice enhance performance? *Journal of Applied Psychology, 79*(4), 481–492.

Druckman, D. and Bjork, R. A. (1991). *In the Mind's Eye: Enhancing Human Performance.* Washington, DC: National Academy Press.

Druckman, D. and Swets, J. A. (1988). *Enhancing Human Performance: Issues, Theories, and Techniques.* Washington, DC: National Academy Press.

Dywan, J. (1988). The imagery factor in hypnotic hypermnesia. *International Journal of Clinical and Experimental Hypnosis,* 36, 312–326.

Dywan, J. and Bowers, K. (1983). The use of hypnosis to enhance recall. *Science,* 222, 184–185.

Egner, T. and Gruzelier, J. H. (2001). Learned self-regulation of EEG frequency components affects attention and event-related brain potentials in humans. *NeuroReport, 12*(18), 4155–4159.

Egner, T. and Gruzelier, J. H. (2003). Ecological validity of neurofeedback: Modulation of slow wave EEG enhances musical performance. *NeuroReport, 14*(9), 1221–1224.

Egner, T. and Gruzelier, J. H. (2004). EEG biofeedback of low beta band components: Frequency-specific effects on variables of attention and event-related brain potentials. *Clinical Neurophysiology, 115,* 131–139.

Egner, T., Zech, T. F. and Gruzelier, J. H. (2004). The effects of neurofeedback training on the spectral topography of the healthy electroencephalogram. *Clinical Neurophysiology, 115,* 2452–2460.

Eich, E. (1988). *Learning During Sleep.* Washington, DC: National Academy of Sciences.

Emmons, W. H. and Simon, C. W. (1956). The non-recall of material presented during sleep. *American Journal of Psychology, 69*(1), 76–81.

Evans, F. J., Gustafson, L. A., O'Connell, D. N., Orne, M. J. and Shor, R. E. (1966). Response during sleep with intervening waking amnesia. *Science, 152,* 666–667.

Evans, F. J., Gustafson, L. A., O'Connell, D. N., Orne, M. J. and Shor, R. E. (1970). Verbally induced behavioural responses during sleep. *Journal of Nervous and Mental Disorders, 150,* 171–187.

Fehmi, L. G. and Collura, T. F. (2007). Effects of electrode placement upon EEG biofeedback training: The monopolar–bipolar controversy. *Journal of Neurotherapy, 11*(2), 45–63.

Fehr, T. G. (2006). Transcendental meditation may prevent partial epilepsy. *Medical Hypotheses, 67*(6), 1462–1463.

Feltz, D. and Landers, D. (1983). The effects of mental practice on motor skill learning and performance: A meta-analysis. *Journal of Sport Psychology, 5,* 25–57.

Fergusson, L. C. (1993). Field independence, transcendental meditation, and achievement in college art: A reexamination. *Perceptual and Motor Skills, 77,* 1104–1106.

Fink, A., Grabner, M. B., Benedek, M. and Neubauer, A. C. (2006). Divergent thinking training is related to frontal electroencephalogram alpha synchronization. *European Journal of Neuroscience, 23,* 2241–2246.

Fisher, R. (2006). Still thinking: The case for meditation with children. *Thinking Skills and Creativity*, *1*(2), 149–151.

Fox, B. H. and Robbins, J. S. (1952). The retention of material presented during sleep. *Journal of Experimental Psychology*, *43*, 75–79.

Fox, P. T. and Raichle, M. E. (1985). Stimulus rate determines regional blood flow in striate cortex. *Annals of Neurology*, *17*, 303–305.

Frederick, J. A., Lubar, J. F., Rasey, H. W., Brim, S. A. and Blackburn, J. (1999). Effects of 18.5 auditory and visual stimulation on EEG amplitude at the vertex. *Journal of Neurotherapy*, *3*(3/4), 23–28.

Frederick, J. A., Timmerman, D. L., Russell, H. L. and Lubar, J. F. (2004). EEG coherence effects of audio-visual stimulation (AVS) at dominant and twice dominant alpha frequency. *Journal of Neurotherapy*, *8*(4), 25–42.

Fredrikson, M. and Engel, B. T. (1985). Learned control of heart rate during exercise in patients with borderline hypertension. *European Journal of Applied Physiology*, *54*, 315–320.

French, S. N. (1980). Electromyographic biofeedback for tension control during fine motor skill acquisition. *Biofeedback and Self Regulation*, *5*(2), 221–228.

Fudin, R. (1993). Final comments on Hudesman, Page, and Rautiainen's (1992) subliminal psychodynamic activation experiment. *Perceptual and Motor Skills*, *77*(2), 367–370.

Gable, S. L. and Haidt, J. (2005). What (and why) is positive psychology? *Review of General Psychology*, *9*(2), 103–110.

Gallwey, W. T. (1974). *The Inner Game of Tennis*. New York: Random House.

Garza, D. L. and Feltz, D. L. (1998). Effects of selected mental practice on performance, self-efficacy, and competition confidence of figure skaters. *Sport Psychologist*, *12*, 1–15.

Gauld, A. (1992). *A History of Hypnotism*. Cambridge: Cambridge University Press.

Gazzaniga, M. S., Ivry, R. B. and Mangun, G. R. (2002). *Cognitive Neuroscience: The Biology of the Mind*. New York: Norton.

Gelderloos, P., Goddard, P. H., Ahlstrom, H. H. B. and Jacoby, R. (1987). Cognitive orientation toward positive values in advanced participants of the TM and TM-sidhi program. *Perceptual and Motor Skills*, *64*, 1003–1012.

Gernsback, H. (1911). Ralph 124C 41+. *Modern Electrics*, *4*, 165–168.

Gevins, A. S., Smith, M. E., McEvoy, L. and Yu, D. (1997). High-resolution EEG mapping of cortical activation related to working memory: Effects of task difficulty, type of processing, and practice. *Cerebral Cortex*, *7*, 374–385.

Ghandi, B. and Oakley, D. A. (2005). Does 'hypnosis' by another name smell as sweet? The efficacy of 'hypnotic' inductions depends on the label 'hypnosis'. *Consciousness and Cognition*, *14*, 304–315.

Giray, M. and Ulrich, R. (1993). Motor coactivation revealed by response force in divided and focused attention. *Journal of Experimental Psychology, Human Perception and Performance*, *19*(6), 1278–1291.

Goldstein, D. S., Ross, R. S. and Brady, J. V. (1977). Biofeedback heart rate training during exercise. *Biofeedback and Self Regulation*, *2*(2), 107–125.

Goleman, D. (1972). The Buddha on meditation and states of consciousness, part II: A typology of meditation techniques. *Journal of Transpersonal Psychology*, *4*(2), 151–210.

Goss, S., Hall, C., Buckolz, E. and Fishburne, G. J. (1986). Imagery ability and the acquisition and retention of movements. *Memory and Cognition*, *14*(6), 469–477.

Graf, R. G. (1973). Speed reading: Remember the tortoise. *Psychology Today*, 7(7), 112–113.

Green, D. M. and Swets, J. A. (1966). *Signal Detection Theory and Psychophysics*. New York: Wiley.

Greenwald, A. G., Draine, S. C. and Abrams, R. L. (1996). Three cognitive markers of unconscious semantic activation. *Science*, 273, 1699–1702.

Greenwald, A. G., Spangenberg, E. R., Pratkanis, A. R. and Eskenazi, J. (1991). Doubleblind tests of subliminal self-help audiotapes. *Psychological Science*, 2, 119–122.

Grouios, G. (1992a). Mental practice: A review. *Journal of Sport Behaviour*, 15(1), 42–59.

Grouios, G. (1992b). On the reduction of reaction time with mental practice. *Journal of Sport Behaviour*, 15(2), 141–157.

Grouios, G. (1992c). The effect of mental practice on diving performance. *International Journal of Sport Psychology*, 23, 60–69.

Gruzelier, J. H., Egner, T. and Vernon, D. (2006). Validating the efficacy of neurofeedback for optimising performance. In C. Neuper and W. Klimesch (eds), *Progress in Brain Research*, 159, 421–432.

Hale, B. (1982). The effects of internal and external imagery on muscular and ocular concomitants. *Journal of Sport Psychology*, 4, 379–387.

Hall, P. D. (1999). The effect of meditation on the academic performance of African-American college students. *Journal of Black Studies*, 29(3), 408–415.

Hanslmayr, S., Sauseng, P., Doppelmayr, M., Schabus, M. and Klimesch, W. (2005). Increasing individual upper alpha power by neurofeedback improves cognitive performance in human subjects. *Applied Psychophysiology and Biofeedback*, 30(1), 1–10.

Harris, D. and Robinson, W. (1986). The effects of skill level on EMG activity during internal and external imagery. *Journal of Sport Psychology*, 8, 105–111.

Hashimoto, K., Tokunaga, M., Tatano, H. and Kanezaki, R. (1987). A study on reducing competitive anxiety in sport: The change in pre-competitive state anxiety and the effect of biofeedback training on anxiety. *Journal of Health Science*, 9, 89–96.

Hatfield, B. D., Landers, D. M. and Ray, W. J. (1984). Cognitive processes during self-paced motor performance: An electroencephalographic profile of skilled marksmen. *Journal of Sport Psychology*, 6, 42–59.

Hauck, P. D., Walsh, C. C. and Kroll, N. A. (1976). Visual imagery mnemonics: Common vs. bizarre mental images. *Bulletin of the Psychonomic Society*, 7, 160–162.

Herbert, R. and Tan, G. (2004). Quantitative EEG phase evaluation of transcendental meditation. *Journal of Neurotherapy*, 8(2), 120–121.

Herrmann, C. S. (2001). Human EEG responses to 1–100Hz flicker: Resonance phenomena in visual cortex and their potential correlation to cognitive phenomena. *Experimental Brain Research*, 137, 346–353.

Hiew, C. C. (1995). Hemi-Sync into creativity. *Hemi-Synch Journal*, 13(1), 3–6.

Higbee, K. L. (1979). Recent research on visual mnemonics: Historical roots and educational fruits. *Review of Educational Research*, 49(4), 611–629.

Higbee, K. L. (2001). *Your Memory: How It Works and How to Improve It*. New York: Marlowe.

Hilgard, E. R. (1965). Hypnosis. *Annual Review of Psychology*, 16, 157–180.

Hilgard, E. R. (1979). *Personality and Hypnosis: A Study of Imaginative Involvement*. Chicago, IL: University of Chicago Press.

Hilgard, E. R. (1992). Dissociation and theories of hypnosis. In E. Fromm and M. R. Nash (eds), *Contemporary Hypnosis Research*. New York: Guilford Press, pp. 69–101.

Hill, R. D., Allen, C. and McWhorter, P. (1991). Stories as a mnemonic aid for older learners. *Psychology and Aging*, 6(3), 484–486.

Hill, R. D., Storandt, M. and Simeone, C. (1990). The effects of memory skill training and retrieval incentives on free recall in older learners. *Journal of Gerontology*, 45, 227–232.

Hinshaw, K. (1991). The effects of mental practice on motor skill performance: Critical evaluation and meta-analysis. *Imaginations, Cognition and Personality*, 11, 3–35.

Hobson, J. A. (1989). *Sleep*. New York: Scientific American Library.

Homa, D. (1983). An assessment of two extraordinary speed-readers. *Bulletin of the Psychonomic Society*, 21(2), 123–126.

Hoskovec, J. and Cooper, M. (1969). A critical review of methodology of sleep learning experiments. *Activitas Nervosa Superior*, 2(3), 161–164.

Hudesman, J., Page, W. and Rautiainen, J. (1992). Use of subliminal stimulation to enhance learning mathematics. *Perceptual and Motor Skills*, 74(3), 1219–1224.

Huxley, A. L. (1932). *Brave New World*. New York: Doubleday Doran.

Hyona, J. and Nurminen, A. (2006). Do adult readers know how they read? Evidence from eye movement patterns and verbal reports. *British Journal of Psychology*, 97, 31–50.

Jacobs, G. and Lubar, J. F. (1989). Spectral analysis of the central nervous system effects of the relaxation response elicited by autogenic training. *Behavioural Medicine*, 15, 125–132.

Jacobs, S. B. and Salzberg, H. C. (1987). The effects of posthypnotic performance-enhancing instructions on cognitive-motor performance. *International Journal of Clinical and Experimental Hypnosis*, 35(1), 41–50.

James, R. J. (1987). Comparative effects of different modes of augmented feedback on striate muscle strength scores. Paper presented at the Annual Meeting of the Biofeedback Society of America, Boston.

James, W. (1890). *The Principles of Psychology*. New York: Dover Publications.

Jangid, R. K., Vyas, J. N. and Shukla, T. R. (1988). The effect of the transcendental meditation programme on the normal individuals. *Journal of Personality and Clinical Studies*, 4(2), 145–149.

Jarus, T. and Ratzon, N. Z. (2000). Can you imagine? The effect of mental practice on the acquisition and retention of a motor skill as a function of age. *Occupational Therapy Journal of Research*, 20(3), 163–178.

Jaseja, H. (2005). Meditation may predispose to epilepsy: An insight into the alteration in brain environment induced by meditation. *Medical Hypotheses*, 64, 464–467.

Jaseja, H. (2006). A brief study of a possible relation of epilepsy association with meditation. *Medical Hypotheses*, 66, 1036–1037.

Jaseja, H. (2007). Meditation and epilepsy: The ongoing debate. *Medical Hypotheses*, 68(4), 916–917.

Jasper, H. H. (1958). Report of the committee on methods of clinical examination in electroencephalography. *Electroencephalography and Clinical Neurophysiology*, 10, 370–375.

Jausovec, N. (1996). Differences in EEG alpha activity related to giftedness. *Intelligence*, 23, 159–173.

Jevning, R., Anand, R., Biedebach, M. and Fernando, G. (1996). Effects on regional cerebral blood flow of transcendental meditation. *Physiology and Behaviour*, *59*, 399–402.

Jha, A. P., Krompinger, J. and Baime, M. J. (2007). Mindfulness training modifies subsystems of attention. *Cognitive, Affective, and Behavioural Neuroscience*, *7*(2), 109–119.

Jones, D. H. and Carron, T. J. (1965). Evaluation of a reading development program for scientists and engineers. *Personnel Psychology*, *18*(3), 281–295.

Joyce, M. and Siever, D. (2000). Audio-visual entrainment program as a treatment for behaviour disorders in a school setting. *Journal of Neurotherapy*, *4*(2), 9–25.

Juola, J. F. (1988). The use of computer displays to improve reading comprehension. *Applied Cognitive Psychology*, *2*(1), 87–95.

Just, M. A. and Carpenter, P. A. (1987). *The Psychology of Reading and Language Comprehension*. Needham Heights, MA: Allyn and Bacon.

Kabat-Zinn, J. (2003). Mindfulness based interventions in context: Past, present and future. *Clinical Psychology: Science and Practice*, *10*, 144–158.

Kamiya, J. (1968). Conscious control of brain waves. *Psychology Today*, *1*, 57–60.

Kanfer, R. (1987). Task-specific motivation: An integrative approach to issues of measurement, mechanisms, processes, and determinants. *Journal of Social and Clinical Psychology*, *5*(2), 237–264.

Karino, S., Yumoto, M., Itoh, K., Uno, A., Yamakawa, K., Sekimoto, S. and Kagal, K. (2006). Neuromagnetic responses to binaural beats in human cerebral cortex. *Journal of Neurophysiology*, *96*, 1927–1938.

Karlin, R. (1958). Machines and reading: A review of research. *Clearing House*, *32*, 349–352.

Kavussanu, M., Crews, D. J. and Gill, D. L. (1998). The effects of single versus multiple measures of biofeedback on basketball free throw shooting performance. *Journal of Sport Psychology*, *29*(2), 132–144.

Keele, S. W. (1982). Learning and control of coordinated motor patterns: The programming perspective. In J. A. S. Kelso (ed.), *Human Motor Behavior: An Introduction*. Hillsdale, NJ: LEA, pp. 161–186.

Kelly, B. D. (2008). Meditation, mindfulness, and mental health. *Irish Journal of Psychological Medicine*, *25*(1), 3–4.

Kennerly, R. (1996). An empirical investigation into the effect of beta frequency binaural beat audio signals on four measures of human memory. *Hemi-Synch Journal*, *14*(3), 1–4.

Kennerly, R. (2004). QEEG analysis of binaural beat audio entrainment: A pilot study. *Journal of Neurotherapy*, *8*(2), 122.

Khil'chenko, A. E., Moldavskaya, S. I., Kol'chenko, N. V. and Shevko, G. N. (1965). Investigations of the functional state of the cerebral cortex in people receiving hypnopaedia instruction. *Voprosy Psikhologii*, *11*(4), 133–139.

Kihlstrom, J. F. (1987). The cognitive unconscious. *Science*, 237, 1445–1452.

Kihlstrom, J. F. and McConkey, K. M. (1990). William James and hypnosis: A centennial reflection. *Psychological Science*, *1*, 174–177.

Kilpatrick, J. (1985). Doing mathematics without understanding it: A commentary on Higbee and Kunihira. *Educational Psychologist*, *20*, 65–68.

King, G. and Coney, J. (2006). Short-term effects of meditation versus relaxation on cognitive functioning. *Journal of Transpersonal Psychology*, *38*(2), 200–215.

Klimesch, W. (1999). EEG alpha and theta oscillations reflect cognitive and memory performance: A review and analysis. *Brain Research Reviews, 29*(2–3), 169–195.

Klimesch, W., Schimke, H., Ladurner, G. and Pfurtscheller, G. (1990). Alpha frequency and memory performance. *Psychophysiology, 4*, 381–390.

Konareva, I. N. (2005). Modifications of the EEG frequency pattern in humans related to a single neurofeedback session. *Neurophysiology, 37*(5/6), 388–395.

Konstant, T. (2000). *Successful Speed Reading in a Week*. Oxford: Hodder and Stoughton.

Kosslyn, S. M., Margolis, J. A., Barret, A. M. and Goldknopf, E. J. (1990). Age differences in imagery abilities. *Child Development, 61*, 995–1010.

Kosslyn, S. M., Thompson, W. L., Constantini-Ferrando, M. F., Alpert, N. M. and Spiegel, D. (2000). Hypnotic visual illusion alters color processing in the brain. *American Journal of Psychiatry, 157*, 1279–1284.

Kraemer, D. J., Macrae, C. N., Green, A. E. and Kelly, W. M. (2005). Sound of silence activates auditory cortex. *Nature, 434*, 158.

Krinsky, R. and Krinsky, S. G. (1996). Pegword mnemonic instruction: Retrieval times and long-term memory performance among fifth-grade children. *Contemporary Educational Psychology, 21*, 193–207.

Kugler, J. and Kaumann, A. (1967). The effect of acoustic stimulation during sleep. *Electroencephalography and Clinical Neurophysiology, 22*, 98.

Kuo, A. A. (2001). Does sleep deprivation impair cognitive and motor performance as much as alcohol intoxication? *Journal of Western Medicine, 174*(3), 180.

Kurita, M. (2001). Change in intellectual and physiological functions of 832 persons who learned Kurita's speed reading system for two days. *Journal of International Society of Life Information Science, 19*(1), 47–53.

Kurita, M. (2003). Improvement of the degree of understanding through a five-day class in the beginning level of Kurita's speed reading course. *Journal of International Society of Life Information Science, 21*(2), 464–465.

Lal, S. K., Henderson, R. J., Carter, N., Bath, A., Hart, M. G., Langeluddecke, P. and Hunyor, S. N. (1998). Effect of feedback signal and psychological characteristics on blood pressure self-manipulation capability. *Psychophysiology, 35*(4), 405–412.

Landers, D. M. (1985). Psychophysiological assessment and biofeedback: Applications for athletes in closed-skill sports. In J. H. Sandweiss and S. L. Wolf (eds), *Biofeedback and Sports Sciences*. New York: Plenum Press, pp. 63–105.

Landers, D. M. (1988). Improving motor skills. In D. Druckman and J. A. Swets (eds), *Enhancing Human Performance*. Washington, DC: National Academy Press, pp. 61–101.

Landers, D. M., Petruzzello, S. J., Salazar, W., Crews, D. J., Kubitz, K. A., Gannon, T. L. and Han, M. (1991). The influence of electrocortical biofeedback on performance in pre-elite archers. *Medicine and Science in Sports and Exercise, 23*(1), 123–129.

Landsberger, H. A. (1958). *Hawthorne Revisited*. Ithaca, NY: Cornell University Press.

Lane, J. D., Kasian, S. J., Owens, J. E. and Marsh, G. R. (1998). Binaural auditory beats affect vigilance performance and mood. *Physiology and Behaviour, 63*(2), 249–252.

Lansing, R. W. and Barlow, J. S. (1972). Rhythmic after-activity to flashes in relation to the background alpha which precedes and follows the photic stimuli. *Clinical Neurophysiology, 32*(2), 149–160.

Lasaga, J. I. and Lasaga, A. M. (1973). Sleep learning and progressive blurring of perception during sleep. *Perceptual and Motor Skills, 37*, 51–62.

Lawson, M. J. and Hogben, D. (1998). Learning and recall of foreign language vocabulary: Effects of keyword strategy for immediate and delayed recall. *Learning and Instruction, 8*(2), 179–194.

Lawther, K. S. (1968). *The Learning of Physical Skills*. Englewood Cliffs, NJ: Prentice Hall.

Lazar, S. W., Kerr, C. E., Wasserman, R. H., Gray, J. R., Greeve, D. N., Treadway, M. T. *et al.* (2005). Meditation experience is associated with increased cortical thickness. *Neuroreport, 16*(17), 1893–1897.

Leach, J., Bulpin, K., Rahman, S., Rass, A., Nelson, C., Chamorro-Premuzic, T. and Gruzelier, J. H. (2006). Controlled study of neurofeedback with novice singers. Paper presented at the Society of Applied Neuroscience, Swansea, Wales, 19–26 September.

Ledford, B. R., Robison, L., Miller, T. and Wright, C. D. (1988). The effects of preconscious visual symbolic and linguistic cues upon the academic achievement of college students. *Imagination, Cognition and Personality, 7*(3), 251–264.

Lee, C. (1990). Psyching up for a muscular endurance task: Effects of image content on performance and mood state. *Journal of Sport and Exercise Psychology, 12*, 66–73.

Lehrl, S. and Fischer, B. (1990). A basic information psychological parameter (BP) for the reconstruction of concepts of intelligence. *European Journal of Personality, 4*, 259–286.

Lejeune, M., Decker, C. and Sanchez, X. (1994). Mental rehearsal in table tennis performance. *Perceptual and Motor Skills, 79*, 627–641.

LeShan, L. (1942). The breaking of habit by suggestion during sleep. *Journal of Abnormal and Social Psychology, 37*, 406–408.

Leuba, C. and Bateman, D. (1952). Learning during sleep. *American Journal of Psychology, 65*, 301–302.

Levin, J. R., Morrison, C. R., McGivern, J. E., Mastropieri, M. A. and Scruggs, T. E. (1986). Mnemonic facilitation of text-embedded science facts. *American Educational Research Journal, 23*(3), 489–506.

Levin, J. R., Pressley, M., McComick, C. B., Miller, G. E. and Schriberg, L. K. (1979). Assessing the classroom potential of the keyword method. *Journal of Educational Psychology, 71*, 583–594.

Levin, M. E. and Levin, J. R. (1990). Scientific mnemonomies: Methods for maximizing more than memory. *American Educational Research Journal, 27*, 301–321.

Levy, C. M., Coolidge, F. I. and Staab, L. C. (1972). Paired associate learning during EEG defined sleep: A preliminary study. *Australian Journal of Psychology, 24*(2), 219–225.

Lewis, S. A. (1968). Learning while asleep. *Bulletin of the British Psychological Society, 21*, 23–26.

Lieber, R. L. (2002). *Skeletal Muscle Structure, Function and Plasticity: The Physiological Basis of Rehabilitation*, 2nd edition. Pittsburgh, PA: Lippincott Williams and Wilkins.

Liebert, R. M., Rubin, N. and Hilgard, E. R. (1965). The effects of suggestions of alertness in hypnosis on paired-associate learning. *Journal of Personality, 33*(4), 605–612.

Lim, S. and Lippman, L. G. (1991). Mental practice and memorization of piano music. *Journal of General Psychology, 118*(1), 21–30.

Linden, C. A., Uhley, J. E., Smith, D. and Bush, M. A. (1989). The effects of mental practice on walking balance in an elderly population. *Occupational Therapy Journal of Research*, 9(3), 155–169.

Lofflin, J. (1988). Help from the hidden persuaders. *New York Times*, 20 March.

Lubar, J. F. and Shouse, M. N. (1976). EEG and behavioural changes in a hyperkinetic child concurrent with training of the sensorimotor rhythm (SMR): A preliminary report. *Biofeedback and Self Regulation*, 1(3), 293–306.

Lutz, A., Greischar, L. L., Rawlings, N. B., Ricard, M. and Davidson, R. (2004). Long-term meditators self-induce high amplitude gamma synchrony during mental practice. *Proceedings of the National Academy of Science, USA*, 101(46), 16369–16373.

McCarty, D. L. (1980). Investigation of a visual imagery mnemonic device for acquiring face–name associations. *Journal of Experimental Psychology: Learning, Memory and Cognition*, 6(2), 145–155.

McConkie, G. W., Raynor, K. and Wilson, S. J. (1973). Experimental manipulation of reading strategies. *Journal of Educational Psychology*, 65, 1–8.

McDaniel, M. A. and Pressley, M. (1984). Putting the keyword method in context. *Journal of Educational Psychology*, 76, 598–609.

Machida, K. and Carlson, J. (1984). Effects of verbal mediation strategy on cognitive processes in mathematics learning. *Journal of Educational Psychology*, 76(6), 1382–1385.

McNamara, D. S. (2000). Preliminary analysis of photoreading (No. NAG2–1319). NASA Ames Research Center.

Mahoney, M., Gabriel, T. and Perkins, T. (1987). Psychological skills and exceptional athletic performance. *Sport Psychologist*, 1, 181–199.

Mandler, G., Nakamura, Y. and Van Zandt, B. J. (1987). Nonspecific effects of exposure on stimuli that cannot be recognised. *Journal of Experimental Psychology: Learning, Memory and Cognition*, 13, 646–648.

Marcel, A. J. (1983). Conscious and unconscious perception: Experiments on visual masking and word recognition. *Cognitive Psychology*, 15, 197–237.

Marks, D. F. (1977). Imagery and consciousness: A theoretical review from an individual differences perspective. *Journal of Mental Imagery*, 2(2), 275–290.

Martin, K. and Hall, C. (1995). Using mental imagery to enhance intrinsic motivation. *Journal of Sport and Exercise Psychology*, 17, 54–69.

Martindale, C. and Armstrong, J. (1974). The relationship of creativity to cortical activation and its operant control. *Journal of Genetic Psychology*, 124, 311–320.

Martindale, C. and Hines, D. (1975). Creativity and cortical activation during creative, intellectual and EEG feedback tasks. *Biological Psychology*, 3, 91–100.

Mau, W. and Lynn, R. (2001). Gender differences on the Scholastic Aptitude Test, the American College Test and college grades. *Educational Psychology*, 21, 133–136.

Maxwell, M. J. (1973). Cognitive aspects of skimming: Evidence and implications. *Reading World*, 12(4), 229–238.

Mayer, B. and Merckelbach, H. (1999). Unconscious processes, subliminal stimulation, and anxiety. *Clinical Psychology Review*, 19(5), 571–590.

Merikle, P. M. (1988). Subliminal auditory messages: An evaluation. *Psychology and Marketing*, 5(4), 355–372.

Merikle, P. M. and Daneman, M. (1998). Psychological investigations of unconscious perception. *Journal of Consciousness Studies*, 5(1), 5–18.

Merzenich, M., Nelson, R. J., Stryker, M. P., Cynader, M. S., Schoppmann, A. and Zook, J. M. (1984). Somatosensory cortical map changes following digit amputation in adult monkeys. *Journal of Comparative Neurology*, *224*, 591–605.

Meyers, A., Cooke, C., Cullen, J. and Liles, L. (1979). Psychological aspects of athletic competitors: A replication across sports. *Cognitive Therapy and Research*, *3*, 361–366.

Middleton, A. E. (1885). *All about Mnemonics*. London: Simpkins (chapters available at: http://stepanov.lk.net/mnemo/all3e.html).

Miller, G. R. and Coleman, E. G. (1972). The measurement of reading speed and the obligation to generalise to a population of reading material. *Journal of Reading Behaviour*, *3*, 48–56.

Mollen, J. D. (1998). *Acquisition and Processing of Information During States of REM Sleep and Slow-Wave Sleep*. Cambridge: Cambridge University, Department of Experimental Psychology.

Moore, T. M. (1992). Subliminal perception: Facts and fallacies. *Skeptical Inquirer*, *16*, 273–281.

Moore, T. M. (1995). Subliminal self-help auditory tapes: An empirical test of perceptual consequences. *Canadian Journal of Behavioural Science*, *27*(1), 9–20.

Morasky, R. L., Reynolds, C. and Sowell, L. E. (1983). Generalization of lowered EMG levels during musical performance following biofeedback. *Biofeedback and Self Regulation*, *8*(2), 207–216.

Morris, P. E., Fritz, C. O., Jackson, L., Nichol, E. and Roberts, E. (2005). Strategies for learning proper names: Expanding retrieval practice, meaning and imagery. *Applied Cognitive Psychology*, *19*, 779–798.

Moses, J., Clemens, W. J. and Brene, J. (1986). Bidirectional voluntary heart rate control during static muscular exercise: Metabolic and respiratory correlates. *Psychophysiology*, *23*(5), 510–520.

Murphy, S. M. (1994). Imagery interventions in sport. *Medicine and Science in Sports and Exercise*, *26*(4), 486–494.

Murphy, S. T. and Zajonc, R. B. (1993). Affect, cognition and awareness: Affective priming with optimal and suboptimal stimulus exposures. *Journal of Personality and Social Psychology*, *64*, 723–739.

Natale, J. (1988). Are you open to suggestion? *Psychology Today*, *2*, 28–30.

Noel, R. (1980). The effect of visuo-motor behaviour rehearsal on tennis performance. *Journal of Sport Psychology*, *2*, 220–226.

Nogrady, H., McConkey, K. M. and Perry, C. (1985). Enhancing visual memory: Trying hypnosis, trying imagination, and trying again. *Journal of Abnormal and Social Psychology*, *94*(2), 195–204.

Norman, D. A. and Bobrow, D. B. (1975). On data-limited and resource-limited processes. *Cognitive Psychology*, *7*, 44–64.

Norris, P. (1986). Biofeedback, voluntary control, and human potential. *Biofeedback and Self Regulation*, *11*(1), 1–20.

Olmstead, R. (2005). Use of auditory and visual stimulation to improve cognitive abilities in learning-disabled children. *Journal of Neurotherapy*, *9*(2), 49–61.

Orlick, T. and Partington, J. (1988). Mental links to excellence. *Sport Psychology*, *2*, 105–130.

Orme-Johnson, D. (2006). Evidence that the transcendental meditation program prevents or decreases diseases of the nervous system and is specifically beneficial for epilepsy. *Medical Hypotheses*, *67*, 240–246.

Oster, G. (1973). Auditory beats in the brain. *Scientific American, 229*(4), 94–102.

Oswald, I., Taylor, A. M. and Treisman, M. (1960). Discriminative responses to stimulation during human sleep. *Brain, 83*, 440–453.

Pan, W., Zhang, L. and Xia, Y. (1994). The difference in EEG theta waves between concentrative and non-concentrative qigong states: Power spectrum and topographic mapping study. *Journal of Traditional Chinese Medicine, 14*, 212–218.

Parker, K. A. (1982). Effects of subliminal symbiotic stimulation on academic performance: Further evidence on the adaptation-enhancing effects of oneness fantasies. *Journal of Counselling Psychology, 29*(1), 19–28.

Parks, P. (1997). Psychophysiologic self-awareness training: Integration of scientific and humanistic principles. *Journal of Humanistic Psychology, 37*(2), 67–113.

Pates, J., Cummings, A. and Maynard, I. (2002). The effects of hypnosis on flow states and three-point shooting performance in basketball players. *Sport Psychologist, 16*, 34–47.

Pates, J., Oliver, R. and Maynard, I. (2001). The effects of hypnosis on flow states and golf-putting performance. *Journal of Applied Sport Psychology, 13*, 341–354.

Patton, G. W. R. (1994). Testing the efficacy of name mnemonics during conversation. *Psychological Reports, 75*, 131–142.

Peigneux, P., Laureys, S., Delbeuck, X. and Maquet, P. (2001). Sleeping brain, learning brain: The role of sleep for memory systems. *Neuroreport, 12*(18), 111–124.

Pelletier, K. R. (1974). Influence of transcendental meditation upon autokinetic perception. *Perceptual and Motor Skills, 39*(3), 1031–1034.

Peper, E. and Schmid, A. B. (1984). The use of electrodermal biofeedback for peak performance training. *Somatics, 4*(3), 16–18.

Perrott, D. R. and Nelson, M. A. (1969). Limits for the detection of binaural beats. *Journal of the Acoustical Society of America, 46*, 1477–1481.

Persinger, M. A. (1984). People who report religious experiences may also display enhanced temporal-lobe signs. *Perceptual and Motor Skills, 58*(3), 963–975.

Persinger, M. A. (1993). Transcendental meditation (TM) and general meditation are associated with enhanced complex partial epileptic-like signs: Evidence for cognitive kindling. *Perceptual and Motor Skills, 76*(1), 80–82.

Perski, A. and Engel, B. T. (1980). The role of behavioural conditioning in the cardiovascular adjustment to exercise. *Biofeedback and Self Regulation, 5*(1), 91–104.

Perski, A., Tzankoff, S. P. and Engel, B. T. (1985). Central control of cardiovascular adjustments to exercise. *Journal of Applied Physiology, 58*(2), 431–435.

Petruzzello, S. J., Landers, D. M. and Salazar, W. (1991). Biofeedback and sport/exercise performance: Applications and limitations. *Behaviour Therapy, 22*, 379–392.

Petsche, H., Richter, P., von Stein, A., Etlinger, S. C. and Filz, O. (1993). EEG coherence and musical thinking. *Music Perception, 11*(1), 117–151.

Poetzl, O. (1960). The relationship between experimentally induced dream images and indirect vision. *Psychological Issues, 2*, 46–106 (originally published 1917).

Powell, G. (1973). Negative and positive mental practice in motor skill acquisition. *Perceptual and Motor Skills, 37*, 312.

Pratkanis, A. R. (1992). The cargo-cult science of subliminal persuasion. *Skeptical Inquirer, 16*, 260–272.

Pratkanis, A. R., Eskenazi, J. and Greenwald, A. G. (1994). What you expect is what you believe (but not necessarily what you get): A test of the effectiveness of subliminal self-help audiotapes. *Basic and Applied Social Psychology, 15*(3), 251–276.

Pressley, M. and Dennis-Rounds, J. (1980). Transfer of mnemonic keyword strategy at two age levels. *Journal of Educational Psychology, 72*, 575–582.

Pressley, M. and Levin, J. R. (1978). Developmental constraints associated with children's use of the keyword method of foreign language vocabulary learning. *Journal of Experimental Child Psychology, 26*, 359–372.

Pressley, M., Levin, J. R. and Delaney, H. D. (1982). The mnemonic keyword method. *Review of Educational Research, 52*(1), 61–91.

Pressley, M., Levin, J. R. and Miller, G. E. (1982). The keyword method compared to alternative vocabulary-learning strategies. *Contemporary Educational Psychology, 7*, 50–60.

Privette, G. (1983). Peak experience, peak performance, and flow: A comparative analysis of positive human experiences. *Journal of Personality and Social Psychology, 45*(6), 1361–1368.

Randerson, J. (2008). One in five admit using brain drugs. *The Guardian*, April 10th, p. 10.

Rasey, H. W., Lubar, J. F., McIntyre, A., Zoffuto, A. C. and Abbott, P. L. (1996). EEG biofeedback for the enhancement of attentional processing in normal college students. *Journal of Neurotherapy, 1*(3), 15–21.

Raugh, M. R. and Atkinson, R. C. (1975). A mnemonic method for the learning of a second language vocabulary. *Journal of Educational Psychology, 67*(1), 1–16.

Rawlings, E. I., Rawlings, I. L., Chen, S. S. and Yilk, M. D. (1972). The facilitating effects of mental rehearsal in the acquisition of rotary pursuit tracking. *Psychonomic Science, 26*, 71–73.

Raymond, J., Sajid, I., Parkinson, L. and Gruzelier, J. H. (2005). Biofeedback and dance performance: A preliminary investigation. *Applied Psychophysiology and Biofeedback, 30*(1), 65–73.

Rayner, K. and Duffy, S. A. (1986). Lexical complexity and fixation times in reading effects of word-frequency, verb complexity, and lexical ambiguity. *Memory and Cognition, 14*(3), 191–201.

Regan, D. (1989). *Human Brain Electrophysiology: Evoked Potential and Evoked Magnetic Fields in Science and Medicine*. New York: Elsevier.

Register, P. A. and Kihlstrom, J. F. (1987). Hypnotic effects on hypermnesia. *International Journal of Clinical and Experimental Hypnosis, 35*, 155–179.

Richardson, A. (1967a). Mental practice: A review and discussion. *Research Quarterly, 38*, 95–107.

Richardson, A. (1967b). Mental practice: A review and discussion, part II. *Research Quarterly, 38*(2), 263–273.

Richardson, A. and McAndrew, F. (1990). The effects of photic stimulation and private self-consciousness on the complexity of visual imagination imagery. *British Journal of Psychology, 81*(3), 381–394.

Robazza, C. and Bortoli, L. (1994). Hypnosis in sport: An isomorphic model. *Perceptual and Motor Skills, 79*, 963–973.

Robinson, A. J. and Snyder-Mackler, L. (1995). *Clinical Electrophysiology: Electrotherapy and Electrophysiologic Testing*. Pittsburgh, PA: Lippincott, Williams and Wilkins.

Robinson, F. P. (1934). The tachistoscope as a measure of reading perception. *American Journal of Psychology, 46*(1), 132–135.

Roediger, H. L. and McDermott, K. B. (1993). Implicit memory in normal human

254 *References*

subjects. In F. Boller and J. Grafman (eds), *Handbook of Neuropsychology, Volume 8*. New York: Elsevier, pp. 63–131.

Roland, P., Larsen, N. and Skinhoj, E. (1981). Supplementary motor area and other cortical areas in organisation of voluntary movements in man. *Journal of Neurophysiology*, *43*, 118–136

Rosenfeld, J. P., Reinhart, A. M. and Srivastava, S. (1997). The effects of alpha (10 Hz) and beta (22 Hz) entrainment stimulation on the alpha and beta EEG bands: Individual differences are critical to prediction of effects. *Applied Psychophysiology and Biofeedback*, *22*(1), 3–20.

Rosenthal, B. G. (1944). Hypnotic recall of material learner under anxiety and non-anxiety-producing conditions. *Journal of Experimental Psychology*, *34*, 369–389.

Ross, S. L. (1985). The effectiveness of mental practice in improving the performance of college trombonists. *Journal of Research in Music Education*, *33*(4), 221–230.

Rossiter, T. R. and LaVaque, T. J. (1995). A comparison of EEG biofeedback and psychostimulants in treating attention deficit hyperactivity disorders. *Journal of Neurotherapy*, *1*(1), 48–59.

Roth, M., Decety, J., Raybaudi, M., Massarelli, R., Delon-Martin, C., Segebarth, C., Morand, S., Germingani, A., Decorps, M. and Jeannerod, M. (1996). Possible involvement of primary motor cortex in mentally simulated movement: A functional magnetic resonance imaging study. *NeuroReport*, *7*, 1280–1284.

Rubin, G. S. and Turano, K. (1992). Reading without saccadic eye movements. *Vision Research*, *32*, 895–902.

Rummel, N., Levin, J. R. and Woodward, M. W. (2003). Do pictorial mnemonic text-learning aids give students something worth writing about? *Journal of Educational Psychology*, *95*(2), 327–334.

Russell, T. G., Rowe, W. and Smouse, A. D. (1991). Subliminal self-help tapes and academic achievement: An evaluation. *Journal of Counselling and Development*, *69*, 359–362.

Ruuskanen-Utoi, H. and Salmi, T. (1994). Epileptic seizure induced by a product marketed as a brainwave synchronizer. *Neurology*, *44*(1), 180–181.

Ryan, E. D. and Simons, J. (1983). What is learned in mental practice of motor skills? A test of the cognitive-motor hypothesis. *Journal of Sport Psychology*, *5*(4), 419–426.

Ryan, E. D., Blakeslee, T. and Furst, D. M. (1986). Mental practice and motor skill learning: An indirect test of the neuromuscular feedback hypothesis. *International Journal of Sport Psychology*, *17*(1), 60–70.

Sabourin, M. and Rioux, S. (1979). Effects of active and passive EMG biofeedback training on performance of motor and cognitive tasks. *Perceptual and Motor Skills*, *49*, 831–835.

Sackett, R. S. (1934). The influence of symbolic rehearsal upon the retention of a maze habit. *Journal of General Psychology*, *10*, 376–398.

Sackett, R. S. (1935). The relationship between amount of symbolic rehearsal and retention of a maze habit. *Journal of General Psychology*, *13*, 113–130.

St Louis, E. K. and Lansky, E. P. (2006). Meditation and epilepsy: A still hung jury. *Medical Hypotheses*, *67*, 247–250.

Salazar, W., Landers, D. M., Petruzzello, S. J., Myungwoo, H., Crews, D. J. and Kubitz, K. A. (1990). Hemispheric asymmetry, cardiac response, and performance in elite archers. *Research Quarterly for Exercise and Sport*, *61*(4), 351–359.

Sappey-Marinier, D., Calabrese, G., Fein, G., Hugg, J. W., Biggins, C. and Weiner,

M. W. (1992). Effect of photic stimulation on human visual cortex lactate and phosphates using 1H and 31P magnetic resonance spectroscopy. *Journal of Cerebral Blood Flow and Metabolism, 12*(4), 584–592.

Savoy, C. and Beitel, P. (1996). Mental imagery for basketball. *International Journal of Sport Psychology, 27*, 454–462.

Scheele, P. R. (1993). *The PhotoReading Whole Mind System.* Wayzata, MN: Learning Strategies.

Schindler, A. F. and Poo, M. (2000). The neurotrophin hypothesis for synaptic plasticity. *Trends in Neurosciences, 23*(12), 639–645.

Schreiber, E. H. (1991). Using hypnosis to improve performance of college basketball players. *Perceptual and Motor Skills, 72*, 536–538.

Schultz, R. B., Etnyre, B., McArther, J. M. and Brelsford, J. W. (1987). Effects of electromyographic biofeedback on reaction time and movement time. *Perceptual and Motor Skills, 65*(3), 855–859.

Schwab, K., Ligges, C., Jungmann, T., Hilgenfeld, B., Haueisen, J. and Witte, H. (2006). Alpha entrainment in human electroencephalogram and magnetoencephalogram recordings. *Neuroreport, 17*(17), 1829–1833.

Schwartz, M. S. and Andrasik, F. (2003). *Biofeedback: A Practitioner's Guide,* 3rd edition. London: Guilford Press.

Schwarz, D. W. F. and Taylor, P. (2005). Human auditory steady state responses to binaural and monaural beats. *Clinical Neurophysiology, 116*, 658–668.

Seligman, M. E. P. (1990). *Learned Optimism.* New York: Knopf.

Seligman, M. E. P. and Csikszentmihalyi, M. (2000). Positive psychology: An introduction. *American Psychologist, 55*(1), 5–14.

Senter, R. J. and Hoffman, R. R. (1976). Bizarreness as a nonessential variable in mnemonic imagery: A confirmation. *Bulletin of Psychonomic Society, 7*, 163–164.

Shanks, D. R. and Cameron, A. (2000). The effect of mental practice on performance in a sequential reaction time task. *Journal of Motor Behaviour, 32*(3), 305–313.

Shapiro, S. L. and Walsh, R. (1984). *Meditation: Classical and Contemporary Perspectives.* New York: Aldine.

Sharp, H. C. (1959). Effect of subliminal cues on test results. *Journal of Applied Psychology, 43*(6), 369–371.

Sheehan, P. W. (1988). Memory distortion in hypnosis. *International Journal of Clinical and Experimental Hypnosis, 36*, 296–311.

Shields, I. W. and Knox, V. J. (1986). Level of processing as a determinant of hypnotic hypermnesia. *Journal of Abnormal and Social Psychology, 95*(4), 358–364.

Shor, R. E. and Orne, E. C. (1962). *Harvard Group Scale of Hypnotic Susceptibility, Form A.* Palo Alto, CA: Consulting Psychologists Press.

Silverman, L. H. (1983). Subliminal psychodynamic activation: Overview and comprehensive listing of studies. In J. Masling (ed.), *Empirical Studies of Psychoanalytic Theories, Volume 1.* Hillsdale, NJ: Erlbaum, pp. 69–100.

Simon, C. W. and Emmons, W. H. (1956). Responses to material presented during various levels of sleep. *Journal of Experimental Psychology, 51*, 89–97.

Slagter, H. A., Lutz, A., Greischar, L. L., Francis, A. D., Nieuwenhuis, S., Davis, J. M. and Davidson, R. J. (2007). Mental training affects distribution of limited brain resources. *PLoS Biology, 5*(6), 1228–1235.

Smith, H. P. and Tate, T. R. (1953). Improvements in reading rate and comprehension of subjects training with the tachistoscope. *Journal of Educational Psychology, 44*(3), 176–184.

Smyth, M. M. (1975). The role of mental practice in skill acquisition. *Journal of Motor Behaviour*, 7, 199–206.

Spache, G. D. (1962). Is this a breakthrough in reading? *Reading Teacher*, 15, 258–263.

Spangenberg, E. R., Obermiller, C. and Greenwald, A. G. (1992). A field test of subliminal self-help audiotapes: The power of expectancies. *Journal of Public Policy and Marketing*, 11, 26–36.

Spanos, N. P. (1992). Compliance and reinterpretation in hypnotic responding. *British Journal of Experimental and Clinical Hypnosis*, 9(1), 7–15.

Spiegel, H. and Spiegel, D. (1987). *Trance and Treatment: Clinical Uses of Hypnosis.* Washington, DC: American Psychiatric Press.

Start, K. B. and Richardson, A. (1964). Imagery and mental practice. *British Journal of Educational Psychology*, 34, 280–284.

Stephens, J. H., Harris, A. H., Brady, J. V. and Shaffer, J. W. (1975). Psychological and physiological variables associated with large magnitude voluntary heart rate changes. *Psychophysiology*, 12(4), 381–387.

Sterman, M. B. and Friar, L. (1972). Suppression of seizures in an epileptic following sensorimotor EEG feedback training. *Electroencephalography and Clinical Neurophysiology*, 33(1), 89–95.

Stevens, G. L. and Orem, R. C. (1967). Characteristic reading techniques of rapid readers. *Reading Teacher*, 17, 102–108.

Striano, S., Meo, R., Bilo, L., Ruosi, P., Soricellis, M., Estraneo, A. and Caporella, A. (1992). The use of EEG activating procedures in epileptology. *Acta Neurologica*, 14, 275–289.

Suinn, R. M. (1997). Mental practice in sport psychology: Where have we been, where do we go? *Clinical Psychology: Science and Practice*, 4(3), 189–207.

Taguchi, K. (2006). Should the keyword method be introduced in tertiary foreign language classrooms? *Electronic Journal of Foreign Language Teaching*, 3(1), 22–38.

Taktek, K. (2004). The effects of mental imagery on the acquisition of motor skills and performance: A literature review with theoretical implications. *Journal of Mental Imagery*, 28(1), 79–114.

Tang, Y., Ma, Y., Wang, J., Fan, Y., Feng, S., Lu, Q., Yu, Q., Sui, D., Rothbart, M. K., Fan, M. and Posner, M. I. (2007). Short-term meditation training improves attention and self-regulation. *Proceedings of the National Academy of Sciences*, 104(43), 17152–17156.

Tani, K. and Yoshi, N. (1970). Efficiency of verbal learning during sleep as related to the EEG pattern. *Brain Research*, 17, 277–285.

Tansey, M. A. (1993). Ten-year stability of EEG biofeedback results for hyperactive boy who failed fourth grade perceptually impaired class. *Biofeedback and Self Regulation*, 18(1), 33–44.

Tansey, M. A. and Bruner, R. L. (1983). EMG and EEG biofeedback training in the treatment of a 10-year-old hyperactive boy with a developmental reading disorder. *Biofeedback and Self Regulation*, 8(1), 25–37.

Tellegen, A. and Atkinson, G. (1974). Openness to absorbing and self-altering experiences ('absorption'), a trait related to hypnotic susceptibility. *Journal of Abnormal Psychology*, 83(3), 268–277.

Teplan, M. and Stolc, S. (2006). Short-term effects of audio-visual stimulation on EEG. *Measurement Science Review*, 6(2), 67–70.

Theiler, A. M. and Lippman, L. G. (1995). Effects of mental practice and modeling on guitar and vocal performance. *Journal of General Psychology*, 122(4), 329–343.

Theus, K. T. (1994). Subliminal advertising and the psychology of processing unconscious stimuli: A review of research. *Psychology and Marketing, 11*(3), 271–290.

Tilley, A. J. (1979). Sleep learning during Stage 2 and REM sleep. *Biological Psychology, 9*, 155–161.

Timmerman, D. L., Lubar, J. F., Rasey, H. W. and Frederick, J. A. (1999). Effects of dominant and twice-dominant alpha audiovisual stimulation on the cortical EEG. *International Journal of Psychophysiology, 32*, 55–61.

Toman, J. (1941). Flicker potentials and the alpha rhythm in man. *Journal of Neurophysiology, 4*, 51–61.

Twining, W. E. (1949). Mental practice and physical practice in learning a motor skill. *Research Quarterly, 20*, 432–435.

Uldo, W. and Berg, E. (2007). Brain wave synchronization and entrainment to periodic acoustic stimuli. *Neuroscience Letters, 424*(1), 55–60.

Underwood, B. J. (1972). Are we overloading memory? In A. Melton and E. Martin (eds), *Coding Processes in Human Memory*. New York: Wiley, 1–23.

Ungerleider, S. and Golding, J. (1991). Mental practice among Olympic athletes. *Perceptual and Motor Skills, 72*, 1007–1017.

Valentine, E. R. and Sweet, P. G. (1999). Meditation and attention: A comparison of the effects of concentrative and mindfulness meditation on sustained attention. *Mental Health, Religion and Culture, 2*(1), 59–70.

Vandell, R. A., Davis, R. A. and Clugston, H. A. (1943). The function of mental practice in the acquisition of motor skills. *Journal of General Psychology, 29*, 243–250.

Vernon, D. (2005). Can neurofeedback training enhance performance? An evaluation of the evidence with implications for future research. *Applied Psychophysiology and Biofeedback, 30*(4), 347–364.

Vernon, D. (2008). Neurofeedback: Using computer technology to alter brain functioning. In F. Orsucci and N. Sala (eds), *Reflexing Interfaces: The Complex Coevolution of Information Technology Ecosystems*. New York: IGI Press, pp. 94–108.

Vernon, D. and Gruzelier, J. H. (2008). Electroencephalographic biofeedback as a mechanism to alter mood, creativity and artistic performance. In B. N. DeLuca (ed.), *Mind–Body and Relaxation Research Focus*. New York: Nova Science.

Vernon, D., Ahmed, F. and Gruzelier, J. H. (2004). The effect of low-beta EEG biofeedback training on cognitive performance: A null result. Paper presented at the International Society for Neuronal Regulation, Winterthur, Switzerland, 24–28 February.

Vernon, D., Egner, T., Cooper, N., Compton, T., Neilands, C., Sheri, A. and Gruzelier, J. H. (2003). The effect of training distinct neurofeedback protocols on aspects of cognitive performance. *International Journal of Psychophysiology, 47*(1), 75–85.

von Gizycki, H., Jean-Louis, G., Snyder, M., Zizi, F., Green, H., Froanconeri, S., Gaglio, J., Troia, S., Speilman, A., Nunes, J. and Taub, H. (1997). Photic stimulation produces a hypnogogic state. *Sleep Research, 26*, 269.

von Gizycki, H., Jean-Louis, G., Snyder, M., Zizi, F., Green, H., Giuliano, V., Speilman, A. and Taub, H. (1998). The effects of photic driving on mood states. *Journal of Psychosomatic Research, 44*, 599–604.

von Stein, A. and Sarnthein, J. (2000). Different frequencies for different scales of cortical integration from local gamma to long range alpha/theta synchronisation. *International Journal of Psychophysiology*, *38*, 301–313.

Wachholtz, A. B. and Pargament, K. I. (2005). Is spirituality a critical ingredient of meditation? Comparing the effects of spiritual meditation, secular meditation, and relaxation on spiritual, psychological, cardiac, and pain outcomes. *Journal of Behavioural Medicine*, *28*(4), 369–384.

Wadhwani, S., Radvanski, D. C. and Carmody, D. P. (1998). Neurofeedback training in a case of attention deficit hyperactivity disorder. *Journal of Neurotherapy*, *3*(1), 42–49.

Wagner, M. J. (1975). Effect of music and biofeedback on alpha brainwave rhythms and attentiveness of musicians and non-musicians. *Journal of Research in Music Education*, *23*(1), 3–13.

Wagstaff, G. F. (1991). Compliance, belief and semantics in hypnosis: A non-state sociocognitive perspective. In S. J. Lynn and J. W. Rhue (eds), *Theories of Hypnosis: Current Models and Perspectives*. New York: Guilford Press, 362–398.

Wagstaff, G. F., Brunas-Wagstaff, J., Cole, J., Knapton, L., Winterbottom, J., Crean, V. and Wheatcroft, J. (2004). Facilitating memory with hypnosis, focused meditation, and eye closure. *International Journal of Clinical and Experimental Hypnosis*, *52*, 434–455.

Wahbeh, H., Calabrese, C., Zwicky, H. and Zajdel, D. (2007). Binaural beat technology in humans: A pilot study to assess neuropsychologic, physiologic, and electroencephalographic effects. *Journal of Alternative and Complementary Medicine*, *13*(2), 199–206.

Walker, J. E., Norman, C. A. and Weber, R. K. (2002). Impact of qEEG-guided coherence training for patients with a mild closed head injury. *Journal of Neurotherapy*, *6*(2), 31–43.

Wallace, W. H., Turner, S. H. and Perkins, C. C. (1957). *Preliminary Studies of Human Information Storage*. University of Pennsylvania, Signal Corps Project No. 1320, Institute for Cooperative Research.

Wang, A. Y. and Thomas, M. H. (1995). Effect of keywords on long-term retention: Help or hindrance? *Journal of Educational Psychology*, *87*(3), 468–475.

Wang, A. Y., Thomas, M. H. and Ouellette, J. A. (1992). Keyword mnemonic and retention of second-language vocabulary words. *Journal of Educational Psychology*, *84*, 520–528.

Wechsler, D. (1931). The incidence and significance of fingernail biting in children. *Psychoanalytical Review*, *18*, 201–209.

Weinberg, R. S. (1982). The relationship between mental preparation strategies and motor performance: A review and critique. *Quest*, *33*, 195–213.

Weitzenhoffer, A. M. and Hilgard, E. R. (1962). *Stanford Hypnotic Susceptibility Scale, Form C*. Palo Alto, CA: Consulting Psychologists Press.

Weller, L., Weller, A., Koresh-Kamin, H. and Ben-Shoshan, R. (1999). Menstrual synchrony in a sample of working women. *Psychoneuroendocrinology*, *24*, 449–459.

White, R. W., Fox, G. F. and Harris, W. W. (1940). Hypnotic hypermnesia for recently learned material. *Journal of Abnormal and Social Psychology*, *35*, 88–103.

Whitehouse, W. G., Dinges, D. F., Orne, E. C. and Orne, M. T. (1988). Hypnotic hypermnesia: Enhanced memory accessibility or report bias? *Journal of Abnormal Psychology*, *97*, 289–295.

Wilkinson, L. and APA Task Force on Statistical Inference (1999). Statistical methods in psychology journals: Guidelines and explanations. *American Psychologist*, *54*, 594–604.

Willerman, B. and Melvin, B. (1979). Reservations about the keyword mnemonic. *Canadian Modern Language Review*, *35*, 443–453.

Williams, J. H. (2001). Frequency-specific effects of flicker on recognition memory. *Neuroscience*, *104*(2), 283–286.

Williams, J. H., Ramaswamy, D. and Abderrahim, O. (2006). 10Hz flicker improves recognition memory in older people. *BioMed Central Neuroscience*, *7*(21), 1–7.

Wilson, V. E. and Bird, E. (1981). Effects of relaxation and/or biofeedback training upon hip flexion in gymnasts. *Biofeedback and Self Regulation*, *6*, 25–34.

Witkin, H. A., Oltman, P. K., Raskin, E. and Karp, S. A. (1971). *A Manual for the Embedded Figures Tests*. Palo Alto, CA: Consulting Psychologists Press.

Wollman, N. (1986). Research on imagery and motor performance: Three methodological suggestions. *Journal of Sport Psychology*, *8*, 135–138.

Wood, G. (1967). Mnemonic systems in recall. *Journal of Educational Psychology*, *58*(6), 1–27.

Woodworth, R. S. and Schlosberg, H. (1954). *Experimental Psychology*. New York: Holt.

Woolfolk, R., Murphy, S., Gottesfeld, D. and Aitken, D. (1985). The effects of mental rehearsal of task and mental depiction of task outcome on motor performance. *Journal of Sport Psychology*, *7*, 191–197.

Woolfolk, R., Parrish, W. and Murphy, S. (1985). The effects of positive and negative imagery on motor skill performance. *Cognitive Therapy and Research*, *9*, 335–341.

Wyatt, J. K. and Bootzin, R. B. (1994). Cognitive processing and sleep: Implications for enhancing job performance. *Human Performance*, *7*(2), 119–139.

Wyra, M., Lawson, M. J. and Hungi, N. (2007). The mnemonic keyword method: The effects of bidirectional retrieval training and of ability to image on foreign language vocabulary recall. *Learning and Instruction*, *17*, 360–371.

Yerkes, R. M. and Dodson, J. D. (1908). The relation of strength of stimulus to rapidity of habit-formation. *Journal of Comparative Neurology and Psychology*, *18*, 459–482.

Yuille, J. C. and Sereda, L. (1980). Positive effects of meditation: a limited generalization? *Journal of Applied Psychology*, *65*(3), 333–340.

Zaichkowsky, L. D. and Fuchs, C. Z. (1988). Biofeedback applications in exercise and athletic performance. *Exercise and Sport Sciences Reviews*, *16*, 381–421.

Zecker, S. G. (1982). Mental practice and knowledge of results in the learning of a perceptual motor skill. *Journal of Sport Psychology*, *4*, 52–63.

Zuckerman, M. (1960). The effects of subliminal and supraliminal suggestion on verbal productivity. *Journal of Abnormal and Social Psychology*, *60*, 404–411.

Zukhar, V. P., Kaplan, E. Y., Maksimov, Y. A. and Pushkina, I. P. (1965). A group experiment in hypnopaedia. *Voprosy Psikhologii*, *11*(1), 143–148.

Index

Note: *italic* page numbers denote references to figures/tables.

264   *Index*